Learning the Arts of Linguistic Survival

TOURISM AND CULTURAL CHANGE
Series Editors: Professor Mike Robinson, *Centre for Tourism and Cultural Change, Leeds Metropolitan University, UK* and Dr Alison Phipps, *University of Glasgow, Scotland, UK*

Understanding tourism's relationships with culture(s) and vice versa, is of ever-increasing significance in a globalising world. This series will critically examine the dynamic inter-relationships between tourism and culture(s). Theoretical explorations, research-informed analyses, and detailed historical reviews from a variety of disciplinary perspectives are invited to consider such relationships.

Other Books in the Series
Irish Tourism: Image, Culture and Identity
  Michael Cronin and Barbara O'Connor (eds)
Tourism, Globalization and Cultural Change: An Island Community Perspective
  Donald V.L. Macleod
The Global Nomad: Backpacker Travel in Theory and Practice
  Greg Richards and Julie Wilson (eds)
Tourism and Intercultural Exchange: Why Tourism Matters
  Gavin Jack and Alison Phipps
Discourse, Communication and Tourism
  Adam Jaworski and Annette Pritchard (eds)
Histories of Tourism: Representation, Identity and Conflict
  John K. Walton (ed)
Cultural Tourism in a Changing World: Politics, Participation and (Re)presentation
  Melanie K. Smith and Mike Robinson (eds)
Festivals, Tourism and Social Change: Remaking Worlds
  David Picard and Mike Robinson (eds)
Tourism in the Middle East: Continuity, Change and Transformation
  Rami Farouk Daher (ed)

Other Books of Interest
Progressing Tourism Research
  Bill Faulkner, edited by Liz Fredline, Leo Jago and Chris Cooper
Recreational Tourism: Demand and Impacts
  Chris Ryan
Shopping Tourism: Retailing and Leisure
  Dallen Timothy
Sport Tourism Development
  Thomas Hinch and James Higham
Sport Tourism: Interrelationships, Impact and Issues
  Brent Ritchie and Daryl Adair (eds)
Tourism Collaboration and Partnerships
  Bill Bramwell and Bernard Lane (eds)
Tourism and Development: Concepts and Issues
  Richard Sharpley and David Telfer (eds)

For more details of these or any other of our publications, please contact:
Channel View Publications, Frankfurt Lodge, Clevedon Hall,
Victoria Road, Clevedon, BS21 7HH, England
http://www.channelviewpublications.com

TOURISM AND CULTURAL CHANGE 10
Series Editors: Mike Robinson and Alison Phipps

Learning the Arts of Linguistic Survival
Languaging, Tourism, Life

Alison Phipps

> Existir, humanamente, é *pronunciar* o mundo, é modificá-lo.
> To exist, humanly, is to *name* the world, to change it.
>
> Paulo Freire: *Pedagogy of the Oppressed*

CHANNEL VIEW PUBLICATIONS
Clevedon • Buffalo • Toronto

For Ruth

Library of Congress Cataloging in Publication Data
Phipps, Alison M.
Learning the Arts of Linguistic Survival: Languaging, Tourism, Life/Alison Phipps.
Tourism and Cultural Change; 10
Includes bibliographical references and index.
1. Language and languages–Study and teaching. 2. Tourism. I. Title. II. Series.
P51.P455 2006
910.01'4–dc22   2006022376

British Library Cataloguing in Publication Data
A catalogue entry for this book is available from the British Library.

ISBN 1-84541-054-8 / EAN 978-1-84541-054-4 (hbk)
ISBN 1-84541-053-X / EAN 978-1-84541-053-7 (pbk)

Channel View Publications
An imprint of Multilingual Matters Ltd

UK: Frankfurt Lodge, Clevedon Hall, Victoria Road, Clevedon BS21 7HH.
USA: 2250 Military Road, Tonawanda, NY 14150, USA.
Canada: 5201 Dufferin Street, North York, Ontario, Canada M3H 5T8.

Typeset by Saxon Graphics Ltd.
Printed and bound in Great Britain by MPG Books Ltd.

Contents

Acknowledgements vii

Introduction 1

1   Languages, Tourism and Life 15
2   Educating Tourists 29
3   Risks 48
4   Way Finding 65
5   Pronunciation 81
6   Conversations 97
7   Games 113
8   Rehearsing Speech 128
9   Breaking English 142
10 Tourist Language Learners 156
11 Surviving 171

Afterword 186
Bibliography 189
Index 198

Acknowledgements

This book has been sustained by a number of colleagues and friends over several years. Amongst them I particularly wish to thank Gavin Jack, Manuela Guilherme and Mike Gonzalez who acted as the best of critical friends, reading the manuscript and offering invaluable, illuminating and incisive comment. My debt to them is incalculable. Our previous shared writing projects mean that this book is very much part of a wider conversation and web of ideas. John Corbett patiently accompanied me in my language learning enthusiasms and, with Augusta Alves, saw to their continuation after the main work was completed. To both, thanks.

As series editor Mike Robinson contributed both wisdom and critical insight, combined with a generosity and humour that are rare indeed. I am very fortunate in *Channel View* as publishers, and especially wish to thank Sami Grover and Sarah Williams in overseeing the series and the process. I am also indebted to my tutors and all those who learned languages alongside me in numerous locations at home and in Portugal, and to Kath Bateman of Caledonia Languages Abroad, for advice and inspiration.

The University of Glasgow and the Arts and Humanities Research Council granted me both funding and research leave to complete this manuscript. I gratefully acknowledge their contribution and record my particular thanks to the anonymous reviewers of this project for their encouragement and suggestions. I am indebted to Elizabeth Moignard for her sustained support throughout.

I was fortunate to be invited to give papers at the Universities of Cornell, Durham, Aberdeen, Stirling, at The Open University, The Centre for Tourism and Cultural Change, Sheffield Hallam University, in New Orleans, at the Ludwig Maximillian University in Munich, The Centro Estudos Sociais, Universidade de Coimbra, Ecole Superior, Viseu, the Ecole Francisco Ferrer in Brussels and at close of the Society for Research into Higher Education's annual conference in Edinburgh during 2005. I am grateful to all for their generous hospitality, especially to the British Council in Coimbra, and to the different audiences for their lively engagement with the ideas in this book. In particular, but in no particular order, I wish to thank: Luís Mendes, Gillian Moreira, Georgina Hodge, Ana Matos, Clara Keating, Rosa Chaves, Antonio Ribeiro, Maria del Carmen

Mendes Garcia, Ronald Barnett, Ralf St. Clair, Jan Parker, Tim Ingold, Michael Cronin, Veronica Crosbie, Shirley Jordan, Abhik Roy, John O'Regan, Anselma Gallinat, Jim Coleman, Inma Alvarez, Sharon Macdonald, John Joseph, Richard Johnstone, Jane Wilkinson, Philippe Pourhashemi, Catherine Steel, Judith Still, Susan Bassnett, Henry Giroux, Norman Shanks, Kathy Galloway.

Robert remains my most ardent critic, faithful friend and loving companion.

This book is dedicated to Ruth, who accompanied its genesis with compassion.

Arts & Humanities
Research Council

The AHRC funds postgraduate training in the arts and the humanities, from design and dance to archaeology and English Literature. The quality and range of research supported not only provides social and cultural benefits but also contributes to the economic success of the UK. For further information on the AHRC, please see our website *www.ahrc.ac.uk*.

Introduction

'Quick' is an old English word used to refer to vibrancy and to anything characterised by the presence of life.

What happens when we ignore the 'quick', when our habitual ways of researching social, cultural and linguistic practices fail to search out the presence of life? The 'quick' of human relationship, the interstices of life, energy and freshness are repeatedly and systematically excluded from research into languages and from research into tourism. In the discourses of endangered languages, skills-shortages and language crisis we find little to suggest vibrancy. Equally in many of the dystopian accounts of tourism as a blight on the planet, or in the critical voices that consider its effects, we find little to suggest a freshness and liveliness that may come through relationship and encounter. And yet holidays – shaped into tourism, touched by languages – we know, offer refreshment, renewal and a revitalisation. Tourism has become one of the greatest repositories for our imagination of happiness.

There is much that is 'quick' when a tourist steps out of her habitual ways of speaking and viewing the world, and has a go at speaking the language of her hosts. And yet, in the literature on languages and the languages crises, we find virtually no mention at all of the wide practice of learning other languages, or of what I term the *languaging* practices of tourists – having a go, trying to make sense and getting somewhere against all the odds. Life. Energy. Freshness. In the same way in the research into tourism we find a massive multilingual phenomenon boiled down to a few articles bemoaning the lack of language skills in its servants, and a few more critically assessing the patterns of discourse and the potential symbolic violence inherent in such representations. Modern linguists ignore tourism in their research, with one or two exceptions making forays into the study of travel writing, and tourism scholars ignore the main medium of tourism – not language, but languages.

And yet all the time there is life, energy and freshness in the 'quick' of human – tourist – relationships worked out in the learning of languages. The crisis in mainstream modern languages other than English may well be real, but in tourist language classes there is life and freshness. The problem is that such life and energy is not present in ways that are easily quantifiable.

1

The UK Nuffield Foundation report *A New Landscape for Languages* (Kelly & Jones, 2003) documented a significant change in when and where and who was engaged in language learning activities:

> [...] there is a growing tendency for languages to be provided on the margins of the mainstream curriculum in schools, colleges and universities. Language learning may be marginal in the amount of teaching time allocated, in being timetabled outside the main teaching hours, and in being located in less well suited premises. It may be marginal in terms of accreditation arrangements and staffing provision. (Kelly & Jones, 2003: 39)

Changes in patterns of learning and languages don't just happen. They index much wider phenomena and aspects of social and cultural change. Although there may appear to be a certain logic to this particular change, as a response to the multilingual phenomenon and experiences of tourism, there are also certain paradoxes associated with this change. It is my contention that analysing what happens when people bother to invest time and energy in learning to speak a tourist language reveals much about the experience and process of both becoming and being a tourist, its material, social and linguistic dimensions. It is equally my contention that framing such research in functional terms, looking only at the efficacy of language pedagogy or of tourism and failing to analyse the social and intercultural dimensions of language and tourism experience, as it is encountered through everyday life, will not get us very far in terms of understanding the human importance of learning to engage with others, in different contexts and in different languages. Skills-based paradigms dominate the literature on tourism and on language learning, burdening the human activities of those learning with performance criteria and failing to consider the 'quick' of human relationships.

Languages are not just skills, even if they enable skilful interaction and an efficacy in human activity. To find a way of thinking that does not simply rehearse the commonplaces of language pedagogy, communicative learning and intercultural communicative competence requires a shift away from the discourses of performance and competency and skills. It also requires a different perspective to be taken, one that does not seek to write of language learning and teaching as two sides of the same coin, one that does not insist on language acquisition and focus on the measured and tested outcomes of the inputs of a curriculum and its production through assessment.

Furthermore, to examine the context of languages learned for and by tourists, rather than by school pupils or modern language students equally shifts the focus away from the dominant literature in the study of language pedagogy, language acquisition and, more recently, of the crisis that has beset the formal teaching of languages other than English in schools and universities. Tourist language learning is precisely the activity that the majority of mainstream language teaching defines itself against. Serious language teaching is 'more than just learning to order a cup of coffee' I hear and read, repeatedly. Maybe. But to take seriously the multilingual, intercultural concentrations that accompany the world's largest industry – tourism – then learning to order a cup of coffee has to be taken more seriously than has hitherto been the case in the literature on languages.

Throughout this book I write not as a language pedagogue, but as a tourist language learner. I am not interested in the kinds of pedagogies used or the methods employed in tourist language classes, but rather in the social life and everydayness of the worlds brought into being and imagined through the activity of learning a language for tourist purposes. I am also interested in what 'tourist purposes' might actually be, when subject to more than superficial analysis. As well as demonstrating the need to 'arrive and survive', what might the learning of languages and their actual use – the *languaging*, as I term it – tell us about wider social and cultural phenomena in an age of globalisation and of cultural change?

Consequently, in this book I am concerned with the 'quick', with the messy, complex and often contradictory work of learning to speak a language for tourist purposes. What happens when tourists learn other languages? What constitutes a curriculum shaped by the collective energy and desires of tourists learning languages? How important is the perception and the minimising of risk to tourist language learning? What effort is involved in moving from the learning environment of the classroom to the actual contexts of *languaging* as a tourist? What is occurring through way finding, role playing, lessons in pronunciation and language games? Instead of focusing on skills and competences as detached add-on languages to be acquired through language classes that will help with the finding of hotel rooms, visiting museums and buying tickets, I take a phenomenological perspective.

I argue throughout this book that languages are fully embodied, not detached and 'acquirable', in easily measurable ways. Furthermore, when the focus of language scholars is only on the acquisition and the measurement of competences, of success spooned out according to numbers applying to mainstream courses or reasons for learning, we miss out on seeing what goes on in the 'quick' of human relatedness, through languages. There can be no speaking of a tourist language in which the person is not fully engaged. It is never just skills that are 'performed'. People speak – to and with each other. Discourses of performance and competence simply mask and technologise the variedness and complexities of felt languages, from within the human person.

Languages in Crisis

If undergraduate students are voting with their feet, and avoiding studying modern languages unless they happen to come from an elite background where such luxuries in accomplishment can be afforded, it is because they are forced to make their choices in the framework of utilitarian criteria that directly link decisions about education to the shape of the labour market. Languages, increasingly are being pushed out of secondary and higher education into primary education and onto the margins. Languages, as taught both to tourists and those studying for qualifications to work in the tourism industry, are sold as packaged commodities and skills sets for basic training and in the lifelong learning market (Kelly & Jones, 2003). Those studying languages in these contexts – usually on the margins of the working day, after hours or in lunch breaks, or as part of vacation courses – are of diverse ethnic and social backgrounds. This is in marked contrast to the demographics of those studying modern languages in mainstream contexts. The democratisation of travel in the west has brought about a democratisation in the learning of languages for tourist purposes, but not yet in mainstream study.

In adult and lifelong learning there is a long tradition of engaging people from diverse social and ethnic backgrounds. In many ways my own attempts to dwell alongside those learning a language and languaging as tourists simply add to the numbers of those adults wishing to do the same. Others have documented the important social contribution of popular adult education in other places and it is not my intention to write here within that particular, and honourable, tradition (Crowther *et al.*, 1999). I am far more interested in the tourist languaging phenomenon. The growth in tourist language learning and the particular and peculiar questions that tourism raises for languaging are the ones that detain me here. Why bother to put your whole body through an often humiliating and difficult, unwieldy and socially awkward learning experience where the rewards are slow and meagre at best and why do this for the sake of interactions that, if truth be told, will be fleeting and impersonal for the most part?

Over the past three years I have engaged in an empirical ethnographic study of the phenomenon of languages for tourist purposes. Certain languages pitch themselves in the languages market, outside of standard university courses and within the 'training' context of courses taught as foreign languages across the curriculum, or institutional wide language programmes; as useful not as intellectual endeavours. I have engaged in a variety of different courses, as participant observer, beginning with a six-week course in Tourist Italian, and following this up with a year-long course in Portuguese. I continued this work through taking a language holiday that involved *in situ* language courses and home stays with families in Lisbon.

Some of those who bothered, alongside me, might be introduced as follows:

Pat: Retired, former nurse who loves Italy. She has been going there on coach tours with her neighbour ever since her husband died. She loves the opera too. She travels in to class by public transport from the suburbs. It is the first time she has really engaged with another language.

Anja: A graduate student of Spanish who loves Capoeira, Brazilian literature and art history. She is German, speaks impeccable English with a Glaswegian accent. She just loves learning languages and Portuguese attracts her because of its relationship to Spanish.

Pascal: A French Jesuit missionary. He has lived and worked in the French colonies of Africa for much of his ordained life. He is now of retirement age and is to be placed in Mozambique. He has been sent on holiday to Lisbon to begin learning the language and to mark the end of one phase in his life.

Catriona: Speaks French and German fluently. Teaches at a local university. A keen gardener as we discover through the classes. She travels a lot with her work, increasingly to Portugal, but also with connections to Brazil and Mozambique. She had a trip to Portugal last year and it got under her skin.

Graham: A community worker from one of the housing schemes and an ardent supporter of the local football team. He is spending his holidays at the European Cup Final in Portugal and it is football that brings him to the classes. He hasn't learned a language before.

Regina: A Dutch musician who loves learning about the music of other countries through their languages. She often goes on holidays that combine language and cultural activities. She has spent time in Brazil and is now in Portugal.

Betty: Goes to Spain and Portugal regularly on holiday. Began learning Spanish through the evening class access scheme for senior citizens. Wants to expand her repertoire.

Rhona: Has been to the same resort on the Algarve for the last 13 years and knows lots of people there. She goes back to the same place every year. It's beautiful. Has never learned a language before. It is a real challenge. Comes to class on the bus from one of the schemes.

Sita: Has just finished her first degree and is about to go travelling, starting with South America, especially Brazil, for a year. Portuguese could come in handy.

At a time when language degrees are in crisis in languages other than English, modern language professionals have spent much time and energy demonstrating that 'languages are about much more than learning to order a coffee'. This is the constant refrain. There are hierarchies that are constantly appealed to by those who teach other languages in which tourism is the lowest of the low. The last thing languages are about is ordering coffee, we are repeatedly told (Byram, 1997; Méndez García, 2005). It is easy to understand this perspective. It is clear that languages are indeed about more than ordering coffee. But it is my contention, in this book, that far from being the first aspect of language learning to be dismissed, as is so often the case, the desire and willingness to order a coffee in another language, to step outside one's habitual ways of speaking, to let go of one's normal fluency and linguistic power point to aspects of social and moral life that are of fundamental significance.

To find ways in which the experiential struggles of tourist languages and intercultural communication may be captured, described and analysed – rather than dismissed out of hand or modelled to enable ever increasing profits – we need other methodologies and frameworks.

Languages, both generally and within the context of tourism, have come to be understood as functional necessities that may solve some of the myriad problems of intercultural communication and the mastery of which will provide basic skills, increase economic profit and personal pleasure. This is the common sense position, the position that asset-strips languages of their life and of all other human relationships beyond those that guarantee value for money. This is the position that fails to notice the 'quick' of human relationships in languages and the way that languages inhabit others and offer others spaces in which to dwell and to encounter the world. If, as I contend in this book, there is more to languages than economics and the training of the labour market, then how might we find ways of uncovering alternative language economies, other ways in which human beings may exchange stories, words, encouragement, meaning and come to work through and change their own ways of being as they encounter different possibilities for language and for life?

Languages for Tourist Purposes

This book presents the data, stories, memories and experiences that I have gathered through participant observation, mainly through reflective journal entries of my own. As a language learner myself I write deliberately from my own place of 'dwelling' – a concept to which I shall return – in the world of tourist language learning. The narrative entries – italicised to mark them out stylistically – punctuate the main line of the text and argument. Other course participants and course or holiday providers described remain anonymous composites throughout according to the now standard ethical conventions of such research. The tourist sites, however, and tourist destinations have not been anonymised. They remain publicly available and present as destinations that form part of the stock of the tourist imagination.

Throughout I attempt to reflect the relationship I evolved with language, participants, activities and the process of learning. My concentrated identity throughout the tourist language courses and holiday was always primarily that of a tourist language learner. Learning to speak another language – like the learning of other skills, as Ingold notes (Ingold, 2000) – is an absorbing activity. It is often exhausting and as a process of 'enskilment' (Ingold, 2000: 5) it involves attuning 'the whole organic being (indissolubly mind and body) situated in a richly structured environment' (Ingold, 2000: 5). This is not, following Ingold, a process of enculturation, of learning the Italian or Brazilian or Portuguese language as if this exists as an entity separately from its context, and as if it is acquirable by being observed, or through understanding symbolic systems. Far more it involves a full education of attention in which learning is constituted by doing, breathing, living, languaging – dwelling in the world and being practically engaged with it:

> It involves an embodied skill, acquired through much practice. It carries forward an intention, but at the same time is continually responsive to an ever-changing situation. [...] The attentive quality of the action is equivalent to what, in relation to musical performance, I have called 'feeling': to play is to feel; to act is to attend, The agent's attention, in other words, is fully absorbed in the action. (Ingold, 2000: 414)

As such I would not wish to over play claims for aspects of this work as an ethnography of tourist language learners. Undoubtedly I owe a debt to the ethnographic method and training I have had in the past. But my field notes – the ethnographic present of a fully native tourist language learner – are actually language learning notes, vocabulary lists, phrases for booking hotel rooms or buying the right size of shoes, of knowing how to order a coffee. It is in the nature of such an all-encompassing, absorbing learning activity that the reflection is a reconstruction, created in the ethnographic past tense and in a time of introspection and aloneness, diametrically opposed to the collective cut and thrust of a communicative language classroom.

I write at times as an ethnographer, at other times as an anthropologist, sometimes I write as a tourist, sometimes as a language teacher, often as a language learning subject. This work may be considered a form of auto-anthropology. I move in and out of tropes, moods, memories and registers in order to use language and languages to capture something of the complexity of languages learned for intercultural communication in tourism. All the time this work remains firmly and resolutely in the Derridean prison house of language, but also happily, even celebratorily so – for the limits of language enable much richness and diversity too.

As such I attempt to make the 'double break' that Bourdieu speaks of (Bourdieu, 1977) in *Outline of a Theory of Practice*. Bourdieu remarks:

> [...] that linguistic research takes different directions according to whether it deals with the researcher's mother tongue or with a foreign language, emphasizing in particular the tendency to intellectualism implied in observing language from the standpoint of the listening subject rather than that of the speaking subject. (Bourdieu, 1977: 1)

The first break seeks, phenomenologically, to make explicit the primary experience of the social world of language learning for tourist purposes. As such my primary experience has been that of language learning and then of languaging. The second break, here, is that of considering the nature of this practice of tourist language learning and the conditions that make it possible, which enable people to actually bother. As such I seek not to establish rules, models, grammars and vocabularies for tourist language learning but rather to enter the social world of this experience, to describe the phenomena of this primary experience and then to consider its wider relations to the conditions of life. This approach produces experiences and produces language. It is performative. The reality is that I have learned languages for tourist purposes, alongside others embarked on similar activities. The difference between us is that I have dwelt on the experience in particular and practiced, crafted ways, taking time to write and read and consider, in order to offer a partial, yet nonetheless academic narrative of that experience. These may bring what Law describes as 'resonances' to aspects of tourism and languages that remain unavailable to us when engaged in routine practice (Law, 2004: 145).

As the stories told in this book unfold, much will also be revealed about the working method. Methodologically this work may be characterised as ethnography, or auto-ethnography but the boundaries around ethnography and its possibilities are presently fraught with much self-criticism and reflexive angst. The method is primarily that of tourist language learning. For learning another language under the highly circumscribed conditions of a tourist language class as the primary focus of methodological practice is, following Law, to practice methods that are slow, uncertain, which stutter to a stop, which have to be quiet, listen, be patient, and also then step out and make many, many mistakes (Law, 2004: 151).

As I work to weave together a narrative and critical analysis of what I have found, experienced and observed in my intercultural and linguistic encounters with other languages and other people, I return to common tropes and questions of anthropology and ethnography and I also add to some of the possibilities for such messy research.

Aims and Purposes

The purpose of this book, then, is to enter into the 'quick' of the language learning and languaging of tourists. In asking the question: 'Why bother?', I seek to consider the processes in play, the transformational process that comes when a new language is learned, possessed, inhabited and performed, put more succinctly; when it is *languaged*. I therefore focus on the practices of what I term *linguistic guesting* in varied western tourist contexts. In so doing I am concerned to capture, through stories and reflective practice, something of the changes that occur as people come to language, to use that language both in the learning context of the classroom and in the wider social world, and to do this whilst imagining themselves as tourists, and then as being tourists themselves.

Marketing and consumer behaviour models of tourism have focused largely on tourists as consumers, attempting to understand the motivations and the markets in order to increase the potential 'take' in the name of customer satisfaction. The anthropology of tourism has largely focused on the impacts of tourism on host communities, with anthropology, worrying, rightly, about the environmental and cultural devastation that tourism can cause, and about the impact on relationships with other human beings in situations of great wealth inequality (Burns, 1999; Nash, 1978; Nash, 1996). In addition, it has been anthropology's concern to document the decline of ways of life in places reached now by western capitalism and modernity but that in the past have been the object of the anthropologist's concern, career and nostalgia. Anthropology tends to view tourism as responsible for the destruction of cultural and linguistic diversity and its biases in this respect are well documented (Dann, 2004; Russell & Wallace, 2004; Snow, 2004; Turton, 2004).

In tourism studies, influenced largely by sociology, the now seminal texts of MacCannell and Urry (MacCannell, 1975; Urry, 1990) have seen the tourist as a semiologist, interpreting signs and developing the now famous 'tourist gaze' – focused on the personal and collective aesthetic experience of tourism (Bauman, 1996).

Although these traditions of tourism research inform this study and have provided considerable and important insights, this work breaks with these modes of analysis in important ways, ways driven by the subject matter of tourist languages and their learning.

Firstly, the questions that relate to motivation are focused on educational questions of inspiration and relationship. They are not primarily seeking to ask economic questions.

Secondly, the focus here is not on the hosts but on the guests, not on the erosion of others' languages in host communities so much as on the countercultural engagement of tourists with the languages spoken in a destination. This is an anthropology of guests, not an anthropology of hosts, and methodologically it works from the perspective of auto-anthropology, examining my own view as tourist language learner, and that of other tourist language learners, learning destination languages. More than this, however, this is an anthropology of the 'quick' of learning and languaging when guests attempt to be good guests, and to engage, courteously, with their hosts.

Finally, this study breaks with the long tradition of privileging sight, of the tourist gaze, in tourism studies. Cronin has argued persuasively that other faculties come in to play in tourism, particularly that of language and its imaginative potential (Cronin, 2000). The anthropology of the senses has also developed new prospects for understanding the embodied, sensuous responses available within the modalities of tourism (Taussig, 1993). An anthropology of the guest, a focus on linguistic guesting, enables a shift from examining what it is that tourists privilege visually. In its place, I work with the dwelling perspective outlined by Heidegger and developed latterly by Ingold and then by Urry and Crouch in order to describe something of the phenomenological world of the tourist and the worlds in which he/she dwells (Crouch, 2002; Ingold, 2000; Urry, 1990; Urry, 2000). The interest here is not in what it is that the tourist sees, but in seeing the tourist as someone who has the potential to *do* tourism, *to language*, to engage with the world through the languages of others, to be intercultural, momentarily, in the fleeting, ordinary yet highly symbolic instances of human relation and encounter that tourism may afford.

Conceptual Terrain

Understanding and experiencing the ways in which bothering with languages as tourists is part of what Ingold terms 'a movement of becoming' (Ingold, 2000: 200) or, in Heidegger's terms a 'letting dwell', operates at various different levels. It may begin with the common sense practicalities of phrase book language, taking these seriously for what they are and for what they tell us about tourists and language. However, it quickly moves into other questions that have historical, political and ethical resonance and that gnaw away at the question of the place and status of languages, tourist languages and other world languages. It is clear that the models and skills agendas of much of intercultural and language training and education can only take us so far and that other tropes and conceptual frameworks will necessarily be mobilised, critiqued and developed in order to discover the breadth and depth of the connections here.

The questions that this work poses do not relate so much to the functioning and structuring of language and linguistic systems as to a phenomenology of cultural and intercultural dimensions of languages. To this end, languages are considered as artefacts. Languages are seen as both fashioned and as being fashioned by tourist users and by those they encounter. For the purposes of this study, languages are considered rather as material objects, or as markers of identity, rather like those that form the classic trinity of cultural studies: race, gender and class. Languages mark us out in certain and specific ways. Our attempts to speak other languages, as tourists, do things to how we are understood and to how we are interpreted by others. It is clear that languages destabilise us, mark us out as different when, as tourists, we travel from a place where our languages fit with the local landscape, to a place where they sit more uneasily, awkwardly with other ways of living and of speaking. It is also clear that languages get things done, that they function pragmatically and relationally to accomplish the work of culture and the labour of leisure. Languages, then, are seen as embedded in the contexts and processes of intercultural communication that operate within tourism.

It is therefore important at this juncture to clarify my use of three separate terms: language learning, languaging and tourist language learners.

(1) *Language learning*: I make a fundamental distinction between language learning and languaging. Language learning for me signifies the activities that occur in the language classroom, that are bounded

by the timeframe of the classroom work and also marked out by the homework exercises, the listening to tapes, watching videos etc. in order to practice and reinforce communicative learning of the language. Language learning is focused on the world of the classroom, even though, as we shall see, the tourist world and tourist imaginings regularly break in to this world. It is focused on performance, often also on assessment, even in adult learning classes, and it tends to posit culture as a body of knowledge about a people of a place or a destination that is a fixed entity, and one which needs to be learned about. I am not against these activities, but I find it helpful to understand them as distinct from the using of a language in the context of the whole social world, rather than with a limited and predictable number of other social actors, in a scaffolded learning environment.

(2) *Languaging*: The term 'languaging' is one that I have developed together with my colleague Mike Gonzalez. It has been used before in different contexts and at different times in history. It emerged for us out of the process of struggling to find a way of articulating the full, embodied and engaged interaction with the world that comes when we put the languages we are learning into action. We make a distinction between the effort of using languages that one is learning in the classroom contexts with the effort of being a person in that language in the social and material world of everyday interactions. 'Languagers', for us, are those people, we may even term them 'agents' or 'language activists', who engage with the world-in-action, who move in the world in a way that allows the risk of stepping out of one's habitual ways of speaking and attempt to develop different, more relational ways of interacting with the people and phenomena that one encounters in everyday life. 'Languagers' use the ways in which they perceive the world to develop new dispositions for poetic action in another language and they are engaged in developing these dispositions so that they become habitual, durable. Languaging, then, is an act of dwelling.

(3) *Tourist language learners*: In order to make a distinction between language learning that occurs as part of formal degree programmes, or as a bilingual upbringing, or in a variety of other educational settings, and the processes of learning involved in courses for tourists and for tourist purposes, I use the term tourist language learners. I do so deliberately and somewhat provocatively vis-à-vis the prejudiced discussions of language professionals when referring to those who 'just want to learn how to order a coffee'. I am a tourist language learner. Tourism and business travel afford me a great many

opportunities to use my languages. There are many occasions when I am using my languages that also corresponded to times of being a tourist. This connection is a vital one for me for it is both at the heart of the paradox identified at the start of this chapter and it enables me to focus on the processes of learning, of enskilling of attunement and of becoming a tourist that are not rendered by speaking simply of language learners.

It is tempting to suggest that the outcome of the development of a differentiated conceptual terrain will be more small-scale stories, such as those that Koshar calls for (Koshar, 2000) when he maintains that what tourism studies requires is not grand narratives but 'a set of more general conceptual markers that will bring organisation into a field that is at present dispersed and without direction' (p. 13). In the relatively short intervening period much has been achieved in tourism studies attempts to find such markers and to begin to elucidate something of the relationship between them.

Getting Personal

I come to this work as a passionate and accomplished linguist. I have been learning the languages offered to me in secondary school aged 11 for over 25 years now. I am considered to be fluent, nearing 'native-speaker' competence in both German and French. I have lived, worked and travelled extensively in Germany and in France. I have taught both these languages and I have also taught my own mother tongue – English – whilst working abroad. I also come to this work with an academic training in both language and literary studies and in anthropology. My interests in tourism have grown out of my love of creative interaction with speakers of other languages, out of being hosted and hosting myself, in my own home, in my classes and through academic work and travel of many kinds over the years.

In previous collaborative work I have been keen to understand cultural phenomena and everyday life, to examine the current crisis in modern languages and to work, conceptually and empirically, with understandings of languages for intercultural communication. Themes of entertainment, travel, interaction and communication in many forms have fascinated me over the years, all of which I find studied in the emerging field of tourism and cultural change. In addition the formative and crucial role of education, and in particular of critical pedagogic approaches to culture, has remained a strong concern. This particular study is rooted in my long-standing concerns, but is also an attempt to make explicit the connections between languages and tourism, which I feel and live out constantly in my daily life and work, and to subject them to a more critical gaze.

In being present to the problematics of languages and tourism I also feel and perceive a powerful set of possibilities for human life in the human imagination, in its localisation and in its mobility, and in the way words evoke something of the facticity of an experiencing self in big and small stories alike. I come to this work of language influenced both by literary and narrative theory and by the work of linguistic anthropologists – again, moulded at this present moment by new linguistics and grasping towards a *felt* aspect to language, a sensory and sensing dimension where tourism is one significant and symbolic place or mode of being, where the rooted-ness of languages in particular places and in the environment, comes into fresh relief.

This work is, in some sense post-disciplinary, involving the use of concepts such as performance, script, narrative, habit, body, translation, mobility, place, touch and hospitality. These have been added to the larger markers and tiring concepts that began to befuddle the field as they became grander narratives – of culture, geography, anthropology, consumption, gaze, hosts, guests, liminality and most latterly globalisation.

But as the dynamics of intellectual work and community unfold, and as I attempt to tell this particular story of languages, tourists and social miracles in action, I too am moved to gently suggest some grander narratives that emerge from this work. These pertain to the values, virtues and stories that my tourist language learners live by – not necessarily grand narratives, but ones that play within the contexts of globalisation and community, which seek to find meaning and relationship in the extraordinary ordinariness of speaking with others.

But first, there are stories to tell.

Chapter 1
Languages, Tourism and Life

I think I must be entirely mistaken. I must be in the wrong place. I'm here to enroll in a six-week course in Tourist Italian. The place is mobbed. We are queuing up outside the classroom door. It's like being in a vortex of the over-60s. There are no men anywhere to be seen. All is chatter and excitement and umbrellas. The contrast to my day job could not be more marked.

Why Bother?

Why do people bother to learn another language for tourist purposes? On the surface of things the answer would appear to be simple. Tourism concentrates multilingual and intercultural experiences significantly. It does so at times of great symbolic significance to tourists, times that are anticipated and that are associated, socially, culturally and often personally, with happiness. In order to survive in the multilingual, intercultural worlds of tourism being able to speak the language is an obviously advantage.

But in a globalising world that speaks English and assumes English to be a lingua franca there is nothing obvious about learning other languages. I teach languages to undergraduate students on degree programmes and our programme, like programmes in modern languages across the western world – languages other than English that is – is in crisis. The number of students applying for undergraduate courses is declining, and the siren voices asking what 'use' such courses are grow more shrill by the minute. The past decade has simultaneously seen an unprecedented growth in mobility across international borders and a decline in the learning of languages other than English in the mainstream of higher education across the globe.

At the same time the learning of languages for tourist purposes has become a growth industry. New beginner, intermediate and advanced courses proliferate across the spectrum of adult education and so-called lifelong learning.

Thick with Languages

Tourist destinations and sites are marked places, thickened through the actions of tourists and the work of hospitality. To the grounded, placed, rooted nature of beaches or museums or cathedrals or exhibitions, tourism brings people, with their personal belongings, their modes of attire and with their languages. Destinations undergo material change in cultural, social and physical ways in order to accommodate visitors and their needs. Tourists, put simply, are temporarily leisured people (Bauman, 1996) out of place (Robinson & Andersen, 2002). Although tourists are recognisable as such visually – their attire and belongings point to their mobility and leisure – they are also audibly different, speaking in languages and accents that are also out of place, often clumsy or inappropriate or loud.

Mary Douglas argued that 'dirt is matter out of place' (Douglas, 1966). As matter 'out of place' languages and tourists are invariably perceived to be problems, to be dirt, out of place, requiring solutions that will tidy up the linguistic confusion and cultural disorder that threaten the order of things, the way things are habitually carried on. As such languages have come to be considered as basic skills required by the tourist industry for its smooth, efficient running and by tourists for 'getting by' successfully. Part of the way in which the perceived disorder of multilingual tourism is dealt with by the travel industry is to train and pay people to act as a translation interface with those who arrive at a place where their native language is not spoken. Addressing the 'skills-shortage in languages' is a tourism management refrain. To be a good host, these days, is to be able to speak words of welcome – be it on websites, in tourist brochures, and as tour guides – in languages that are comprehensible, and even native to the tourists. To be a good host – in Cronin's terms (Cronin, 2003) – is to also be a translator.

But there is another side to this equation. However thick an intercultural and multilingual experience tourism may be, the opportunities for speaking the languages of the hosts are often so limited and so systematically and even technologically frustrated as to force the question again: why bother? Why bother to learn another language as a tourist? Why bother, when brochures, guidebooks and service staff speak the common languages of the tourists. Because people do. Large numbers of people – many more than those studying for language degrees in universities – attend classes in adult and continuing education in order to learn languages that they might be able to use when on holiday. This is the key paradox which is the catalyst for the explorations in this book.

The air is full of strange sounds. Snatches of conversation reach my ears. Some enter.... German... Austrian... French... American... Australian... Italian...

Spanish... English... Scots... Lancastrian... Portuguese... Swabian... Dutch... Japanese... and are locatable, sometimes they are comprehensible, taking me off into other worlds away from this one, through the trigger of sound on memory. I turn to my friends and speak to them in French. My partner speaks to me in English. I listen to the guide, and the commentary is German. Another guide moves forward and the place is animated with Portuguese. The tourists around me are speaking, listening, reading, some are writing. This is an intensely multilingual place.

Tourism is an intensely multilingual, intercultural experience in which the opportunities for speaking the language of the destination are often very limited. Even in an age when English is used as one of the most common languages of tourist communication, opportunities for speaking English in London, or Edinburgh or New York or Cape Town, are often limited to the moments of meeting members of the service industry – ordering coffees, buying stamps or tickets, booking in to a hotel or camp site. And, again as Cronin argues, such destinations are multilingual places, where the inhabitants may well not speak English themselves, as migrant workers in the service industry (Cronin, 2003). Linguistic and also economic power is involved in the languages used by hosts and guests alike within the tourism industry. The dominant situation is comparable to the one characterised by Nuñez:

> Perhaps the most striking example of the asymmetry in host-guest relationships is to be found in linguistic acculturation in which the usually less literate host population produces numbers of bilingual individuals, while the tourist population generally refrains from learning the host's language. The cadre of bilingual individuals in a tourist-orientated community or country are usually rewarded. The acquisition of a second language for purposes of catering to tourists often results in economic mobility for people in service positions. Interpreters, tour guides, bilingual waiters, clerks, and police often are more highly compensated than the monolinguals of their communities. (Nuñez, 1977: 208)

The question that detains me in this chapter is not so much the one pertaining to the injustices inherent in the asymmetries of language power that Nuñez describes, or at least not direclty. Rather I am interested in what happens when the normal language dynamic is reversed and tourists are the ones who speak the language of the destination. What happens when tourists take the time to learn to speak with their hosts? Why do some people bother to learn the languages of the places they go to on holiday? What happens when an intercultural moral imperative works itself out in the 'quick' of tourists learning languages and languaging?

In this sense I am following the logic of the argument advanced by Crouch who criticises tourism studies for seeing space and place as inert and merely available for the inscriptions that tourism brings along

(Crouch, 2002: 208). The multilingual soundscapes of tourism render touristic spaces anything but inert. Place and languages *speak back* and meet with tourists as part of their embodied experience of doing tourism.

Tourists are not tourists all the time, any more than hosts are only ever hosts, but in the asymmetries of languages and power the encounters within tourism are symbolically significant. Memories of tourist soundscapes and imaginations of future encounters pervade everyday life. The music, we might say, lingers on. The motivations for the tourism industry – for the hosting destination – are relatively clear. A smoother linguistic process, a warmer, easier, accommodating welcome – so the logic goes – will help develop the destination, help increase the profits. Smooth processing of large numbers of people helps keep the tourism industry efficient. But what happens to relationships, the ones so often characterised as dehumanising, massified, alienated in the tourism literature (MacCannell, 1975; Meethan, 2001; Smith, 1977) when good hosting, good linguistic hospitality, to use Ricoeur's phrase (Ricoeur, 2004), encounters what we might term good linguistic guesting, encounters people who have taken it upon themselves to learn *and to use* the language of the destination? What happens when tourists taken it upon themselves to step outside of their own everyday language habits, when tourists don't assume that everyone will speak English, or that theirs will be the language spoken, but when they bother to deepen their potential for relations with another place and people?

Beyond this, other questions are raised: Do the multilingual, intercultural environments of tourism encompass wider, and more complex modes of being? Urry asks the question 'what happens when people travel?' (Urry, 2002). Here, I ask, in the contexts of complex mobilities and intercultural encounters: What happens to us and to others when we attempt *caffè* over coffee, *se faz favor* over please? Why is it that that most maligned of language tasks – learning to order or offer a cup of coffee or a beer in a tourist language – is an enduring feature of tourist life? Who are we and who are others in this expression of a relationship?

Languages, Tourism and Everydayness

In focusing on tourist language learning and on an anthropology of the guest, it is worth stating that I understand intercultural communication as an everyday quest, amongst many other things, for alterity and as an encounter with other ways of living and speaking and acting. Such a quest, or engagement with the shifting realities of social life leads to a re-attunement of the whole being, to an education of attention that does not change who we are, but expands our horizons and enskills us to dwell in different worlds. Intercultural communication *is* the process of embodied learning with languages. It is embedded in everyday life and takes on particular material and cultural shape within tourism. It is not, to repeat, a set of competences or add-on skills.

I am consequently interested in the ways in which languages and tourism, as forms of intercultural learning, shape the everyday life of tourism, its tactics and strategies (de Certeau, 1984). I see intercultural communication not as some nirvana of toleration and harmony where all people will perfectly comprehend each other's different patterns of behaviour with a high degree of self reflexivity, but rather that intercultural communication *is* the human struggle to make meaning culturally and dialectically out of relationships between people, places and praxis. And culture, following Ingold, does not lie in 'some shadowy domain of symbolic meaning, hovering aloof from the hands on business of practical life, but in the very texture and pattern of the weave itself' (Ingold, 2000: 361). As such, this dialectical process indexes the crafting of new patterns and forms of social and material life and of language, out of our dwelt relationships with all around us and to hand.

Other languages, in other people and in other places, offer a change from the routines of our everyday language and our everyday lives. They offer new perspectives and new places to dwell, temporarily. They offer new homes in an age when home is no longer fixed but is made up – as hooks says (hooks, 1991) of multiple locations or as Said says: 'Homes are always provisional' (Said, 1999: 185). Some aspects of the routines and habits of our lives are suspended and remade in fresh yet familiar ways whilst on holiday. We may still wish for our morning coffee, but we will ask for it in a different way, using different words and gestures, paying for it perhaps at a different point in the procedure, feeling a different weight of cup or thickness of crockery in our hands and against our lips, a different taste in our mouths and other sounds of language in the conversations around us and in the newspapers opened at the bar. The first time we try to make our order it may be difficult, a risk, with no real expectation of success, but as time passes, we become more practised, even fluent, in this simple routine language task of daily tourist life.

But this is not the only direction to cultural change that we may trace here. Through the things seen and done, the habits changed, the people encountered, the food tasted and the language spoken, changes may enter life back at home. The world and its languages are brought home. Diets may change subtly, food tasted at a distance may be sought out and purchased at home, shared with friends and family, souvenirs may be of an everyday practicality – bowls, cups, cookware, modifying the modalities of everyday life. And the languages may linger. It is in the utter ordinariness of everyday life that we might find signs of newness and of transformation. There may be a new relationship with people and places that has been fostered through the intercultural encounters that inevitably come with tourism. These may lead to the resolve, for our purposes, to take up language classes or persevere with home language learning kits, tapes, videos, books and the internet. All of these aspects bring with them changes that pursue other, better ways of living life. They are often quite subtle. It may take years of return trips to the same place for the language learning to begin, or it may happen quickly and determinedly, as a result of a desire to enter more deeply into relation with people and place.

Under such a view of the possibilities afforded in tourism for cultural change, I regard attempts to manage away intercultural difference and linguistic diversity as removing certain crucial dimensions and opportunities for encounter and for imagination from the tourist experience. In short, smoothing out the intercultural bumps in languages and tourism itself places significant obstacles in the path of the creative processes of culture, closing down options and imaginative possibilities for cultural change in favour of the single of trope of well-meaning or not so well-meaning economic progress.

And there is much more to tourism and to languages, and the learning of both.

Dwelling Perspective

In the chapter 'Building, Dwelling, Thinking' Heidegger reflects on the relationship between language, building and dwelling, by pointing to the German word *bauen* – to build, as originally meaning to dwell:

> What, then, does *Bauen*, building, *mean*? The Old English and the high German word for building, *buan*, means to dwell. This signifies: to remain, to stay in place. The real meaning of the verb *bauen*, namely, to dwell, has been lost to us. But a covert trace of it has been preserved in the German word *Nachbar*, neighbour. The neighbour is in Old English the *neahgebur; neah*, near, and *gebur*, dweller. The *Nachbar* is the *Nachgebur*, the *Nachgebauer*, the near-dweller, he who dwells nearby. The verbs *buri, bueren, beuren, beuron*, all signify dwelling, the abode, the place of dwelling (Heidegger, 1971: 144–5).

The older meanings of dwelling, encompassing neighbourliness, safe keeping, remaining at peace in a place, have fallen in to oblivion. Any attempt at construction, at building – physically or through thought – argues Heidegger is inescapable from dwelling as 'to build is in itself already to dwell (Heidegger, 1971: 146).' To see tourism and language learning simply as constructed, cultural activities – activities of building – is to miss the deeper significance of the ways in which tourists and tourist language learners, set apart temporarily in another place, begin by finding ways of dwelling, of preserving and sparing. 'The fundamental character of dwelling is this sparing and preserving. It pervades dwelling in its whole range. That range reveals itself to us as soon as we reflect that human being consists in dwelling and, indeed, dwelling in the sense of the stay of mortals on the earth' (Heidegger, 1971: 147).

A cornerstone of the argument of this book, in addressing the paradox of tourist language learning in an English language world, and the quick of human relatedness, has to do with the ways in which both tourist language learners and tourists themselves dwell in language and with language. How does dwelling, 'being on the earth, under the sky, belonging to one another in neighbourliness, being accountable' to paraphrase Heidegger, require languages as well as whatever is physically to hand. One cannot dwell – one can only build – in Portugal, as a tourist, if one does not work at the textures of being with a different language, with Portuguese. Only through the action of languaging, from language learning as a way of preparing to dwell in other places, can the sense of dwelling as 'remaining at peace and preserving of the integrity of being' be accomplished and respected. 'This means that in dwelling in the world, we do not act *upon* it, or do things *to* it; rather we move along *with* it. Our actions do not transform the world, they are part and parcel of the world's transforming itself' (Ingold, 2000: 200).

Tourism as Intercultural Communication

The research to date in languages and tourism falls into three categories (1) research taking a discourse analytic approach looking inside language for the ways in which tourism constructs and represents worlds in language (Dann, 1996; Jaworski & Pritchard, 2005; Jaworski *et al.*, 2003; Snow, 2004); (2) an applied, model based approach (Pearce, 2005) purporting to offer ways of enabling the tourism industry to deal with the supposed problem of monolingual, monocultural tourists through intercultural training (Baysan, 2001; Leclerc & Martin, 2004; Pearce, 2005); and (3) an emergent literature addressing the teaching and training in languages and intercultural communication in the tourism industry (Fighiera & Harmon, 1986; Russell & Leslie, 2004; Winslow, 1997) and, conversely, a literature addressing the teaching of intercultural communicative competence in language students (Byram, 1997; Corbett, 2003; Guilherme, 2002; Kramsch, 1998).

In the last three decades discourse analysis – 'the study of how stretches of language take on meaning, purpose, and unity for their uses' (Cook, 1994: 1) – has contributed much to the understanding of the social nature of communication, of contexts for speech and interaction, of the negotiations of meaning and the ways in which social relationships and social identities determine and are determined in and by language. The research undertaken at the University of Cardiff under the auspices of the Leverhulme Language and Global Communication Project (http://www.global.cf.ac.uk/index.asp) has gone some way towards documenting the discursive qualities of tourism as a form of global communication. Such analysis helps us understand some of the wide-ranging concerns at play in discussions of tourism and language and in the concerns, particularly of macro-level structures, institutions and agencies that aim to protect and legislate on behalf of the rights of peoples, languages and cultures, and on behalf of global capitalism (Urry, 2000).

In recent years attention in the tourism literature has turned in particular to questions of intercultural communication in an attempt to document and model practices that may help with easing the flow of people, their languages and their cultural difference. Several articles have engaged with the question of managing intercultural communication, of cultural sensitivity for those who work in the tourism industry (Leclerc & Martin, 2004). These articles have argued for the insertion of intercultural training in tourism contexts as part of maximising the customer experience and the 'take' that accompanies customer satisfaction. The empirical and theoretical research that unpins this new strand of research in the tourism research field is largely quantitative and aims at modelling behaviour and tourist types according to typologies developed in the 1980s by intercultural communication theorists Hofstede and Hall, Trompenaars and Bennett, amongst others.

Without wishing to prolong a review of the intercultural communication theories, developed largely in the US at a point in history when consumer capitalism was taking off as a major and revolutionary political project, it may be useful here to highlight some of the key elements and premises of this stand of intercultural communication literature. Much critical ink has been spilled already on the problems inherent in the intercultural projects of Hofstede and Hall, amongst others, and on the difficulties and even the desirability of modelling intercultural and cultural behaviours and of testing for certain behavioural norms. However, the intercultural training industry has been built upon these foundational texts and many training programmes have recourse to the models and ideas that these researchers produced. It is therefore no surprise that, in tourism contexts where the key questions that are posed are those of managing diversity to the benefit of the tourism industry and for customer satisfaction, the pieces of research chosen to enable this practical work are those that grew out of consumer capitalist concerns and from the emerging mobilities of global capitalism.

A more critical intercultural literature exists in the field of modern languages, particularly examining the need to train teachers and language pedagogues to operate within the challenges and concerns of globalisation, multilingualism, plurilingualism, the frameworks of the European Council and the emergent concerns of citizenship education. Here there is, yes, a concern with competency and performance and employability, but the notes sounded are critical and practical, and intercultural communication is seen as vital to harmonious engagement between peoples and languages in the future, be this within a multicultural, multilingual nation state, or in tourism (Byram, 1997; Corbett, 2003; Guilherme, 2002; Kramsch, 1998).

Of course it is important for those who enjoy the benefits of tourism, from the refreshment it promises, to the return on investment, to ensure that all may go smoothly. In the communication challenges posed in tourism, from ordering coffee to attending to medical emergencies, the possession of some key phrases or some awareness of how other cultures do things, in either direction, can considerably help things along. The problem with these models, to return to the point I made at the end of the Introduction, is that they see intercultural communication models and language learning as models to solve problems, rather than as the manner of movement, of dwelling, learning and engagement with the world.

I believe that the impulse to help and to communicate well and effectively, to get along with others rather than just to get by, is an important one and one that deserves greater attention than models and responses would suggest. It is therefore my contention that many of the studies of intercultural communication in tourist settings, while addressing issues that are of immediate practical concern, exacerbate the problem by creating intercultural communication, languages and translation to be a problem, one which an industry of technological fixes may then grow to serve, rather than taking a dwelling perspective, one which is heavier, messier, requires time to be taken in and with languages, places, people and praxis.

It is no surprise, in the supply and demand models that dominate intercultural and linguistic training in the tourism industry, that the languages learned to be spoken *for* tourists are those deemed to be the most welcoming of the rich, the rich-world, colonial languages. It is therefore clear that any intercultural assessment of languages and tourism needs to reflect upon the post-colonial condition of tourism and connections between continuing colonialism and languages practised under conditions of tourism. In short, it is important to realise that there is something of a political, language economy at work in this field of intercultural analysis. Equally the documentation, by organisations such as UNESCO, of what is variously termed 'language death', or 'language genocide' (Skutnabb-Kangas, 2000) makes the learning of any language – endangered, or powerful, depending on its situation and context vis-à-vis other languages – anything but a neutral activity.

No languages come with innocent histories but they are carriers of cultural legacies and tourists, as language carriers and language makers, are themselves embedded in an ongoing process of telling and writing of other cultures and other experiences, in and through languages. Tourism, as a crucial site of intercultural encounter and linguistic endeavour sustains and resists these language economies, and what Jaworski and Thurlow (2003), more hopefully term the language ecologies of tourism.

These language economies do not equate simply with cultural economies (Anderson, 1991). There are indeed powerful connections between languages and cultures and these are particularly in evidence in tourism: Tourist Spanish for Spain, Italian for Italy, French for travelling in France. But of course whereas, as tourists, we expect to find French culture in France and Japanese culture in Japan, the languages, following the former patterns of trade, travel, exploration and colonialism, do not equate with culture in the same way. So one may learn Portuguese for holidays in Portugal, Brazil, Angola, Macao. And English will be spoken in many places that are far removed from English culture. Indeed we may find it necessary, in order to reflect this relation, to speak of the *cultures* of English, of French, of Portuguese to avoid the metonymical, partial and often essentialist aspects that pervade our intercultural imaginations as tourists.

Cultures are not static or simple nor are the actions performed by cultural beings, as tourists or as services, neutral actions. Advice given on what to do and how to do it in tourist language courses, phrase books, tourist guides and in the curricula of hospitality industry degree programmes as cultural advice is, of course, ideologically freighted. This political, language economy is not simply confined to languages learned and spoken by tourists. Language of all kinds marks travel writing, travel guides and travel literature, the stories told of trips taken, of life in the destination. All of these find their way into the communicative syllabi of tourist language courses of all kinds, recast for use in tourism. From the enduring stories that shape the canons of our cultures to backs of tickets and the leaflets handed out by tour guides in information booths we find resources for tourist languages in profusion.

Technologies

Intercultural dialogue in much of the literature surveyed above masquerades as a moral imperative but is in point of fact a technological solution to problems of globalisation – be they the problem of trying to address the languages skills-shortage in the tourism industry, saving endangered languages, or trying to find ways of bringing speakers of different languages together in such a way as to enable *effective* communication:

> Technical devices originated as prosthetic aids for the human organs or as physiological systems whose function it is to receive data or condition the context. They follow a principle, and it is the principle of optimal performance: maximizing output (the information or modifications obtained) and minimizing input (the energy expended in the process). Technology is therefore a game pertaining not to the true, the just, or the beautiful, etc., but to efficiency: a technical 'move' is 'good' when it does better and/or expends less energy than another (Lyotard 1984: 44).

When turning to intercultural dialogue and modern languages we find a literature, political structures and international agencies seeking solutions to a vast range of human difficulties, but presenting not a solution in any practical sense, but a moral imperative in the terms of conflict avoidance, mutual understanding and co-operation. From within tourism languages are seen as a technological fix to the difficulties of increasing the global 'take' in a market that no longer only speaks English. Where tourism is perceived as a threat then intercultural dialogue, training in languages and education are seen as the technological fix.

This raises questions for moral philosophy. Alasdair MacIntyre, the philosopher of ethics, maintains that searching questions should be asked of moral statements, made impersonally and conjuring up a sense of objective justice. He identifies certain characteristics of moral statements and debates today, a salient feature of which is that they purport to be '*impersonal* rational arguments [...] usually presented in a mode appropriate to that impersonality' (MacIntyre, 1985: 8). This feature is the kind we find in the intercultural pronouncements of UNESCO and of The Council of Europe, for example. 'Its use presupposes the existence of *impersonal* criteria – the existence, independently of the preferences or attitudes of speaker and hearer, of standards of justice or generosity or duty' (p. 9).

Such statements are, says MacIntyre 'only a masquerade' but they beg the question 'Why this masquerade?' (p. 9). Not only do we appear to equate morality with high-flown rationalism and universalism, but, in the traditions of ideas, if not of politics, we need to be vigilant and ask carefully in whose interest such masquerades are made. We might conclude that for transnational political institutions and international agencies, the interests are those of perpetuating massive internationalist bureaucracies, and in the case of research into 'skills-shortages' – less veiled as moral it has to be said – is of increasing the 'take'. But even in the critical fields – and I include myself in this – there is a tendency to see intercultural communication as a fix. Critical awareness and intercultural communication, as part of an education for peace and for global citizenship, can usher in toleration and mutual understanding. That such education can be transformational is not at issue here, rather that it also runs the risk of the 'quick fix' for the future, instead of an acceptance of the 'quick' of the here and now, which includes the all mess of human relatedness in languages.

And so it is, within the contexts of globalisation and intercultural communication, that I come to examine the exception to these rules. Although my concern is with intercultural communication and consequently fits with the aims of organisations such as the The Council of Europe or UNESCO and their view of the potential threats to cultural diversity of tourism, I do not seek to add further technological weight to the calls for intercultural dialogue.

Such calls for intercultural engagement, for massive training in intercultural awareness, I believe, fail to take account of the ways in which people actually become tourists, become linguists, come to bother to learn another language. They fail to understand intercultural communication as I presented it earlier – as the human struggle to make meaning, and to *language*. The moral imperative as expressed and generated by macro-level institutions is not what brings people to bother. It is my contention, throughout this study, that partial, situated answers to some of the questions of intercultural dialogue, cultural diversity and endangered languages may be found in the quick of human relatedness, in the contexts of neighbourliness and of learning together as an everyday process of dwelling in the real world. For the world presented by the agencies and demanding the technological fixes of languages and intercultural dialogue is ignoring everyday communication practices. It sets up the work of languages and intercultural dialogue to be work, not only for the technologically gifted, but also for the Nobel Peace Prize winners, for 'extraordinary' people, not for 'mere tourists'. As such it conjures up big pictures of global scenarios, suggesting that intercultural work is out of the reach of the many, rather than being found in the here and now.

Smaller Pictures

> *We meet after our second lesson together in the early afternoon, to take the bus in to town for our afternoon tour. Suddenly there were new people (Italians, Spanish and French) all students at different levels, and all happy to speak to beginners and ask questions in their newly acquired Portuguese. This felt kind and encouraging, as well as encouraging them. If I was here for four weeks I'd be able to manage this...was the thought I had, often. Our guide, João, sat next to me and let me try and ask questions. I realised how hard it must be for him to constantly have to entertain those of us struggling with sentences and mangling his language.*

> *Rest seems to be a key aspect of languaging...moments of generosity as people listen and correct and allow the mistakes, other moments of generosity when we do the same for others, but also lots of moments of rest from languaging because it is tiring work.*

Here we find an emergent ethics, in the 'quick' of the human, languaging relations of a class of learners on holiday. MacIntyre is keen for us to hold fast to a core of values or virtues that he sees as a tradition 'at variance with central features of the modern economic order and more especially its individualism, its acquisitiveness and its elevation of the values of the market to a central social place' (MacIntyre, 1985: 254). His argument is not one of cultural or moral relativism, or one that attempts to operate at the level of pat universals and moral imperatives. 'What matters at this stage is the construction of local forms of community within which civility and the intellectual and moral life can be sustained through the new dark ages which are already upon us' (p. 263).

It is such local forms of community, such as emerge under the conditions of what Bauman terms liquid modernity (Bauman, 2000), where tourism and languages, intersect that have become a source of fascination for me and hold the focus throughout this book. I am not interested in sheering up the vast bureaucracies of intercultural citizenship programmes and economic accountability dressed up as intercultural dialogue. Nor am I interested in improving the ways in which we do business and increase our 'take' from the tourism market, how we may take what others have not yet got, how we may continue year on year in increasing our profits – as if this and this alone will lead us to human flourishing. Neither of these macro-level stories are where my story started in this book, though both cut through the narrative in different ways, as both form the context of the world in which tourism and languages intersect in tourists and linguists.

My stories are smaller, ordinary. They start in the quick of human relatedness, in the dwelling perspective, in turning the key of an unfamiliar wardrobe door, eating home-made guava jam and feeling the spectres of colonialism in life and language. And my story starts before this too, it begins in rooms built of concrete breeze blocks, where the heating doesn't always work, and where a group of people, initially strangers, gather week by week to learn to speak Italian and Portuguese as tourists.

Chapter 2
Educating Tourists

Educational Tourism

Why bother learning another language? An answer perhaps is that travel broadens the mind. Travel is good for us. It is educational. Or so the story goes. To visit other places, to see sites will give us more breadth of experience. We will learn to put ourselves in other places, not just through our imaginations, but through our memories of places we have already encountered. Travel has long functioned as a rite of passage for elites. The king and queen travelled to see the extent of their kingdom and where they rested, or paused to see the view, often becomes a place for today's tourists to visit. Those working to extend the reach of Christendom would travel; monks and courtiers would move between monasteries and European courts. And those in the service of the king, the soldiers and sailors, would see the world and return with stories that entered the common imagination, in song and tales. Benjamin (1973b) speaks of the tale of the traveller as story teller describing the difference between those who stay at home and the tales of those who travel and return.

The fabric of cultural life is shot through with a variety of teachings on the powerful magic of travel and its ability to bring change, adventure, new perspectives and renewal of wearisome lives, and in the last two hundred years these have become carriers of significant symbolism. The growing work in the field of literature and tourism (Robinson & Andersen, 2002) or of film- and media-induced tourism (Chaney, 1993) points to the wide variety of ways in which tourism and culture inform each other's myths and practices, changing perspectives and practices on the ways in which social life is lived. Raymond Williams expresses this as follows:

> From the later eighteenth century onwards, it is no longer from the practice of community but from being a wanderer that the instinct of fellow-feeling is derived. Thus an essential isolation and silence and loneliness become the carriers of nature and community against the rigours, the cold abstinence, the self ease of ordinary society (cited in de Botton, 2002: 60).

Travel, the experience of detachment from places we call 'home', from 'community', from the normal locations of our work, comes to provide a strong symbolic and experiential set of possibilities through which we can develop common-feeling with others, both at home and abroad.

I am concerned with the ways in which tourists learn to be tourists, to imagine tourism, and how they do this as tourist language learners. As in the previous chapter the concern is with the in-betweenness and subtle changes in perspective that occur when people engage in learning languages and languaging, as tourists, and with this as their point of engagement. I am interested in the embodied, slow movement of the whole being into the worlds opened up by a new language and the ways in which this movement is structured and framed, on the margins of the educational system, for adult learners, as tourism. This chapter is consequently interested in how, when people bother to learn another language for tourism, this mode of travel broadens the mind.

When it comes to the massified, democratised, consumer-oriented form of travel we call tourism, there is less certainty about the mind-broadening benefits. Crik, for instance, maintains that:

> Little detailed empirical work has been done on the effects of travel on attitudinal change, but a study by two educational anthropologists (Brameld & Matsuyama, 1977) concludes with serious reservations about the educational benefits of tourism. Tourists, for a start, are poor 'culture-carriers', being stripped of most customary roles through which their culture could be understood by others. In any case, for most people tourism involves more hedonism and conspicuous consumption than learning or understanding (Crik, 1996: 33–4).

To claim that tourism broadens the mind is a step too far perhaps. We are not quite sure about tourism and about its ability to transform us, change our ideas, give us a stock of awe-inspiring, morally superior narratives even if the experiences and memories we have as tourists often ended up as dramatic narratives of obstacles overcome, bodies in transition, and triumph in the face of adversity. We can go further here, however, for not only are we not quite sure of the status of travel in broadening the mind, we are also clear that some forms of travel have educative, knowledge-enhancing and transformative potential and others are not even contemplated in that category. Tourism, as a commonplace of life in the affluent ends of modern western democracy, is perceived negatively when juxtaposed with other, higher forms of travel, in this regard.

In referring to the critical work on cosmopolitanism Featherstone, for instance, uses the term 'cultural tourist' to invoke a sense of dilettante-dabbling in the cultures of others (Featherstone, 2002: 1). In the field of education we find the same perspective. In his now seminal development of the concept of intercultural communicative competence and the value for learners of other languages of experiences of residence abroad – of short or long duration, Byram makes a fundamental distinction between the figure of the tourist and that of the sojourner (Byram, 1997: 1).

Byram's tourist

- hopes that what they have travelled to see will not change, for otherwise the journey would lose its purpose;
- hopes that their own way of living will be enriched, but not fundamentally changed by the experience of seeing others.

Byram's sojourner

- is either a member of the social elite or a displaced person;
- produces effects on society that challenge unquestioned and unconscious beliefs;
- is in turn changed and challenged by encounters with others;
- has an experience that is potentially more valuable, both for societies and for individuals.

This opposition between the tourist – 'bad' – and other forms of travel, such as sojourning – 'good' – is one found regularly in various forms of writing across the arts, humanities and social sciences (Hennig, 1997; Méndez García, 2005; Shaules, 2004). It is clear that it evidences a widely held prejudice and one which, to be fair, also reflects the experience of concern of those who see tourism as in need of redemption, as a blight on the planet, destructive of habitats of both flora and fauna and erosive of the diversity of local culture. There is much in the tourism studies literature to support this dichotomy, and also much in terms of reflection on the assumptions scholars and others make regarding tourism. Crik maintains that the plethora of negative representations of tourism that populate the literature in the arts, humanities and social sciences points to its fundamental significance as a social practice: 'A trivial activity could not generate such religiously constructed, lopsided and ambivalent representations as exist about tourism' (Crik, 1996: 17–18). This echoes the view of Barnard and Spencer who maintain that: 'To ignore tourism in our accounts of culture contact in the twentieth century is probably as great an omission as to ignore slavery in the eighteenth century or colonialism in the nineteenth' (Barnard & Spencer, 1996: 552).

I do not have any wish to re-open this debate around the representation of tourism here, other than to lay foundations for a discussion of the educational dimension of tourism. For in arguing that tourism is about 'us' not about 'them', and allowing for the possibility that tourism may produce strengthening cultural materials through its practices, Crik opened a space for a consideration of ways in which tourism may broaden the mind, and may be seen as an educational practice. The Weberian binary order of work as separate from leisure still has a powerful hold and entertaining the idea that tourism, leisure, may be a significant locus of learning needs pressing home.

For, despite all our prejudices, tourism provides us with a fund of knowledge about other people, places, habitats and languages and it does so, for those fortunate enough to participate in it, from a very early age. And this is not all. Tourism is embedded into the wider educational curriculum in astonishing ways – school trips, visits to museums, field courses, exchanges – all have a touristic dimension that is rarely the focus of scholarly attention (Hecht, 2004; Fordham, 2005). The literature on languages and residence abroad nowhere includes a discussion of tourism as a key feature in encounters with other cultures. This is not to denigrate this literature at all, but to point to an absence that reveals something of a scholarly prejudice, or a blind spot, when it comes to actually 'seeing' tourism in action and as a valid mode of critical, reflective, educational engagement with the world.

The literature on modern languages, born as it is out of a time of acute crisis for languages other than English does not reflect the powerful role that tourism plays in motivating language learners, or even, with one or two exceptions (Gallagher-Brett, 2004), on its usefulness for future employment. Business, not tourism is one of the preferred categories – as to work in tourism still appears to have the status of a 'student summer job' and is not a serious and valuable mode of intercultural experience or engagement. In a field that has readily, even hungrily embraced the functional arguments for languages as having the potential to stem the flow of undergraduates away from its courses, this omission is somewhat startling. In short, tourism is now such a feature of our everyday lives that we fail to see it.

Tourist Language Programmes

It is already growing dark outside, it does that in early October this far North. I'm a bit early, a bit keen perhaps. I don't know if I've actually come to the right place here but I have a sense that this is probably it – a dark classroom, dimly lit, chalky, cold and with no one present. I decide not to go in. Its too uninviting and somehow a bit embarrassing – like being the first one to arrive at a party. I wait around in the corridor outside and a young man arrives, beanie hat, also soaked by the rain. He tries the classroom door, looks in and then joins me lingering in the corridor. We speak to each other – are you here for Gaelic? No – Portuguese – oh, me too. Do you think we are the only ones? No – they have a quota of 10 I think. So, why are you learning Portuguese?

For all of us engaging in the various language courses for tourists, the languages were 'for' something. The range of answers varied but in each case it involved relationships with people through work, family or place. In other words, the choice of which language to learn was never arbitrary and was motivated by a prior sense of connection and purpose that went far beyond functional concerns. Despite all the cynical marketing of languages in schools and universities in the UK as being useful 'because they will get you a job' the reality was different; because of the network and complex of places, people and possibilities that emerge under present cultural conditions, languages present themselves as ways into relationships. Languages are *for* relationships. *For* their maintenance and *for* their communication. This makes the 'quick' of language learning an intimate business.

As language pedagogues know well, the dominant approach to language learning has been predominantly based upon the communicative approach to learning (Corbett, 2003) over the past three decades. This approach can best be understood in opposition to the structural or grammar-based approaches. My own language learning as a school child was largely focused on the learning of grammar and gaining of structures that could then be used to build sentences. The focus was on writing as the main productive skill, and on reading as the main receptive skill with speaking and listening coming in later at the same time as the communicative approach was gaining in popularity. The communicative approach aims to develop productive language skills throughout, through role play, interaction and by bringing extracts of the target language, spoken by native speakers, into the classroom. The shift towards communicative methods has accompanied the cultural changes in mobility, whereby more and more speakers of other rich-world languages are able to encounter each other to do business together, have holidays together, visit each others' country and interact face to face, rather than at a distance. The skills that come to the fore to react to such changes are those of speaking and listening more than those of reading and writing.

To take the instance of tourism we can see how being able to read signs etc. forms a part of the tourist experience, but that writing skills are rarely necessary. Face-to-face contact predominates in tourist relations and, in the main, those courses I took in the UK focused on this aspect of communication. In the language holiday, however, the situation was slightly different. Here the classroom contact was based almost entirely on structural knowledge of the language and on reading and writing skills, with the interactive, communicative aspects being developed, in creative, multilingual settings on tourist visits to sites, restaurants, cafes, etc., and in sampling the local culture, films, art, etc.

We might envisage the placing of communicative and experiential dimensions to tourist language learning in three different ways, based on the three different courses I took. In the Lisbon language holiday the grammatical knowledge was at the core, with touristic, communicative dimensions forming the parallel programme in the afternoon and after hours. In the Tourist Italian class the focus was entirely communicative and all the exercises dealt directly with touristic activity and its communication. In the Portuguese class activities were separated out with a balance between structural learning, using abstract, decontextualised exercises, and communicative approaches drawing on social life and tourism. On the margins of this class, towards the ends of sessions, videos were used that gave a flavour of life as a tourist and of 'authentic' culture for tourists.

Literacy Practices

In home learning, phrase books and other more privatised, less socially orientated modes of learning a language, we find a similar pattern emerging, with some emphasis on basic structures, but a high emphasis on comprehension of spoken language and on the production of reasonably accurate speech in return. Phrase books are perhaps a unique case and they certainly merit further discussion but they too focus on the scripting of communication to facilitate the face-to-face encounter with imagined-yet-real human beings. The materials I was recommended to buy by the language tutors were always pocket grammar books, pocket dictionaries and whatever audio materials accompanied the course book that we were given to use:

> It's the second class and as we arrive we begin to empty our bags. We notice each others dictionaries. Most of us have the Pocket Oxford or the Pocket Collins Gem. One or two have the bigger Portuguese–English version and it sits proudly on their desk. I'd tried to buy a copy on eBay myself, but had settled in the end for the pocket version, once I'd been outbid. We have versions of the course book – some for Brazil, some for Portugal. I have a grammar book. It's a small one, but seems well laid out and it reminds me of the trusted pocket versions that got me a long way with French and German. There is something vaguely comforting about its size and about the way the corners are already curling and making it look used. 'Where did you buy that?' asks someone. 'I got it on Amazon', you can also buy it in the university book shop, the one round the corner, you know where I mean?' 'I got mine in Borders.' 'I've not been able to get one yet, the uni book shop had sold out when I was there.'

The new materials were a source of interest and some anxiety. Certain books that from our enrollment letter we believed to be crucial, were, it turned out, scarce commodities. We put a lot of energy into sharing books in the early weeks, and sharing information on where we had been able to buy what we needed. Portuguese language learning materials were not easy to come by. Invariably however, we never really depended on the course book itself and instead, we took home materials our tutor had produced herself and which we gradually gathered together into folders, with dividers and indexes for ease of studying. Our varied literacy practices and materials were, nonetheless, one of the foundations of our social relations together as a group. We produced together, what Barton terms a literacy ecology, with the common aim of transforming this into a spoken ecology over time (Barton, 1994).

What this discussion of the trends and the materials of language learning highlights is the mismatch between what is imagined – a language *spoken* and embodied more or less fluently in a travel or tourism context – and the pull into literacy practices. The artefacts that underpinned the literacy practices were themselves designed for maximum mobility and portability – A4 sheets of photocopied paper, pocket-sized books. The actual tourism aspects, with the exception of the Italian course, were omnipresent, but were most explicit on the margins of the courses and were much less portable. When the tourist language learners had free reign, however, in written or oral homework assignments or when invited to bring their own artefacts into class, the tourism dimension was the immediate focus again. This tension between literacy and orality practices is worth further exploration.

One of principal mistakes made in the field of modern languages, in the desire to find ways of responding to the crisis in recruitment to largely literary programmes, has been to attempt to see languages as purely functionalist, utilitarian skills that will get young people good jobs at the ends of their studies or schooling. The shift from written to oral modes of communication is confused with skills-deficits and functional requirements of the labour market, with no attention being paid to the wider shifts in social and cultural life. There is a fundamental failure in the embracing of such a skills and employability agenda, to acknowledge the insights of anthropological approaches to culture. When the dominant mode of interaction with other language and cultures was through text, it was important for skills of structure to dominate. But the field of modern languages has failed to understand itself as a site for both the communication and understanding of cultural difference. At a time when it is a common experience for people to encounter other languages, but for the mainstream courses in those languages to furnish learners with none of the skills that may facilitate and enrich such encounters, then it is hardly surprising that such courses become termed as 'irrelevant'. It is because they are.

What the tourist language programmes index, in their pedagogic approaches and in the distribution of their artefacts, is the tension and conflict between the pull towards touristic communication and the recourse to literacy practices. As such we are brought into the in-betweenness, and the 'quick' of the varied relations of the tourist language learner – deepening and moving, writing and reading in order to arrive at a place of speaking and listening in the end, from which the process may begin again, in new directions.

The curricula of language courses for tourists are themselves symbolic artefacts that represent a microcosm of educational, touristic and human communicative concerns that have emerged out of the experience of being tourists and doing tourism in the modern world. To understand more fully what this shows we must look at the curricula themselves and the activities that flow from them.

This is not to say that reading literature, understanding foreign film, etc., cannot be hugely important in the development of critical, skillful, educated citizens. But those voting with their feet and enrolling in their thousands in lifelong learning courses where they may at least practise the basics of human communication: speaking and listening, with others who speak other languages, are absolutely on to something important about cultural life, common-feeling and tourism.

Curricula for Tourists

We may understand a curriculum as a regular course of study or training offered as a set of building blocks designed for the purpose of structuring formal education. Although evening classes and home study courses take place on the margins of more formal educational structures, they are nonetheless socially framed in curricular terms. The curriculum material it is believed will enable tourists to learn the language of the destination culture is organised, packaged and parcelled in certain ways and over time to give a sense of progress and structure that may accompany acquisition and engagement.

An important shift in understanding the nature of the curriculum came with the notion of the 'hidden curriculum' and Giroux's critique of the 'norms, values and beliefs embedded in and transmitted to students' through the curriculum (Giroux, 2001: 47). Barnett and Coate (2005: 3) make a key distinction when considering the idea of the curriculum in higher education. They demonstrate how curriculum design has been understood as the filling of spaces, minds, time, gaps in module outlines, driven more by the administrative framings of educational establishment than by an attention to the space or to the students who inhabit the curricula thus conceived. In addition they distinguish between the *curriculum-as-designed* and the *curriculum-in-action*. They see the curriculum more as an achievement than as a task and one that has to be 'brought off *in situ*' (p. 3). The *curriculum-in-action* becomes a site of contest, conflict, negotiation and activity where a variety of competing desires, ideologies and perspectives meet.

These distinctions prompt interesting lines of thought when considering the shapings and spacings of a tourist language curriculum. The lifelong learning elements of higher education are also formally structured and submitted under similar course design and quality assurance procedures to those of undergraduate or postgraduate university courses. There is, however, a different experience of time and space at work within such courses to those operating in the more 'central', less peripheral zones of learning in the university. These courses are often evening classes, done in addition to the central employment of people's lives.

They take place in leisure time and in rooms that are usually designed and laid out for other, primary purposes, ironically often those of the supposedly 'heavier' curricula. Or, they are part of programmes engaging an ageing population and offered at discount prices as part of a programme to tackle social inclusion. In the case of language holidays, they take place in small office-like establishments, but not now on the margins of the working day but actually in the holiday period itself. The cohorts involved in such programmes of learning either have lots of time on their hands to study, or very little indeed, and such students are thrown together into the spaces of a tourist class and curriculum.

What such groups are offered varies considerably. The *curriculum-as-designed* more often than not is contained in course books adapted for use in home and car study. As mentioned above the books are handy, 'designed' materially as artefacts, for mobility, they come in various portable forms with CDs and cassettes that 'move' easily. The curriculum, like its attendant artefacts, is designed for a mobile population – mobile both in the sense of tourist mobilities and in the sense of the kinds of mobilities that engage the cohorts of such classes, often encouraged to learn and study whilst on the move.

They also work with what we may best conceive as pre-existing templates. The teachers and learners on such courses already have an idea of language courses and learning in mind. All participants have already experienced core language curriculum in various guises and in various incarnations and approaches. This resembles the understanding Barnett and Coate speak of as a space all expect to be filled in and pre-structured

(Barnett & Coate, 2005). Underlying the tourist language curriculum is the template for a beginners' or intermediate language learning programme; a set of grammar, vocabulary and cultural topics may be found in most language programmes. *How* such topics are assessed is a cause for considerable, often heated and ideologically freighted debate. What has been deemed necessary to progress in a language is not so contentious. Greetings, using the simple present tense, moving on to talking about oneself, one's domestic and family circumstances, being able to ask for directions, order food, move around the place – arrive and leave – all of these form a part of standard beginners' language courses and the tourist curriculum is no different.

How they are engaged is a different matter, however.

Our teacher is young, a graduate student funding her way through her study of Calvino by working in this part of the tourism industry. She wants us to work dialogically in more ways than one. She asks us to work in groups in the first class to list all the different things we want to learn during the six-week course and why.

- *Pronunciation: I don't want to sound Glasgow.*
- *If you do make mistakes will they understand you? I was blanked in France when I tried to speak French.*
- *I want to be better mannered and not assume that they'll speak English and are bound to understand me. I got lost in Italy and it was an awful experience.*
- *I want to know what to do in an emergency.*

The list then comes thick and fast:

- *Ordering food in a restaurant, grocers, weights, colours, sizes.*
- *Directions.*
- *Buying petrol.*
- *Courtesy – hello, goodbye, please, thank you.*
- *Meeting and greeting.*
- *Emergencies – doctors, pharmacies, bones and anatomy (the older women all laugh knowingly).*
- *Ancient sites – I want to go sight seeing.*
- *Travelling – buses, trains, airports, cheap flights, buying tickets, exits.*
- *Loos – I stood outside the doors in Holland and I didn't know where to go. What is Gents? What is Ladies?*

This is what I believe Barnett and Coate (2005) have in mind when they talk about the *curriculum-in-action,* and of engaging students through the curriculum. Here the concerns generated by the would-be-tourists in the class index three key things: (1) a shared set of pressing concerns relating to practical and imagined knowledge in action; (2) a common articulation of the kinds of activities that would be expected as part of tourism; and (3) an expression of a pre-existing template of *curriculum-as-designed*. Embedded in here are a set of values, desires for transformation and for an emancipation from 'rude' to 'courteous'.

Tourist *Curriculum-in-Action*

> *The levels of frustration are palpable. We've been here for four days, working away every day. The course book we've been given as part of our course package has been opened once and it was just way too easy for all of us. We could do all the exercises with ease, but for some reason the tutor just dwelled on our pronunciation all the time. And then she brought in lots of photocopied sheets from a different book and started going over things we know already too. Granted, we are all at slightly different levels, but this just feels ridiculous. We have already moaned about this in the breaks and in the afternoon visits and over lunch, in local cafés and on the balcony overlooking the street. Whenever we can get out into the fresh air or drink together from the water cooler we seem to bond over the frustration of it all. In this session we are booking hotel rooms. I begin to be a bit playful, injecting other fun dimensions into the scenario, asking for outrageous things, picking a fight with the receptionist. Everyone is on board and we start to up the ante on what it is we can actually manage to do in this language.*

It is when the *curriculum-as-designed* of Barnett and Coate (2005) butts up against what we might term the *curriculum-as-desired* in the context of a tourist language curriculum, that we find interesting and revealing conflicts in action. In none of the tourist language programmes I participated in was an overtly 'designed' aspect of a curriculum in evidence. We might turn to de Certeau here and his distinction between strategies and tactics to illuminate the kinds of tensions are emerging here between the design and the desire of the curriculum. De Certeau (1984: 37–9) sees 'tactics' as 'a calculated action determined by the absence of a proper locus' as opposed to 'strategies', which he views as Cartesian in attitude: 'an effort to delimit one's own place in a world bewitched by the invisible power of the Other.' He also says 'a tactic boldly juxtaposes diverse elements in order to produce a flash shedding a different light on the language of a place and to strike the hearer' (de Certeau, 1984: 37–9).

In the Italian course the six-week programme was structured around the participants' own desires, with this being the prime structuring device for the activities, materials and programme. In the beginners' Portuguese course an external framing was in evidence at certain key points in the course: in the opening lesson and at times of assessment and course feedback exercises. Here it was clear that, as points could be gained from this course (which was refereed to as a 'module' by the institution's strategists) that might be accumulated, over time, into elements of a degree, then the tutor and class would defer to the central quality frameworks in what was a reluctant acquiescence with bureaucratic accountability. In this class we were informed of the text book to purchase in the pre-course documentation, but in practice, this book was the least preferred and least privileged of the learning resources for the whole class and the tutor.

In the language holiday the first encounter suggested a strong framing, with orientation oral and written tests being taken and glossy text books being handed out to the language holidaymakers. However, again, this book, although being referred to and even worked through meticulously in some classes, was not the preferred classroom or homework resource, and it too was supplemented by worksheets and by objects to hand.

In these three instances, then, we find that the *curriculum-as-designed* articulates in distinctive ways with the *curriculum-as-desired*. Issues of power and resistance – strategies and tactics, in de Certeau's terms – are paramount. In the Italian instance there is a strong collaboration around the learners' own expressed wishes for learning and for topicality. In the beginners' Portuguese class there is a structure formed around grammatical, structural and comprehension content, and dipping in to a text book and other resources, but in practice the class is largely directed by the tutor and a variety of media and of learning activities. There is room in this class for a wider, longer term dialogue about the language and cultural life of Portugal and Brazil and this is part of the dynamic of each classroom and of the *curriculum-as-desired*. In the language holiday the tutor is 'autonomous' but there is no sense of an overall shape or design to the curriculum, despite the intensive nature of grammar and written work in the class.

So what might this tell us about the curriculum for tourist language learners? On the one hand it is clear that the curriculum already exists as a template that bears a considerable resemblance to that of beginners' language courses. However, on the other hand, the touristic purpose of the courses interacts with this template as the course begins and in the pre-course literature and this changes not only curriculum content but also the mode of encounter with the language by those wishing to learn it. The desired fluidity of movement and mobility that is anticipated (if not always practised) in tourism, of freedom to roam, to soak up the sun, to eat and drink and sleep and see, is brought to bear upon the *curriculum-in-action* in tourist language classes.

In this respect a tourist language class, even when following the overt content and patterning of a standard beginners' language class in mainstream pupil, student or adult education, is modified by the presence of tourism and its troping of learning desire. In short, tourism adds, considerably, to the zones of proximal development, identified by Vygotsky

(1978), whereby lifelong processes of learning do not proceed so much in stages as through social interaction, social and cultural contact and shared experiences. Tourism, as a set of knowledge practices and discursive formations, is present in the imaginations of the tourist language learners and those of the tutors, even though the bureaucratic assessment demands on all of the courses do not contain any shred of awareness that tourism may be a key aspect in the course.

Tourism is present as a form of what Ingold terms *non-human agency* (Ingold, 2000) with which tourist language learners interact *interagentically*, that is to say as agent-to-agent, with change occurring in the interstices of the encounter. The tourists are changed and develop through their learning of the language, and tourism, its practices and destinations are changed through the encounter with languages-in-learners. But this is not all. The encounter is also an imaginary one, but nonetheless real for being so. All are involved in fluid visions of what being speakers of Italian, Portuguese may *do* and what tourism under such circumstances may *become*.

The conflicts and concessions that arose in the courses and holidays I participated in occurred at different junctures and in response to different artefacts, around assessment, around text books, around imagined risks, but always around *desire*. I am using the term desire here in place of the more usual framings of learning around a literature and discourse of motivation, and motivational strategies (Chambers, 2000) and models (Dörnyei, 2000). Whilst contributing to an understanding of aspects of motivation relating to language learning it is my belief that these models bracket out many of the areas of social life, and aspects of the messy, instinctual groping that accompanies a dwelling perspective on tourist and languages. Desire, then, is used here to capture something of the dimensions of Eros, of a yearning, a longing, a grasping towards an unknown embodiment, a sensed but not yet felt fluency that come with travels into another language.

The low-status or even non-existence of the text book showed it to be the 'least-desired-artefact' in the *curriculum-in-action*. In contrast, the handouts were lovingly made and lovingly ordered, plastic wallets, ring binders, hole-strengtheners, dividers all came to the aid of these precious ephemeral documents in each of the classes. Bright colours were in evidence: oranges, pinks, reds, blacks, blues in note books and binders. And these objects, not those of the pre-ordained, consumer language learning products, were well thumbed and well used, *trusted tools* in the classes. Packing would occur every Monday evening, or prior to the daily class. Note books, vocabulary lists, files, handouts, a grammar text, the pocket dictionary – all accompanying a day's work for the evening class learners, a morning's work for the senior citizens and the holiday learners.

The *curriculum-as-desired* was colourful, hand-made, full of imagined possibilities. It grew from both real and imagined encounters with the destinations where the language was envisaged to be spoken by the tourist learner, what we might term *language destinations*. The materials brought in to class interacted both positively and negatively with the *curriculum-as-desired* by us as tourist learners. Where there was space for shaping a *curriculum-as-desired*, or at least negotiating with some aspects of subjection to assessment regimes as ordained from outside of the course, then the tourist learners were happy with their engagement. Where this wasn't the case and where there was no real opportunity to bring the *curriculum-as-desired* into the classroom then resistance grew and the *curriculum-as-desired* took shape outside of the classroom, on the language holiday.

> *Class began and the pace and level changed completely from being too easy to being too fast, if not too difficult. I spent most of the morning feeling dreadfully out of control, in need of order, pushed around, tongue-tied and out of my depth. Only Sara was managing easily…I found I was having to actively produce the imperfect tense based on a table at the back of the book and my prior knowledge of other languages, especially French. I just had to assume that this is how the tense would work and then fill in the gaps. All the dot joining feels so infantilising and then I'm having to make this other leap into doing something I can't do and having to guess…knowing that this is a context in which guessing isn't allowed and any aspect that is wrong will be jumped on. It is a very odd mixture.*

> *So I try – get no positive feedback and then find everyone else in the class is helping me out, whispering translations and once again resisting what is happening only this time for different reasons. I notice myself feeling cross, tongue-tied, subjected and dejected. Occasionally I feel close to tears – and on holiday too – and yet I don't feel I can ask others to go slower for me or even that this would be worthwhile, as I am being helped most of all by the whispered learning from them.*

This *curriculum-as-desired* was a common curriculum, one that held in tension the individual desires and *what fors* of the language learning activity, with the common development of the tourist language. The class members wanting to learn to dance Capoeira and to do so in Brazil, in Portuguese, met others wanting to engage in voluntary work, to gap-year travel, to sail round the Portuguese coast, to hear and understand the opera in Verona, or just to be an anthropologist. All had specific interests and questions that related to their desires, but as we, as classmates, came together and came to know of each others' travels and preferred destinations, in important breaks, beginnings and ends of classes, they became of common concern, common interest. They developed in that zone of proximal development through interests shared, if not through shared interests, but always, in the commonly felt desire to travel in the tourist language.

It is my contention here that the fluidity and the communitas (Turner, 1995), or social bondedness possible in these classes, together with the creation of a *curriculum-as-desired*, is created from and reliant upon tourism. Tourism is ever present and inserts itself firmly into the imagination of the tourist learners and tourist tutors alike, making itself manifest in different ways, at different moments in the courses. Tourist learning is not the same as other forms of formal instruction even if it is parasitic upon them. Tourist language learning desires and, if allowed, shapes the curriculum according to the imagined possibilities of the tourist language in action. As such it is an embodied imagining of being a tourist and of learning to let the language dwell in the tourist body – the letting dwell that Heidegger speaks of in *Building, Dwelling, Thinking* (Heidegger, 1971) – of letting the language be possessed by the whole person. That is to say it engages actively with the shared concerns of the tourist group, it enjoys the difference and possibility of the imaginative potential of others' holidays. Meeting others, using the language, surviving, 'getting by' are all important concerns for the learners, they manifest themselves in the learning activities and the creativity that surrounds them.

Learning Activities

Tourist language develops through multiple forms of learning. I do not wish here to engage in the already well-debated field of learning style. What interests me here is the range of activities that are included in tourist language classes (see Table 2.1).

Many of these activities are recognisably the same as those encountered in mainstream language classes, providing a mix of learning activities around the so-called core skills of reading, writing, listening and speaking and doing so either through communicative or through structural grammar approaches. I do not wish to comment in detail on these aspects of learning as this is also an area where much debate has already ensued. What interests me here are the ways in which the tourist learners modify the activities to make them fit their idea of tourist activities and the vocabulary/language that they have already developed in key domains (See Table 2.2). This aspect of creativity in the development of a *curriculum-as-desired* by tourist learners is an important one, as it represents the extent to which the tourist imagination is at work in these contexts and the powerful discursive hold that tourism has on language learning.

Table 2.1 *Tourist language learning activities*

Beginners' Italian (day class, public institution)	Beginners' Portuguese (evening class, public institution)	Private language school holiday (beginners)
Whole class teaching	Whole class teaching	Whole class teaching
Blackboard exercises – oral	Grammar exercises – written and oral	Handout exercises
Pair work – oral	Occasional use of course book	Vocabulary building
Group work – oral	Pair work and role play – oral and written	Grammar exercises – written and oral
Walking around the classroom, partner finding – oral	Pair mixing – oral	Language holiday – tourist programme (all oral)
Games – oral	Games – oral	Tours
Spontaneous oral tests	Videos	Meals
Role play – oral	Audio tapes	Museums
Oral revision activities	Handouts, exercises for written and oral work	Castles
Handout exercises for oral work	Written free composition	Churches
	Assessments	Day excursions

We've all got a bit sick of the kids stuff and the serious stuff. We can all do this already, even I can, and I'm a bit behind on all of the rest. We've been given yet another sheet that is too easy for us and is just boring. So we start to play. I glance at Anja and catch her eye, mischievously, when she follows the initial script for the role play we are to do, and she answers the phone I'm simulating and asks me if she can help. I want a room. She can help and seems to have what I want. What I want becomes increasingly outrageous. I want champagne, breakfast in bed, I want a balcony, a view of the beach, I want a quiet room, I want a big double bed and I want it to be a bargain. We are all helpless by the end of this, giggling like school kids and hugging ourselves with a dual delight in both the vision of an impossible common dream of luxury and the resistance we've shown in the language we can use.

What this aspect of tourist language learning demonstrates is the way in which tourists use the classroom language learning activities to practise being tourists and to play at being tourists in the language. This is an important aspect of language learning activities in this context, I would argue, as it gives a particular focus and texture to the encounters and it unites the learners around the commonly felt cultural importance of tourism in their lives. The fact that all have the ability to push the boundaries of these activities into the times that they most associate with rest and fulfillment, happiness is brought to the fore in the role pay activities, the fun elements in the shopping for clothes or ordering of meals or booking of rooms. The imaginative possibilities keep expanding as lists of vocabulary and grammatical possibilities accrete to the language available and in common action in the classroom.

Table 2.2 *The curriculum-as-designed* and *desired: tourism in the classroom*

Activity	Development
Ordering food	Elaborate development in role play situations into long meals, outrageous pricing strategies, cold soup, etc.
Ordering drinks	Becomes an excuse to order extravagant amounts of alcohol or role playing the leisure of a street café, in the shade.
Booking travel	Leads to stories of journeys taken, delays experienced, difficulties with numbers and destinations.
Booking tickets	Leads to long imagined journeys, a revisiting of favourite museums, sites.
Way finding	Leads to tales of getting completely lost, and recognition of certain sites on maps brought in to class, or located in the course books. Allows sight seeing to be enacted.
Travelling, airports, train stations, buses, metros	Develops into complicated journeys from home to the destination, cancellations, delays, confusion at ticketing strategies.
Shopping	The tourist language learner buys specific souvenirs, certain types of clothes, acquires an air of fashion and leisure, buys postcards, basics from the chemist such as sun cream, headache tablets.
Complaining	The frustrations when things go wrong on holiday, the disappointments are given articulation in outrage, and in the developing ability to express emotion and opinion.
Videos	May lead to some place and site recognition but generally do not produce much activity and development.

This further highlights the cosmopolitan dimensions at play here – the roots and the wings of that the tourist language learners possess (Beck, 2002). At one and the same time they are moving into another dimension of life, through language, through new literacy and new social practices, some of which they bring to the party themselves, others are imposed, often not directly by their tutors but out of the impersonal discursive formations of the educational systems and their bureaucratic control. There is a continual tension between the places of safety – the literature, the materials, anything that is written, and indeed writing practices themselves – and the sense of taking flight that comes with the clumsy attempts to speak. When the learners are on tourist ground, however, there is also a strong sense of commonality – of shared imaginings, shared experiences, shared memories and shared desires. These will form the focus of further explorations throughout this book.

Conclusions

I have begun to open out the question of the relationship between tourism, learning and languages and to do so by addressing the way in which tourist language learners are educated into the ways of being tourists. It is the argument of this chapter that tourism shapes and changes education in important ways. Not only is tourism a major way in which we encounter other languages and cultures but it is also educates us, even before it becomes a major framing device and agent in tourist language classes. The views of tourism as a 'bad' way of learning and sojourning as 'good' are too simplistic to be of value in attempting to understand the relationship, in educational contexts, between languages and tourism.

When the tourist *curriculum-as-designed* meets the tourist *curriculum-as-desired* possibilities are opened up and are developed for tourist language learners to become *languagers* and they do so as a community of practice (Lave & Wenger, 1991; Wenger, 1999). A space is opened, either through co-operation or through resistance for the *curriculum-as-desired* to be made manifest and this curriculum and its attendant activities bear significant hallmarks of tourist tropes. This desire, in its many modalities, enables the experiences of and the desire for tourism to mingle with the motivations that have brought these tourists to learn tourist languages. The tourists begin to imagine themselves and to practise their knowledge in new ways, in the tourist language, and to do so in ways which reveal creativity, engagement and imagination in their lives as tourists.

How this *curriculum-as-desired* develops and what it comes to contain, tells us much about language destinations, as perceived by tourists and about the development of intercultural communication under such dynamic conditions. In particular the activities and the tactical ways in which the tourist language learners develop these activities, when given the opportunity to expand and to role play or to produce free composition, reveal something of the perceived risks associated with being a tourist in another language. This is the subject of the next chapter.

Chapter 3
Risks

Introducing Risk

'So you are walking around an Italian city and now you need a place to stay.' Our tutor begins to write words and phrases on the board:

Desidera?
Posso auitarla
Vorrei una camera...singola, doppia, a tre letti, con bagno, con doccia, con telefone, con televisione
Per quanti notti? Per tre notti, per una notte, una settimana
'And they might ask you....' She continues writing words on the board:
'Half board' mezza pensione
'Full board' pensione completa
'And you might want to ask if breakfast is included...'
'La prima colazione è compresa' or 'non è compresa'
'And then you'll need to be able to ask how much it will cost.'
Quanto costa per una notte?
She turns back to the class.
'And generally when you go to a hotel they ask you for a document...so they'll ask you...' She writes up words and phrases again.
Ha un documento?
Un passaporto
Una patente

The class suddenly stops writing and a stream of comments, stories and questions comes from the floor. All the bodies of the learners are attentive, fight or flight, eager and keen to share their observations, butting in, engaging fully 'isn't there a law about passports? Last year in Italy I nearly couldn't get in to the hotel because I didn't have mine to hand.'

There is puzzlement and sudden anxiety in the class. The methodical work of acquiring phrases and vocabulary for ordering a hotel room now intersects with the world of official papers and new elements of risk and danger are present as memories and anxieties. This is what we might term the 'future present' tense of tourist learning, the moment where the future is indeed present in the here and now of the common-feeling of the class and its situation in each others' stories, fears and memories. The sense of risk is almost palpable in the room. Together we have left the comfort of a nice 'camera doppia con bagno' and we are facing some risk.

Learning the arts of linguistic survival, through tourist language classes, is an activity founded on the perception of risk. Discourses of risk pervade contemporary western life and risk, as a social phenomenon, has been the subject of several major studies. Mary Douglas extended her now seminal work in *Purity and Danger* (Douglas, 1966) into an analysis of the role of risk in modern societies in *Risk and Blame* in response to the prominence of the risk discourse (Douglas, 1994). Douglas, in charting the politicising of risk argues that:

> Risk is the probability of an event combined with the magnitude of the losses and gains that it will entail. However, our political discourse debases the word. From a complex attempt to reduce uncertainty it has become a decorative flourish on the word 'danger' (Douglas, 1994: 40).

In charting a range of fields of social and cultural life in which discourses on risk abound Douglas demonstrates the extent to which the risk profession, the science of analysing risk, is at odds with perceptions of risk in society. '"The public" definitely does not see risks in the same way as the experts' (Douglas, 1994: 11).

Beck (1992; 2002) in the field of sociology and social theory has devoted considerable attention to the analysis of risk and to the creation of 'Die Risikogesellschaft' (Beck, 1986) or 'risk society'. This is Beck's term for describing the nature of what others have called the postmodern, or post- industrial society. Beck argues that in 'advanced modern societies' the production of wealth goes hand in hand, systematically, with the parallel production of risks (Beck, 1986: 25). Beck argues that through their ability to produce a discourse on risk, to become performative, advanced modern societies become reflexive societies. What in its 1986 version he described as a risk society and as a more or less bounded entity, becomes in Beck's later writings (Beck, 2002) the 'global risk society'. The 'global risk society' generates a wide range of risks and representations, as a cosmopolitan society, under conditions of globalisation and mobility.

Nelson Graburn, too, in the more directly related field of anthropology and tourism has also theorised the links between tourism and 'little' deaths maintaining that when we travel we feel we are putting ourselves, our bodies, at risk (Graburn, 1978). For all the statistics on the dangers of the home the unknown or unfamiliar place fills our consciousness and our preparations for travel. Such imagined risks are part of what Urry terms the 'imagined presences' (Urry, 2000), which form part of Beck's reflexive risk society and which required investigation as part of what Beck terms the 'banal cosmopolitanism' of 'advanced modern' societies:

Who today can still feed himself locally or nationally? The product labels may still try to make us believe it, but from yoghurt, to meat and fruit, to say nothing of the globalized hotchpotch of sausage meat, as consumers we are irredeemably locked into globalized cycles of production and consumption. Food and drink of all countries unite – that has long ago become trite reality (Beck, 2002: 28).

In the tourist language classroom, a place of 'banal cosmopolitanism' to follow Beck, we find the imagined presence of a multitude of risks come to a prominence as past and future are triggered into action. Risk, in many different forms and modalities, is present in the activities of tourist language learners. When risks are generated, through narrative and as discourse, they become social phenomena. For the learners in the instance cited above, the need to find a hotel room accompanies that risk of a night with nowhere to stay. Finding shelter, that basic human need, becomes an imagined and situational need for the tourist language learner, and the vocabulary given and learned in order to mitigate against the risk of being left out in the cold indicates the way the right foreign words come to work as a potential charm to ward off the threat of really being without a bed for the night and of being left as 'homeless, banal cosmopolitan tourists' on the streets of Italy's tourist destinations.

At moments such as the one cited here, of perceived risk, past tense and future tense narratives are generated, which add to the imagined presence of tourism in the tourist language class. Bendix in particular, sees tourism as generative of reflexive narratives of perceived and actual risks:

> Tourism is carried, I have tried to demonstrate, through narratives of multiple order. The reflexive narratives that assess tourism's most frightening spoils and the individual's greatest failures are simultaneously critiques and sources for resistance and change (Bendix, 2002: 478).

The pervasive discourses on risk as loss and its 'management' in society – of health and safety, holiday insurance, news of airline failure, coach crashes, stories of holidays that went wrong – are important aspects of perceived and generated risk in our context of tourist language learning. It is, of course, possible to interpret the presence of concerns relating to risk in a Foucauldian manner, arguing that these tourist subjects are positioned by powerful discourses of bureaucratic control that serve the interests of the risk management and insurance businesses. We can see how repeated stories of disastrous holidays in the media together with the regulation of the tourist industry combine to create a heightened awareness of risk to this precious time of projected happiness in the rhythms of tourist life. More than this, we can show even in a vocabulary lesson about hotel rooms that there is a powerful discursive disciplining of the tourist body occurring that is not directly controlled by any one agent of power or control but that is more diffuse and omnipresent to these tourist learners. Under such a reading there is the strong suggestion, often supported by quantitative research, that the belief in the risk is a chimera, a lucrative myth for those who peddle it.

This is not, however, the only way of interpreting the occurrences of risk and its powerful presence in the tourist classes. A different way of understanding this sense of risk might relate to the potential risk to the tourist as travelling subject, the tourist's sense of self and identity, the tourist's sense of well being, and the accomplishment of the tourist's dreams of happiness. This dimension also relates to the question of why people bother learning a tourist language. In the case of our example of risk here, it also opens a space for discussing what happens when tourist language learners engage with another language and its attendant risk-baggage. By opening out the instances of risk (which encompass the discursive), we can see how ontological, epistemological, material and affective aspects of tourist life come into view. Let us take each of these aspects in turn:

(1) *Ontological risk*: The tourist learners here are fearful of the risk to their subjectivity. If they are asked for papers in the hotel and they are not able to present them then they can no longer readily prove that they are who they say they are. The failure to either understand which papers are required, or to actually produce them, renders their status as tourist and as legitimately mobile subject unstable, even invalid. The tourist, in this moment, risks having her status changed from that of tourist to that of a stateless person, from a person with means, to a person with no bed for the night and consequently, inhabiting other cosmologies that have no call on the known world of tourism for orientation. Further, learning to communicate in the language and with the necessary understanding of the specific laws of the land could readily ameliorate such a situation, explanations being given first hand, no reliance on other people to translate, be they friends or officials. The risk could be diminished here, some face saved and a human identity asserted that transcends categories of subject or even of tourist.

(2) *Epistemological risk:* Anxiety in our tourist language learners around passports and documentation also indicates a wider sense of risk: of not complying with rules because these are not part of one's regular practice of knowledge. That different countries have different laws,

and that one comes to know of the operation of these laws as a citizen in ways not available to the tourist visitor, is the basis for the sense of risk here. Whilst guide books may have a handy reference section with factual knowledge the risk here is that without having developed a *habitus* for appropriate and legal action though citizenship, one is vulnerable, as a tourist, to ignorance in terms of factual and in terms of practical knowledge. This risk then intersects with the ontological dimension threatening to turn tourists from law abiding citizens into potential criminals, even prisoners, where ignorance is commonly known to be no defence, or at least this is the fear. Language learning again operates here as a significant gain, able to protect and to offer access to knowledges and its practices that could be occluded by remaining in one's native tongue. It operates as magic.

(3) *Material risk*: This risk in this instance is also a material risk. Passports are intimate and vital possessions for tourists. They make tourism across international borders possible. They contain personal details of height, date of birth, photo-ID etc. and these possessions, whilst often languishing in drawers at home, become intimate and protected documents for a tourist. Accessories designed to protect and to transport such documents form part of the tourist experience. Hotels offer tourists safes for their papers further emphasising the risk to the self if these are lost. The puzzlement and anxiety expressed by our tourist language learners also relates to the surrendering of these intimate, material possessions. Giving up such documentation is perceived as risky and involves trust of other people, of the strangers servicing the holiday. But this material risk extends into other materialist categories most notably that of *linguistic capital*, as defined by Bourdieu. Here not only is there the risk of losing material documents but also of being rendered incapable of action because the language one has learnt is not sufficient to the task of preventing risk in this situation. One does not have the necessary *linguistic currency* here. This represents a perceived loss of status from tourist qua 'banal cosmopolitan' to stateless person.

(4) *Affective risk*: Finally, we see a manifestation here of the risk that the happiness and well being so strongly associated with being on holiday could evaporate. Not having the where with all to find a bed, not managing to do this properly, not being understood or not understanding, worrying about one's passport or other documentation all risk jeopardising the enjoyment. Equally the risks to self of speaking another tongue can operate here, as a potential gain in the form of an 'affective talisman'.

Risk, then, plays an important and varied role in the tourist language learning context. It looms large at key junctures out of the structure of the class. It is present both in the *curriculum-as-designed* but also in the *curriculum-in-action* (Barnett & Coate, 2005). It is one of the aspects of learning that reinforces the work of bothering with the language. It is brought in to the learning context as part of tourism, as closely linked to memories and to the imaginings of those learning the language. Further, I would argue that the tourist language, out of the thick of the language learning situation, takes on a distinctive character and operates as magical talisman with the potential to protect and save from risk, if not from danger (Ong, 1982). As such it follows the pattern, which is one of the sustained points of the argument in this book, of the move into a more oral mode of being – common to Ong's oral cultures.

To understand why this might be, how language comes to have such a magical function in the context of manifestations of risk in tourist language learning, we need to mobilise frameworks that go beyond those of the operations of discursive power and that address the everyday contexts of risk perception, as well as risk narration. For this let me now turn to examine the contributions from the anthropology of perception.

Perception

In recent years the traditional categories used by anthropologists for understanding how we as human beings both perceive and make sense of the world have come under scrutiny. Perception has traditionally been analysed via the Cartesian dualism of a powerful mind processing information in flux 'out there' that falls onto our senses and then constructs it into an ordered schema. Ingold (2000) issues a compelling critique of this Cartesian model when it comes to understanding the ways in which we, as human beings, perceive our environments.

The Cartesian dualism, the separation of the mind as cognitive processor from the body and the devaluing of the body's place in perception, Ingold argues, has developed over a long intellectual period. In anthropology it is made manifest in Durkheim's opposition to psychological explanations for social phenomena and is traced through the work of Edmund Leach and Mary Douglas into the work of the 1970s and 1980s when Kluckhohn, Kroeber and Geertz separated out culture from behaviour. Alongside this development came the later development in intercultural communication and management studies from Hall and Hofstede where we find *The Software of the Mind* and the triumph of the view of the minds of individuals as powerful computers decoding the rules of culture 'out there' (Hofstede, 1996).

To such influential figures in the fields of social and cultural anthropology Ingold brings the contributions of Pierre Bourdieu and his concept of *habitus* together with work from ecological psychology and the work of James Gibson. Both figures, in their different ways, Ingold argues, have taken action or engagement with the world as their starting point and enable different ways of understanding our perception of the environment.

Bourdieu's work and nuanced use of the concept of *habitus* and of *bodily hexis* has been influential across the humanities and social sciences. By *habitus* Bourdieu understands a set of learned dispositions for action in the world. These dispositions are structured, durable, generative and inculcated (Bourdieu, 1991). They relate to the complex ways in which we both learn to act in certain regularised and identifiable ways in the world, but also how we may add to those ways and adapt to other circumstances. Bourdieu, in his own work, was interested in, for instance, how it is people come to be clearly identifiable as members of the aristocracy, or of the bourgeoisie, for instance. What is it about the way we learn to speak, dress, eat, decorate our homes, to move our bodies that symbolises our membership of certain social groups? The way in which one learns, durably, to embody one's body in the world is what Bourdieu refers to as *bodily hexis*: 'Bodily hexis is political mythology realised, *em-bodied* [Bourdieu's emphasis], turned into walking, and thereby of feeling and thinking' (Bourdieu, 1991: 13). Consequently the body indexes an incorporated history of social education, and, importantly here it is worth reminding ourselves that this includes language as embodied.

Bourdieu's work should not be taken at face value. It has been the subject of much attention and indeed the linguistic anthropologist Brenda Farnell maintains that Bourdieu's notions of *habitus* and *bodily hexis* remain bound into Cartesian frameworks:

> Without any deeper understanding of the performative power of action and vocal signs as equally available resources for meaningful action in social life, Bourdieu is stuck on the twin river-banks of objectivism and subjectivism. We can characterize this by saying that although Bourdieu's theoretical resources allow him to include talk *about* the body, he is unable to include talk *from* the body (Farnell, 2000: 413).

Farnell's critique rests on the lack of embodied dynamism in Bourdieu's model and she offers an alternative view 'which locates agency in the causal powers and capacities of embodied persons to engage in dialogic, signifying acts' (Farnell, 1994: 396; Farnell, 2000). For our purposes, and a point to which I shall return later, Bourdieu's link of *habitus* and *bodily hexis* to language and *linguistic capital* provides an important frame of analysis of tourist language learning. Farnell's revisions, however, enable us to think in terms more of movement and dynamism – of what I am terming here *linguistic currency* – in place of Bourdieu's concept of *linguistic capital*. For Ingold, however, and to continue this summary, these observations on embodiment point to the way a history of bodily training means that our senses are attuned to what the environment around us – social and material – may afford, in different ways.

Through his reading of the work of James Gibson, Ingold demonstrates how, far from consisting of the operation of the mind upon data coming in to the body from 'out there', the very 'intentional *movement* [my emphasis] of the whole being (indissolubly body and mind) in its environment' (Ingold, 2000: 166) is the root of perceptual activity. This includes 'talk from the body' – language, new language and changing language habits. The perceiver is not static but moves. For Ingold there are three important implications in Gibson's work for the anthropology of perception:

(1) Perception is a 'mode of action not a prerequisite for action' (Ingold, 2000: 166). The mind is not a processor for sense data from the body, but is an active and exploratory process involving the whole being.
(2) Direct perception is '*practical*, it is knowledge about what an environment offers [in Gibson's terms what it *affords*] for the pursuance of the action in which the perceiver is currently engaged' (p. 166).
(3) 'There is no limit to what can be perceived. [...] Novel perceptions arise from creative acts of discovery rather than imagining, and the information on which they are based is available to anyone attuned to pick it up' (p. 166). Consequently, argues Ingold:

> [...] one learns to perceive in the manner appropriate to a culture, not by acquiring programmes conceptual schemata for organising sensory data [...] but by 'hands-on' training in everyday tasks whose successful fulfillment requires a practiced ability to notice and to respond *fluently* [my emphasis] to salient aspects of the environment. In short, learning is not transmission of information but – in Gibsons's (1979: 254) words – an 'education of attention'. As such, it is inseparable from a person's life in the world, and indeed continues for as long as he or she lives (Ingold, 2000: 166–7).

To apply these insights to our instance of puzzlement and anxiety in the face of a *perceived* risk in the language class we might note the following.

Firstly, the perception of an *imagined* if not an actual risk was associated with a few words being written up on the blackboard and a comment from the tutor. The fear of not having the correct documents to reserve a hotel room was one learned of via experience or via the imagination and

the stories of others and these were then collected together in this particular class, in this social group. These then triggered 'talk from the body' in
the form of perceived risks, and concentrated action, in the form of tourist
language learning.

> *'And generally when you go to a hotel they ask you for a document...so they'll ask*
> *you...'*
> Our tutor writes up words and phrases again:
> *Ha un documento?*
> *Un passaporto*
> *Una patente*

Perceiving the risk was in itself a *mode of dynamic action* for us as language
learning tourists, and an important one. The response to the perceived
risk – imagined, experienced, remembered and potentially material –
caused bodies to move – fight or flight, pupils to dilating, tongues sticking, a leaning forward, a butting in as part of an active and exploratory
process, involving the whole being. It caused us to reach for the Italian,
tourist language, from out of our bodies.

Secondly, in this instance of a directly perceived risk, we see practical
knowledge *and a perceived lack of practical knowledge – linguistic, cultural,*
legal, material – in action. In short, these learners want to know what to say,
what to take, what to do, how to do it in order to negotiate an environment to which their senses are attuned as tourists, but only as tourists, and
in which they are clearly aware of the limitations of such an attunement,
for getting by and for getting a bed. As a tourist language learner I was
risking my English for the sake of epistemological and ontological gains in
tourist Italian.

Thirdly, this instance is an example of a creative act of common discovery. Ingold, we may recall, argues that: 'Novel perceptions arise from creative acts of discovery rather than imagining' (Ingold, 2000: 166). I would
argue that the acts of imagining triggered by the perception of risk – of
imagining oneself out on the streets, spending hours looking for a bed,
suddenly accosted by members of *la Polizia* and of having heard tall tales,
read stories, watched films or documentaries – are as real as actual acts of
discovery. They are Urry's 'imagined presences' (Urry, 2000), together
with the imagined gain of using Italian. Ingold is, I believe, correct in his
thesis on perception, but he privileges the physical over the imaginative in
his desire to ensure that these do not equate with a dualism of the body
versus the mind. What this instance of risk demonstrates, I believe, is that
creative acts of imagining involve the whole being, the *bodily hexis* and
habitus of here the tourist qua language learner.

What these tourist learners are eager for is not facts and information, but a way of developing a new *bodily hexis*, of practising words in their mouths and feeling the practise change the rhythms of their bodies in response to the request for 'une passaporto'. They are keen for such a request to be one to which they can respond *fluently*. They want to be able to respond easily with 'Si, bene, ha un passaporto. Con bagno? Si, con bagno, bene, grazie.'

Real and Imagined Risk

Risk then, for purpose of the argument, is perceived and it takes different forms. Thus far I have focused upon the instance of the perceived risk, of not having the correct documents to ensure the reservation of a room. This triggers deeper fears and perceptions of risk that instantiate the fragility of the tourist subject and the perceived shallow nature of tourist knowledges and perceived skills required for dealing with difficulties when they present themselves. It is important, however, to note that risk is manifest both as *real* and as *imagined*. The response of these learners of tourist Italian is a response that points to their own sense of ignorance, vulnerability and potential danger in situations that are conjured for them in their imaginations as they are engaged in the learning process. The risk is not present in any material way, emerging out of their own environment. It is present in an imagined, remembered and collected form, but is no less 'real' or 'true' for tourist learners than its actual manifestation. Indeed, we might argue, that the risk *feels* greater for these tourists when it takes imagined form than when it is immediate. It is not a real time, actual occurrence, but a concentration of possibilities fuelled by the dynamics of the risk society and its reflexive dimensions (Beck, 1992).

We may recall that Ingold maintains that perception is a mode of action not a prerequisite for action. Even without the necessary vocabulary to negotiate the perceived risk the tourist language learners are already acting in the tourist world they imagine. Earlier in the chapter I evoked the possibility of the language being learned, Italian in this instance, as acting rather like a charm that can *act on* the perceived risk and reduce it or even prevent it occurring. I wish to explore this aspect of language further here, in connection with both the perception of risk and the impulse to language as modes of action in the world.

It is important to note that, despite appearances and even the presentation of Tourist Italian as part of a discrete, preparatory, non-tourist, mode of action, the language classes are already places of leisure, of active touristic imagination, narration and memory, and they are already a mode of action in their own right. The rehearsal space of the classroom (see Chapter 8), the role plays, drills, exercises, games, are not 'second best', but they are part of the practice of what Ingold terms enskillment, or Schechner regards as a 'lengthening strip' of action (Schechner, 1985). These are also lively times, times when language is already being lived socially, physically and imaginatively. This is of the 'quick'.

> *The tutor winds down the blackboard teaching and gives us our instructions. We are to stand up, walk around the classroom and attempt to book hotel rooms from those we meet. I meet an Australian woman in her mid fifties. She asks me what I would like and together, with much humour, we begin to order a room and to prevent each other from having that prized room by using the words on the board. There is much laughter in the room and the seriousness of the moments preceding this exercise have evaporated into play and the clumsiness of using the new words and phrases.*

As the learners perceive a risk through the mention of documents their response becomes more animated, as noted earlier. There is a sense here that what we have as learners is not sufficient for the imagined circumstances. The words on the board act to calm us down and to put in place the first necessary tools for negotiating the risk. The words and the rudimentary grammatical structures that may hold them together lead, in the ensuing role plays, to considerable clumsiness in handling the necessary constructions. As learners we *feel* more in control once we are handling these words and playing with the risk ourselves. The repetition of the role play helps us, we become more confident, our sentences lengthen and we are able to create, through drama, scenarios that are ridiculous in the extent of the risk we present to each other. We call the police, deny each other rooms and laugh. This is risky too, we risk ridicule, but there is much worth bothering with in the risk, if we are to gain the language we are reaching for.

By having the language and taking possession of it with our whole person – as phonetic practice, as part of our breath and the movement of our tongues against our teeth, as part of the slow, fumbling gloopiness of attempting to utter the words that are required by our feelings and needs in the situation we are role playing – we gain a sense of inhabiting the new context and the role it requires. By playing around at the extremes of our perceived risk, by mocking our own powers of imagination, we are able to somehow tame the risk, ridicule it and ourselves, and we manage this only when we leave our native speech – that of questioning and anxiety – and attempt to tackle the risk through play and through another magical, risk-minimising language.

Survival Charms

I could make much of the role of play in this context, and this may indeed be appropriate and is a point to which I shall return (see Chapter 8). For now I wish to focus on the magical role played by language. In *The Spell of the Sensuous* David Abram (1997) makes a powerful case for the connection of language and translation with that of magicians and shamans. Shamans, like magicians, he understands to be skilled, practised communicators with other worlds. Shamans often inhabit the edges of their towns and are called upon to both prevent and to ameliorate the threat of risk from outside, or to calm the fears of risk. Their ritual roles, as liminal beings, are well documented in the anthropological literature. They parallel the roles ascribed to translators, tricksters, fraudsters, magicians.

In his work on orality and literacy Ong (1982) maintains:

> The fact oral peoples commonly and in all likelihood universally consider words to have magical potency is clearly tied in, at least unconsciously, with their sense of the word as necessarily spoken, sounded, hence power-driven. Deeply typographical folk forget to think of words as primarily oral, as events, and hence as necessarily powered (Ong, 1982: 32–3).

Tourist language learning is primarily a move out of literacy – where the written words act as a script to be learned – and into modes of orality, modes in which perceived risks may indeed be checked by the spoken, sounded, power-driven word (see Chapter 4).

It is my contention, following Abram and Ong, that language learning equates, analogously, to magic, in the specific contexts of risk here. Magic, I am understanding here as an action that either 'transforms' or 'traditions' and that involves either a loss of dimensions of the self (a suspension of the native tongue) and a gain of new dimensions (here, Italian phrases). Learning a language and being able to move easily, smoothly, after much practice and rehearsal, does lead to the fluent and fluid negotiation of tricky communicative encounters when moving in worlds that one does not normally inhabit but that one has learned to inhabit. This may, in Bourdieusian terms, lead over time to the development of a new *habitus* and *bodily hexis* out of the encounters with this new environment and all that it affords. In Farnell's view, however, it indexes the dynamic way in which human actors speak from the body into the world, through their 'real activity as such' – here of tourist language learning. Such a view of speaking as 'quick', real action of and *from* the body allows me to move from speaking of linguistic capital to speaking of the dynamics of linguistic currency. It brings to the fore the ways in which currents of fragmented, stumbling tourist language speech *from* the body change the possibilities for action and the nature of perceived risks.

Linguistic Capital and Linguistic Currency

Capital, we know, has a magic status for capitalist societies, or so argued Marx, most notably in his view of the commodity fetish. Capital is given in exchange for goods, goods are alientated from the labour that produced them. As we know, Bourdieu's analysis of forms of capital extends the notion of capital from that of economic capital to other areas of symbolic and cultural life. Capital for Bourdieu may be linguistic, cultural and symbolic, as well as economic. Its effects feel no less 'magical', in the sense of enabling things to happen that would be impossible without such capital, for those who either possess it or are perceived to possess it. Languages, however, are hard to alienate from those who speak them. In many senses languages are inalienable goods. They may indeed be technologised and recorded and may be bought and sold in that sense, but it is not possible to learn a tourist language and then to lose that language in exchange for capital. What does accrue to the tourist language learner, however, is social status in the form of linguistic capital, but when crossing linguistic boundaries, when acting as a tourist, this social status is worth little in terms of linguistic capital.

Bauman, understanding modernity to be a 'melting process' makes a clear distinction between the heavy modernity of the past, when institutions, communities and industries were firmly attached to place, and with the contemporary 'liquid' age, which sees these institutions dissolve and reform as mobile, fluid, intangible:

> Fluids travel easily. They 'flow', 'spill', 'run out', 'splash', 'pour over', 'leak', 'flood', 'spray', 'drip', seep', 'ooze'; unlike solids they are not easily stopped – they pass around some obstacles dissolve some others and bore or soak their through others still. From the meeting with solids they emerge unscathed, while the solids they have met, if they stay solid, are changed – get moist or drenched. [...] These are reasons to consider 'fluidity' or 'liquidity' as fitting metaphors when we wish to grasp the nature of the present (Bauman, 2000: 2).

The argument put forward by Bauman regarding liquid modernity allows us to see the ease of flow of capital, single currencies, international credit cards, the flow of tourist bodies, etc., as having implications for linguistic capital. Following Bourdieu's analysis of the way in which communication functioned in 19th century (Bourdieu, 1991: 46) and his analysis of *linguistic capital*, we may extend the notion of *capital* – a fixed notion – to one of *currency*, which indicates a liquidity of flow and an embodied dynamism.

Consequently, in this context of tourist language learning, rather than speaking just of linguistic capital, I advance the idea of *linguistic currency* as a perceived (and actual) minimiser of risk. A loss in one currency is a gain in another. Gaining in *linguistic currency* is one of the reasons why tourist language learners bother, and in bothering they come, in the situations where their *linguistic currency* functions, to gain also in social status. They are able, also, potentially to act on behalf of others, of friends, members of their families or other tourists.

Currency, like luggage, comes in to being when we move. We may recall that for Ingold at the root of *perceptual activity* is the 'intentional *movement* [my emphasis] of the whole being (indissolubly body and mind) in its environment' (Ingold, 2000: 166). There is much movement in this instance. It begins with the movement of people from their everyday contexts into the environment of the tourist language class, and from there other movements present themselves, most notably that of moving through the imagination into the place where the language will be used for 'real' as well as the movement of the learners around the classroom in the role play. What each environment affords, as a place for *languaging, as an engaged, sensory mode of action*, as the persons move in to it, differs as does the usefulness of the currency.

In a largely anglophone environment the fact that these learners now have some Italian remains largely invisible and is of little practical or even symbolic use. The fact that someone 'speaks' Italian is a matter of mild interest and although there are contexts in which this language may be used in social life in Scotland, they remain largely domestic and intimate – family relations, perhaps ordering food in Glaswegian Italian restaurants, or formal – in the sense of being bounded by the time and space of the language classroom. The linguistic capital is not of much use, it is rather like the kinds of monetary currency that one saves in a drawer for one's next trip and will bring out when it can be put into reliable and genuine use. For the linguistic capital of Italian learned to become linguistic currency of any significance, movement is required. The movement that most regularly affords such an opportunity for capital conversion is that of travel, and for the most part, of tourism.

Having the right *linguistic currency* – rather than capital – though there can be no currency without the base capital, in the first place – is important for our tourist language learners. It can have quite magical effects. It can charm away perceived risks, and actual risks, just as the right currency of money can work in tricky situations. Magic is the effect on other perceivers but, as Peter Brook (1993) maintains, in circumstances of long learning, rehearsal, sifting, weighing, pondering and lingering over words and actions – such as those required for a successful play or those required for a fluent use of a language – there are actually no secrets, there is just a continuing and ongoing relationship with all the environment of the language and the world affords. And this relationship to risk, as we shall see, is not neutral.

Politics of Languages

There is a considerable political dimension at work in the perception of risk. Ingold has been criticised for the lack of political dimensions to his work on the anthropology of perception (Ingold, 2000). Bourdieu, however, to whom Ingold owes a considerable debt, discusses the potential social inequalities that manifest themselves when we come to consider the idea of *linguistic capital*. In his attempts to understand how certain people come to occupy symbolically significant roles and have considerable power and status he demonstrates the kinds of durable learning that are required. It is very difficulty to break out of the linguistic dispositions one has learned as a child, although there are interesting exceptions and 'outliers' who are able to do this, that emerge from empirical studies of language development and acquisition. Accent, dialect, lexis and what we might term phonetic comportment all impact on the way we perceive those we encounter, and how we order them (Douglas & Isherwood, 1996). There can be considerable symbolic violence present in these orderings, as many notable theorists have shown (Bourdieu, 1991; Derrida, 1996; Foucault, 1980; Spivak, 1999; Giroux, 2001).

> Scott has heavily accented English. He has grown up in Scottish working-class environments, has a solid job, lives out in one of the more desirable housing schemes but is acutely aware of his lack of so-called 'good' or 'educated' English. In his home environment he blends in with others. In the classroom he feels odd, different and uneducated. The language being learned is new to everyone and although there are some middle-class, educated linguistics in the class the language is new for all of them. People progress with this language more through determination and motivation than through any particularly innate aptitude. They want this language because it can give ways into living in other ways and other worlds. Scott finds himself enjoying the new language. He finds that he is able to hold his own with others, and, more to the point the other language isn't marking him out in the same ways as his native tongue appears to do. He relaxes, brings sweets to the class, and speaks.

Note how the symbolic violence that can be manifest with regard to *linguistic capital* changes when we speak of *linguistic currency*. It is possible, in ways rarely manifest in first language acquisition, to escape the *bodily hexis* of the first language through acquisition, in a perceiving environment, of a second. This is the way that languaging can enable a critical literacy, one which prompts transformation through the cultural meanings and practices of different groups. The subtleties and orderings of one social and cultural, and in particular class, context are erased in the face of the communicative realities of another (Giroux, 2001: 231). Now all are speakers of a foreign tongue, the social relations are erased and the slate is wiped cleaned, at least linguistically as a new *habitus* and *bodily hexis* develop as a new language grows. But more than this, and following Farnell, Scott is speaking in new ways, from the body. There is movement occurring, and this points to more than a change of *habitus*. This is the magic in the face of perceived risk and of symbolic violence.

Conclusions

Language learning diminishes risks that are ontological, epistemological, material and affective. It does so by enabling the development of a different *habitus* both at home, in the language classroom and as a tourist. It is, following Douglas and Beck, not a neutral social phenomenon but one that is generated by and generative of advanced modern societies. Tourist language learning may be considered as one of the ways in which risk is addressed, narrated and generated. Risk is one of the reasons for bothering to learn another language. The important point here, in the context of perceived risk and its dimensions, is that already in the social context of the language classroom a new *habitus* both emerges and works a particular kind of magic, social, bodily, perceptual, real for the relations at play in the time and space of the classroom and for those that are imagined and role played as part of tourism.

Risk then, and its manifestation in the tourist language classroom, is not a fixed thing, nor is it simply constructed as a discourse of control of the subject. One leaves behind some well-known risks and one plunges into others. Automatic assumptions and gestures are suspended. Risk indexes a complex range of ways tourist language learners perceive their world and that of the tourist world, how they act in the world as 'banal cosmopolitans' to use Beck's term, and then respond to its phenomena – be they remembered, imagined or concrete. Risk is imagined as part of the other tourist presences that are made manifest in the reflexive work of learning a tourist language. But risk in and of its self is not sufficient to explain why people bother to learn another language, in marginalised contexts, where little social capital accrues to the activity, despite the potential exchange rates offered by linguistic currency. Nor is the notion of a risk society sufficient, I would argue, to encompass the many other domains of 'banal', everyday life, which are brought into play through the education of attention, and the speaking from the body that occur when tourists learn and speak other languages.

To demonstrate other dimensions to the phenomenon of tourist language learning that may begin in the context of risk, but which extend beyond it, I now turn to the risk of 'getting lost' and to the perennial activity in tourist language classes of learning to follow directions.

Chapter 4
Way Finding

'We are all on the move and have been for centuries, dwelling in travel' says Clifford (1997: 2). Clifford's view of 'dwelling in travel' returns us to the dwelling perspective, and to the ways in which tourist language learners let other languages dwell in them, alongside others. In *Monolingualism of the Other* Derrida refers to his own monolingualism as follows: 'I am monolingual. My monolingualism dwells, and I call it my dwelling; it feels like one to me, and I remain in it and inhabit it. It inhabits me' (Derrida, 1996: 1).

The question that I am pursuing here relates to the movement of the whole being, through the learning, the 'letting dwell', to return to Heidegger's phrase (Heidegger, 1971), of other languages and, in this particular chapter, how the learning of language in the context of way finding, and following directions changes the way in which the world is perceived and inhabited.

Learning to ask for and follow directions and get to where you have learned you should be plays a key part in the development of a tourist vocabulary. How to gain a sense of place in an unknown environment brings into view the maps and stories used in orienting the tourist around sites and necessities. This also involves the kinds of maps and directions used as examples for learning and the assumptions about the tourist experience and tourist language that these reveal. Language learning as tourists, as we have seen, shows us something of the possibilities of tourism for changing *habitus*, *hexis*, into dynamic movement, bodying-forth.

Learning how to move around, how to get from A to B, how to arrive and depart, how to show up in the right place, at the right time, in a strange tourist environment, so that the sites are actually seen, is an important part of tourism and of the imagined presence of tourism in the language class. Guide books, as apodemic literature, that is to say a literature that instructs, is based upon enabling this movement between co-ordinates (Jack & Phipps, 2003). Maps of the city, timetables, maps of countries and regions are all important geographic matter incorporated into the guide books for tourists. We might make a simple distinction between map-users and those who ask others for directions and it would no doubt be possible to relate this to a taxonomy of tourist-types, but this is not my concern here.

Ingold, in developing his dwelling perspective on perception, proposes a *relational* model as opposed to more genealogical, point-to-point models of connection and communication: 'Every being is instantiated in the world as the line of its own movement and activity: not a movement from point to point, as though the life-course were already laid out as the route between them, but a continual 'moving around', or coming and going' (Ingold, 2000: 142).

I am interested in what happens when people imagine 'moving around', remember 'moving around', and learn how to use spoken language as a way of finding their way. When learning to speak another language, to move around inside another language, the way in which the world is perceived and related to changes. The experience of sitting in a café where the language is a closed curtain of incomprehension, to the gradual movement into dwelling in and being inhabited by that language changes the relationsip to the phenomena of the most everyday things, such as the ordering of a cup of coffee, or the finding of one's way.

Maps and directions are important features of the tourist language class. In any beginners' language course one of the early lessons, whether aimed at tourists or not, will relate to knowing one's left from one's right, and being able to explain the precise location of buildings on a town plan and of how to reach, say, the post office if one is starting from the railway station. The *curriculum-as-designed* (Barnett & Coate, 2005), which we discussed in Chapter 2, introduces learning to ask for directions as one of its primary features, after learning to say one's name and to say hello, and invariably before learning how to secure food and shelter.

Again, drawing on Ingold, we might consider this kind of knowledge as a relational form of knowledge:

> If, however, as the relational model implies, the source of cultural knowledge lies not in the heads of predecessors but in the world that they point out to you – if, that is, one learns by discovery while following in the *path* of an ancestor – then words, too, must gather their meanings from the contexts in which they are uttered. Moving together along a trail or encamped at a particular place, companions draw each other's attention, through speech or gesture, to salient features of their shared environment (Ingold, 2000: 146).

Ingold, following Merleau-Ponty (Merleau-Ponty, 2002), makes an important distinction in his analysis of a relational model of the environment between that of the *globe perspective* and that of the *lifeworld perspective* (Ingold, 2000: 209). He maintains that our modern perspectives of the environment are such that we no longer see ourselves as dwelling and moving in the midst of the lifeworld, the environment, but that we view the environment from the circumference, as if it were a globe and we are positioned outside. In what follows I will show how this view relates to the use of maps and directions in language learning and in the experience of way finding in the tourist environment. Rather than making a simple distinction between maps as literacy objects and asking for directions as the practice of orality, I wish to consider the processes of transition, from literacy practices into the oral modes of being a tourist, the trusting of people rather than of the map-makers technology. I do not see these processes as linear, point-to-point relationships but ones that change, dynamically, as people's relationships with maps, language, and the environment change.

Ingold does not present the globe and the lifeworld as in opposition one to another, but rather, he maintains that 'for any society at any period of its history, we may expect one perspective to be ascendant, and the other to be associated with its more less muted undercurrent' (Ingold, 2000: 216–17). I follow this line of reasoning and contend that in tourism it is the more muted, lifeworld undercurrent that is able to be ascendant. It is not, therefore, just a matter of the period of history, but the modality of everyday life that affects the perception of the environment. Our perceptions are modified through being and engaging with the lifeworld as languaging tourists. Some of this movement may be traced in the activities of tourist language learning.

Learning to Follow Directions

We have brought along tourist maps to our class today. The maps have come from files, drawers, carefully stored souvenirs of past trips to Italy. Our tutor had suggested we might bring these along to learn about directions. I managed to forget mine, though I do have maps that I saved from halcyon days of exploring in Rome, Firenze, Siena, Assisi. Maps of small towns on the itineraries of certain types of holidays to Italy are spread out in front of us on the tables and suddenly we are all inside each others memories of holidays. There is warmth in the sun, there are lemons on the trees and the stories flood out. Many of those in this class are friends and travelling companions: 'Do you remember when we got lost looking for the Therme?' Pat uses the Italian word for baths, thermal springs. The class are mixing more appropriate words for places into their stories, interlingually, evocative, situated.

Our tutor gives us the language – a travel language we might say – we need for the exercise:

'Dov'è la statione, per favore' – where is the station please?
'Scusi' – excuse me
'Avanti diritto' – go straight
'Giri a sinistra' – go left
'Giri a destra' – go right

'*Attravesi il passagio pedonale*' – *cross at the pelican crossing*
'*Vada/arrive a semaforo*' – *go to the lights*
'*Alla chiesa*' – *to the church*
'*All'angolo*' – *to the corner*
'*Segua la strada*' – *follow the street*
'*Per 100 metri*' – *for 100 metres*
'*Prenda la prima strada a destra*' – *take the first right*
'*È sulla sinistra*' – *it's on the left*
'*È qui*' – *it's here*
'*È qui vincino*' – *it's nearby.*

And we begin to lead each other around real places, left, right, straight ahead, oppo-site, behind you, over the bridge. For me the exercise is both real and imagined. I am inhabiting a world being vividly narrated to me by my partner in learning, whose map is before us, but I have never been here. I cannot see this place in my mind's eye, just the lines of the map. It could be just a made up text book map, if it weren't for the warmth and energy of life it is evoking for my learning companion. I'm looking at this town from outside, objectively, in the way Ingold would describe as looking at the environment as a globe rather than as a lifeworld, and yet in the exchange between us and the careful keeping of this souvenir map, this artefact of memory and practical use, I am also able to enter this world as a partial lifeworld. If I ever visit Montecatini Therme I will think of Pat, I will have already visited it in my imagination.

In this example we see a variety of relationships unfolding in the language class: relationships to the immediate interlocutor, relationships across the room with the person who had shared this holiday experience with Pat. In addition to this we see relationships to objects, personal souvenirs of past trips that trigger stories in themselves and whose trails may be traced through object biographies which intermingle with those of tourists (Lury, 1996). The relationships are also ones to the experience of way finding in a tourist desti-nations, to the memories of this shared experience, to the cobble stones, the park, the thermal baths, the sunshine, to the telling of the incidental stories of the trip. And in addition they are relationships with the tourist map, seen from above, from within a global perspective, but from within a language practising activity. These relationships are expressed in the narratives that are triggered, and that in themselves give tourist language learners the change to 'move around' inside both languages in play, and in time, past, present and future, as well as marking their trails with objects that have been actually present in the events. These objects open a space for fiction, as does the activity of learning to ask for directions, emplotting, to use Ricoeur's term (Ricoeur, 1984), the narratives and the tourist imagination.

Michael Cronin (2000: 22) describes pertinently the way in which the privileging of the 'gaze' in tourism studies, notably by Urry (1990), misses 'the more fundamental level at which travel and language are connected'.

Drawing on the linguistic idea of 'displacement' – the ability to talk about things that are distant in place or time – Cronin demonstrates the extent to which an oral tradition of travel narrative constructs our cultural expectations of what might be seen as flat, experienced in other times and places:

> Though people may visit 'sights' they have already 'seen' them in language. This is not to say that visitors will not be disappointed or excited by what they see or real travel is a waste of time but that the places already feature in the prior 'oral tradition' of travel which has staked out the landmarks of cultural identity (Cronin, 2000: 22).

One of the key findings of my recent work with Gavin Jack (Jack & Phipps, 2005) was the way in which tourism, in the contexts of our research, privileged oral as opposed to the written forms of narrative. We were able to identify a particular inversion from everyday life, where written narrative is the privileged form. What we find in this example of the learning of words for directions in this language classroom is both displacement and oral narrative. The Italian words that are crucially and metonymically associated with this particular destination – Italy, Montecatini Therme, with Pat and her friend and the humour of the memory of the this shared experience – demonstrate the way language – oral and written – takes us places in labyrinthine, relational ways. The displacement operates in both the English of the story telling and also in the Italian that triggers memories, powerfully and with appropriate language of the struggle to ask for directions, the fun and the triumph and the difficulty of using Italian to find the way. The narratives and the actual learning activities are examples of a dynamic, relational process with the tourist past, present and future.

Following Ingold we may argue here that when we bother to learn how to ask for directions in another language our situation in the world, the nature of our dwelling, is changed. In addition our sense of direction and movement is changed and our relationship to maps and guide books and to tourist sights is modified by the heightened awareness of place and environment that comes when imagined objects take on a new linguistic form and when their presence is heightened by their being spoken of from the body. As a space is opened for narrative, so the narrative in turn opens a space for movement.

Pat is asserting a very particular role in our task with respect to the activity of narration. It is not equal to the task of role playing way finding, where we pick a building on a made-up map and ask for directions from it to another building on the map, taking turns to move across a map that has no connotations for us. In this instance, with the regalia of travel souvenir maps spread across our desk, Pat has more to offer, she is, in Cronin's words, 'paying her dues to the community through narrative' (Cronin, 2000: 23).

> If bringing back souvenirs can be seen as an act of reparation for the act if betrayal in leaving your native family/community/environment, then the traveller's tale could be interpreted as a form of symbolic mediation that restitutes the gift of story for the temporary loss of the person gone travelling (Cronin, 2000: 23).

This also accords with Bendix's work on narration and tourism and the powerful way in which tourism and narration intertwine, meaning that Pat is continuing here in the tradition of 'travel and tourism's long narrative history' and the tourism industries selling of 'narratable experience' adding to the 'mind-boggling thicket of intersecting and intermeshing stories offered to the potential traveler' (Bendix, 2002: 475).

There is, here, however, a further interesting aspect. Until two weeks previously I had never met Pat. We met in this class as strangers. We have tourist Italian learning in common. We both inhabit the same city. Our *habitus*, following Bourdieu here, is different, as is our generational status. Pat does not have the *habitus* of a linguist – she is not quick to make sense of the written and oral patterning that is second nature to me now, my own enduring and learned disposition as a language professional. I have never *felt* betrayed, as Cronin terms it, by Pat's trip to Montecatini Therme – I never had a sense of temporary loss because she had gone travelling. In the context of this gathered, temporary social group of tourist language learners the gift of oral narration and the experience of loss are ambivalent, and are not the same as in closely bonded familial or community relations. My loss here is more of a lack, a lack of knowledge, a lack of a guide, a lack of someone who can interpret the signs on the ground or the map for me and help it make sense in the language I am learning for the very purpose of being able to get through from A to B.

Such a sense of lack, which bothering to learn a language begins to go some way to address, cannot easily be interpreted in terms of *habitus*. Language learning, as we discussed in the previous chapter, begins to escape from concepts such as *habitus* and becomes, turning here to Farnell again (Farnell, 2000), a bodying-forth, a dynamic embodied 'moving around' that occurs as tourist language learners begin to speak the language, to inhabit it and to let it dwell, from the body, from their place in the world. How then do these dynamic and relational dimensions of maps, directions, tourist imaginings and stories interweave in tourist *languaging* practices, when the language learning contexts are left behind? To consider the transitions between literacy practices and oral practices, the transitions for tourist language learning to languaging, the transitions from imagining or remembering or narrating tourism, to being tourists, let us turn to the tourist map.

The Tourist Map

> *Ordinary wayfinding, then, more closely resembles storytelling than map-using.*
> (Ingold, 2000: 219)

Much ink has been spilled in recent years 'against' the map (Anderson, 1991). De Certeau argues that:

> The map, a totalising stage on which elements of diverse origin are brought together to form a tableau of a 'state' of geographical knowledge, pushes away into its prehistory or into its posterity as if into the wings, the operations of which it is the result or the necessary condition (de Certeau, 1984: 121).

The tourist map and the language learners' map, designed to highlight sites and to practise their language, may, under such a reading, be seen as even more totalising, only choosing to put particular sites on the printed page, ones that are being learned for the purpose of being found, by tourists. Tourist maps make certain aspects of the landscape visible, highlighting things to be seen, whilst ignoring other aspects, ones that may be important for way finding and part of the overall environment, but that are not a part of the tourist map-makers' itinerary. And yet, in this particular instance of tourist language practice there is more going on than encountering the sites on the map and working with its 'totalising' structure.

Firstly, tourist maps are interesting artefacts. They are not simply cartographic abstractions that map features into symbols and precision and grids. They are not really modern maps at all. The maps I am given as a tourist language learner for the purpose of learning the language, and as a tourist for the purpose of finding my way around, have more in common with medieval pictorial maps than with the modern map. De Certeau describes the process by which maps changed from graphically representing features to their current modern form. Early maps, he maintains, were more like history books than geographic maps, illustrating key sites that logged events rather than marked itineraries. From 'Here be dragons' to the pictures of buildings, ships and trees, the illustrations and characters figured on old maps indicate the history and operations or practices of travelling:

> Far from being illustrations, iconic glosses on the text, these figurations, like fragments of stories, mark on the map the historical operations from which it resulted. Thus the sailing ship painted on the sea indicates the maritime

expedition that made it possible to represent the coastlines. [...] But the map gradually wins out over these figures; it colonises space; it eliminates little by little the pictorial figurations of the practices that produce it (de Certeau, 1984: 121).

Brilliant as de Certeau's observations may be here, the process is not as linear and simple as his argument assumes. As a grand theory of map development this may be true, but the tourist map does not fit into this schema. The tourist map also contains pictorial figurations, the places that tell us that other tourists have been to these sites, that these are the things to be seen and that this is how we will know we are in the right place, at the correct building, the place where history happened, art was made, poems were written, where culture or nature occurred, famously, to those who went before. The spatial practices are present in the maps that tourists are given for way finding in their guide books. They are also present in the maps tourist language learners are given to learn by.

The map for tourist learners to *practise* with is a map that contains tourist sites, famous monuments, things that tourists want to go and see. It closely resembles the tourist map. The main object of the role play exercises of describing how to get from Avenida de Liberdade to the Castello S. Jorge is to go there first, through the map, to practise for future trips, to begin to see the tourist languaging world as one that is not flat but one to which the language being learned relates three-dimensionally and as a sensing action, not just as map interpretation, but helped along by the representations of the things that the tourists want to see, and the language in which they may orient themselves more quickly. This relates directly to the second aspect of the way in which maps and languages are related.

So, *secondly*, Pat and I use the map and the language differently, we use it as a point of departure, not as the foundation, for organising our journeys. We do play at finding our way from the hotel to the Therme, via the bridge – and only once I've successfully navigated Pat there, in Italian, does she exclaim that this time she has succeeded in reaching the destination, where once she had failed. The map and the language act to trigger emotions, re-tellings of history, and serve to enable her to take the trip again, this time with the language, and so to navigate successfully. The having of the right language is helping the map reading and the way finding at one and the same time.

The stories that follow from role play exercises in way finding add dramatic action to what is already a drama in itself – a role play; they give the plot a historical twist and raise the stakes in the activity. Pat helps brings the language alive because before, with only the map and no Italian, she had got lost. Being lost, without the language, was her dominant feeling.

The 'gift' then, and the 'loss' are complex here. They involve a more didactic structure than one of reparation. I never missed her when she was away because we had no direct relation, we did not even know of each other's lives. But we are both aware, as we struggle to use this language, of our potential loss and vulnerability in the context of way finding in a strange city and in a different language. Again, some of the sense of risk discussed in the previous chapter is also pertinent here. But it is also the case that the loss involved is one that occurs in the transformation *of a place*, through narration, *into a space*, from fixity and stability, into flux and particularity.

We may be aided considerably here by de Certeau's reflections on 'spatial stories' (de Certeau, 1984: 115). De Certeau argues that 'every story is a travel story – a spatial practice' (p. 115). He makes a crucial distinction between *place* – which he sees as indicating stability – and *space* – which he sees as '*a practised place*', 'occurring as the effect produced by the operations that orient it, situate it, temporalize it, and it make it function' (p. 115). In other words, and to continue our example from previously, the place of the baths in Montecatini Therme, a place that is fixed and relatively stable, a point on a tourist map, becomes a space for Pat as a tourist, a place that is practised, that is transformed, through her narration. As a space the Therme become what she couldn't find, where she got lost or disoriented, it is a place practised previously in tourist time, on holiday, with friends, a place that is shared in memories and that was not, fundamentally understood sufficiently, in Italian, for it to be found as a place. As Pat's practised place, Montecatini Therme becomes a space and it does so, as de Certeau argues, through the action of narration: 'Stories thus carry out a labor that constantly transforms places into spaces or spaces into places. They also organise the play of changing relationships between places and spaces' (de Certeau, 1984: 118).

For me, listening to these stories punctuated as they are with Pat's laughter, memories and experience, my relationship to Montecatini Therme has been transformed. It has become not a space but a place for me. If I go to Montecatini Therme I shall know what I did not know before, that the baths are 'worth visiting', that they are hard to find and having Italian may help considerably, and that Pat and her friend were there before me, enjoyed themselves and got lost. Visiting Montecatini Therme myself, as a tourist and with Italian, will, in turn, however, transform this new place on my itinerary into a space I inhabit in time, orientation and relation, for a while, setting up stories that I too may relate and giving me new vocabulary, in Italian, with which to narrate and to locate myself.

The language learning aspect adds a further dimension to de Certeau's distinction between place and space, however, and one that complicates the matter somewhat. Italian is the language associated with the place, but it is also at one and the same time the language that punctuates the largely English narration of events, in order to add to its piquancy. The loss that Cronin (2000) speaks of, which I am discovering here from Pat is that of being lost, of what happened without the language. In this context this story is changed again as a spatial practice, as it both changes the place into a space but it then adds a further aspect to the spatial practice as it begins to transform the future direction of such stories. It renders the story didactic. It becomes not just a story but a *parable*, a metaphorical moral tale – an Everyman tale told in everyday terms of everyday practices. As such, it points to a wider embodying of a morality, a lesson learned through metaphor and parable; a lesson in Italian, of moving around in Italian, with Italian moving around inside the person. It becomes a lesson in bothering with Italian.

Where Are We? Place-Space Parable

Underlying the argument, thus far, is the claim that through language learning and through the narration of past experiences with way finding and tourist maps, new places becomes spaces and spaces become places, following de Certeau's argument. This process is closely related to the way in which, following Ingold, as introduced in the beginning of this chapter, the globe perspective of the environment may be broken down or broken through, in tourist time and through the engagement with the languages of other places and more 'muted' perspectives, the lifeworld, may emerge. It is this process of transformation and cultural change that is of interest to me here. It is not just that the narration practices change place into space and back again or transform the perspectives language learning tourists have *within* the environment, as opposed to *of* the environment.

These prepositional subtleties are of crucial importance – they are *pre*-positional – i.e. they precede, in some way, the sense we have of our position in the tourist world and vis-à-vis its artefacts. The map is no longer, in this instance, just a map to be seen as a flat surface from above, it becomes a dynamic, three-dimensional narrated, practised and therefore transformable place. But the modality of this shift in world view and perspective is not one that is simply carried by the generic idea of story or narrative as either activities that occur as part of the wider discourse of tourism, or as practices that allow tourism to come into being as an industry (Bendix, 2002). This shift contains within it a cosmological mode, a readiness to change place into space, globe into lifeworld, and the vehicle for this is not simply the story – all stories do not perform such a function

– but the parable. In order to understand this aspect of cosmological shift we need to turn to theology and cosmological readings of parables.

Mcfague (1975) in her seminal work of literary theology, *Speaking in Parables*, maintains that parables are distinctive modes of metaphorical thinking. They are not just radical, poetic metaphors but the basis for 'the way human beings, selves (not mere minds) *move* in all areas of discovery' (Mcfague, 1975: 47). She draws here on Ricoeur's understanding of the Biblical parables (Ricoeur, 1974) and his article 'Listening to the Parables of Jesus' where he maintains that the parables are 'a language which from beginning to end, *thinks through* metaphor and never *beyond*'. Parables are what gives rise to thought, for Mcfague: 'we do not interpret the parable, but the parable interprets us' (Mcfague, 1975: 59). It is, in Pascalian terms, the language of a thinking body.

In order for the parable to interpret us, to change our cosmological outlook Mcfague argues that it must relate to our everyday, embodied worlds aiming at responding to questions, practical difficulties of life, to conundrums, such as how to find our way in a strange place and in a strange tongue. The central tenets of a parable, as opposed to a generic story, are 'its realism and its strangeness' (p. 63). The metaphorical thinking of a parable:

> [...] demands that one partner of the association, at least, be concrete, sensuous, familiar, bodily. It will abide no abstractions, no head without a body, no mystical flights, but because it is the method of *human* movement it insists on taking along the whole human being in all its familiarity, messiness, and concreteness (Mcfague, 1975: 51).

The concreteness, the messiness of being lost, the full familiarity of way finding and of map using are the stuff of Pat's narrative, but it is the parable in her narration which breaks down the globe view – my view as an outsider peering onto Montecatini Therme as an abstracted place on a map, into a practised place, a place where I learn new words, new names, where my sense of a new place is thickened and excited, where I not only *think through* but also *find a way through* seeing this destination and this language as lived, not as seen or as two-dimensional. The parables here are answers to the conundrum and question of how to find the way to the Therme without knowing the place or possessing the language. The parable and the languaging attempt to do precisely this, in tourist Italian, changes the cosmology of the tourist. It effects a transformation. The parable is what interprets our attempts at learning the language and finding our way into a lifeworld.

The Lifeworld

As a tourist language learner, on holiday and both learning and languaging in the space of a walking tour of an area of Lisbon I am both lost in language and found in place and space. In order to make sense of where I am, to tell my left from my right, I both make the following journal entry, and I narrate this tourist story, in a different form, over the phone.

I'm completely lost. We have gathered together for the afternoon's activities that form part of our language holidays. João is our guide. He turns up and all we know is that we are going to go to an old, literary quarter in Lisbon, that of Chiado. We do not know how we will get there, what we will see when we arrive. Some of us have visited Lisbon before, as tourists, negotiating the city in our own languages. We have not done it in Portuguese before, and we don't have much of the language. João notes our names, counts up the group. Some are from our class but we are the neophytes, others are old hands, they are know each other, they are welcoming to us, they are happy to be together, they chat in Portuguese and in Italian, bits of Spanish, German, some English and French. The group is mixed ability. We are the total beginners, many are intermediate, some are advanced. The motivation and sheer exuberance of those who are already at a stage when they can share and talk and move around with their tourist language learning companions is palpable. We are wistful, determined, longing to be where there are, holding on to each instance when something is understood.

We set off. We don't actually have a clue where we are going. We are talking to each other, initially in Portuguese, but, to be frank there are only so many times you can greet each other when that is actually all you are able to do. João seems to be heading for the underground, and we just follow on, taking in the notices, the route, watching him buy his ticket and doing so ourselves. We chat on the underground. I am struck by how clean it all is – others from other places, feel it is dirty. The conversations in the group are multilingual – in and out of all our languages. I'm enjoying my German and French, and am not spending much time in English. This is a surprise.

We join up with the advanced class and the teacher-guide in the metro. He insists on speaking in English, French, German and Portuguese, flitting easily between them, but only speaking Portuguese for his advanced class and not really aiming at us as elementary level. It is a bit frustrating at times. The tour begins in Chiado with the monuments to famous authors including Pessoa. Two churches, rebuilt after the earthquake, are then pointed out. I am struck by the immediacy of the quake in narratives of Lisbon – it is very present because it is the reason for the Pombal layout of the town now and why the architecture looks the away it does, it seems. We walk up and down some streets, see the renovated theatre and opera house, the house where Pessoa was born and then we are taken to the sites of French Occupation under Napoleon and I remember again the French language connection. My landlady had spoken French to me at one point over breakfast.

Then we go into two of the churches in the square. The Jesuit prayed, others walked round. My feet are hurting. I am not used to wearing sandals with no socks and I am _hot and sticky. I keep noting everyone else's feet looked cool and happy in their slip-on sandals – it is annoying and distracting. I want to concentrate and all I can do is melt in the heat and think about my feet, worrying about blisters. We walk up shaded hills around Chiado up to the Carmelite monastery and the site of the start of the Carnation Revolution. We translate individual words between us – 'carnation', 'oeilet', 'Nelken'...and the story of the woman laying carnations and it not being a bloody revolution. We also look at the monastery as an example of one that was taken over by the state and which was not rebuilt after the earthquake. I get a bit confused here between languages and Lisbon history, trying to sort my quakes from my dictators. Everyone is flagging in the heat so we just sit down together on the steps in the shade. The three advanced students who are with us and the guide turn out to be a Spaniard and two Germans. They chat between themselves, asking some questions._

We then go to the Teatro da Trindade and look at an example of early tiles on the Freemason house. And then into a cellar shopping centre to look at the end of the old city walls, before escaping the sun and going into another church. As we come out Sabine asks me what I think about the mix of what she sees as religious kitsch and art. She'd recently been at her first ever mass and was surprised by the incense and the darkness. She asks me if I am Protestant too.

We all end up in a beautiful open air café on high above the banks of the Tejo – ordering juice, iced tea and water as well as some food – 'Pastéis', 'tostas mistas', etc. The conversation is quiet but steady with more questions about the place and the ways of doing things, the words for things and the things we do back home. I am feeling tired, my feet hurt and I have that caged feeling again, of having to listen and listen hard to make sense and not having a way of expressing myself. When we sort out the final bill I present them with Irish Euros – the teacher-guide is excited, he collects the coins and wants to swap his for mine. The connection suddenly came to him between Ireland and Scotland as I took out sterling.

And then the trip was over, we wander back towards the metro – splitting up as we went. I buy ten ride metro tickets with Christina and then get off, with considerable relief to my feet, just outside my lodgings. I spend some time wandering round the supermarket below the apartment block, looking both at the staples of Portuguese food, fish, smoked chorizo, bread, cheese and melons, freshly picked it seems, as well as noting the number of French products and the European reach of the market.

And then it was time to come back, collapse, drink lots of water and spend the evening ordering notes, journaling and winding down.

Phoned home – it cost a fortune! Told this story.

The experience outlined in this long extract from my Lisbon diary is an important one when it comes to understanding something of how it is that language orients and changes the experience of tourism, especially when the tourism is part of learning the language of the place. Here the detachment, the observation role, the clinical movement where left is really left and right is really right and where the answer is a grid reference on a map is changed into a fully embodied experience of way finding, together. Maps are no longer opened out of the table as objects for narration, but tucked away in my bag, in case I can't find my way home. In this lifeworld of tourism and languaging we move in and out of language with increasing intensity and absorption depending on the relative fluencies of those engaged in this form of movement. It becomes a series of stories *in situ*, related to places and people that we, as a group of language learning tourists, are struggling to both understand, repeat and inhabit – to spatialise, in de Certeau's terms. It also becomes its own story for my purposes here. It is a different experience to the role play and the sense of lack and parable that come from the transitional activities of tourist language learning in the classroom space.

If we do indeed make sense of our experiences through the feel of movement, the language comes alive in distinctive ways when we actually are in the lifeworld, *languaging*, rather than accessing it cartographically, imaginatively and even playfully, in a different temporal mode. But one, I would argue, cannot easily exist without another. Increasingly activity holidays

---

New for this season, we are offering the opportunity to explore the Pyrenees, whilst learning French. Justin Major, your bilingual mountain leader and experienced language teacher, will lead the week, taking you up the peaks, through the markets and into the classroom! The course will be tailored to suit the individuals on it so that you can combine the best of the Pyrenees (at your own walking pace) with your own preferences for learning: walking, talking, classroom and exploring the culture of the local villages. Groups will be kept small to ensure individuals get support in their language learning at whatever level of fluency. Language learning activities vary from day to day but are designed to be fun, problem solving, active and to stretch your current level of spoken French.

The approach to teaching will be very practical, enabling you to get out there and use your language skills. The group will be encouraged to speak French most of the time, whether walking in the hills, buying cheese from the market or ordering a meal in a restaurant. Interspersed with being out and about there will be some more formal teaching to help you structure your learning. You will also have the chance to converse with local people – our French friends and acquaintances, local bar owners and farmers are looking forward to meeting you. You might even end up with a Southern accent! Overall the week is designed to be fun and relaxing. However you will definitely go home with better, more confident, French.

http://www.pyrenees.co.uk/2005%20Webpages/Summer2005/speakingfrench2005.html

are offered that give people the chance to learn a language whilst engaged in a tourist activity – cooking, walking, learning about art history, etc.

In such holidays the language is not the destination, as it was in my instance, but a further passion. But in all cases the experience of the language, the early frustration and the growing education of attention and attunement to its sounds, and thus its meaning and life, change the perception of people and place. Sense of direction and the language of place and activity, from where we are and from moving around, rather than of direction from place to place, give us a different feel.

So what might these examples of the direction of movement show us? What is happening when we orient ourselves in our imaginations and through classroom rehearsal and when we do so, with others as *languaging* companions?

Conclusions

In order to find your way you need language and stories, in order for your way to be found, you need parables. In language learning stories become parables, they render the strange familiar, accessible, exciting, messy, but they do so with the message that the world and our position within it was changed. Parables are what point to the shift in thinking from place to space and from the globe view to the lifeworldview, from being detached, apart and away from the activities of languaging and from the life of another place, in tourist time, to being in the midst of this world.

Tourist maps, in this respect, are treasure maps and the treasure is found through the language and its intimate relation to the environment seen in these parables, and seen in real tourist life. The treasure to be found is not so much the souvenir or even the narrative capital, but the cosmological shift experienced as place becomes a parabled, practised, place – a space indeed – and the two dimensions of a map became the three-dimensional, sensory world.

When you know how a place works you need the language of direction, the language of a place less than when you don't know the place. When you don't know the place you need a way of relating to it spatially, of changing your cosmological relationship to it. What makes the difference, between the tourist language learning in the classroom and tourist languaging and way finding out on the streets, is the location of this activity. Maps and asking for directions are both techniques used by tourists for moving around in the new locations, of finding their bearings in a new lifeworld. Seen from the classroom, as an imagined presence, this world is different to the one experienced first-hand through language, where the world of tourist phenomena are brought up close.

Heidegger maintains that the Greek word *techne*, which is the root of the word technique, 'means neither art nor handicraft but rather: to make something appear, within what is present, as this or that, in this way or that way' (Heidegger, 1971: 157). Maps, stories and parables, as features of tourist language learning, all make language appear in varying degrees of sensory intensity depending on where they are experienced from.

This brings us then, to another aspect of the sensing nature of place, space and language – that of sound and pronunciation and the wider ways in which tourist language learners make sense of the tourist lifeworld through their attempts at languaging.

Chapter 5
Pronunciation

We are trying to make a go of the pronunciation rules for 's' and learn about soft voiced constants, hard unvoiced consonants and are given examples of how to pronounce 's' in a variety of different positions. The teacher laughs with us as we look perplexed: 'The first time I heard Portuguese', she says, 'I thought the teacher was kidding on because it sounds so different to English – this is what makes it so interesting. It is really nasally – think nasally – hold your nose', she says.

The first lesson is a lesson in speaking, in actual language production – that of pronunciation and of the relationship of speech to the alphabet. As with other shifts that we have identified so far, there is a concomitant shift from written to oral practice involved here for the tourist language learner. This raises the question as to what extent the relationship of the language to tourism is one of written or of oral modalities. As such this brings into focus different aspects, felt and learned, of making sense to others, and learning how to move around in a new language and it continues the discussions of orientation and attunement from the previous chapter. In this case, however, the attunement is to the language, rather than the directions opened out for movement by the environment. In addition, the question remains on the table as to why it is that such effort may be expended for such seemingly small reward, in the learning of a language for tourist purposes.

In the previous chapter I looked at ways of using tourist maps and understanding the tourist environment through the learning of a tourist language and the way in which this, as a languaging action, becomes a parable of cosmological change. Pronunciation is one of the first lessons in tourist language. In phrase books it is usually part of the introductory chapter, and phonetic transliterations of words are regularly provided to help tourists 'sound right' when they speak. The alphabet and the modulation of vowels and consonants make up key stages in initial lessons. It is here that the *virtues* of good pronunciation and the development of a sensory, embodied ability to speak differently *from* the body, may be traced.

A, B, C...

For the tourist language learners of both Portuguese and of Italian the first classes include an introduction to the pronunciation of the alphabet in

Portuguese and in Italian. In the Portuguese class the letters are written up and a system of phonetic pronunciation (sounds like...) is added to each letter in turn. The sounds of the language produce a reaction, acting as triggers for surprise, laughter and comment, notably the pronunciation of H and J.

a – ah	*o – o*
b – bay	*p – p*
c – say	*q – kay*
d – day	*r – rray*
e – eay/e	*s – s*
f – ff	*t – tay*
g – gay	*u – oo*
h – igha	*v – vey*
i – e	*x – shesh*
j – joka	*z – zay*
l – l	*[k – kappa*
m – m	*w – double u*
n – n	*y – ypsilon]*

The class chants the alphabet in rote learning style following the teacher's lead. There are giggles as strange sounds take a while to form. We are then asked to come up with four names of famous people – first names and surnames and to write them down before finding a partner who will spell out the names in turn for us to write down.

Como é que você escreve isso? – How do you spell/write this?

Pode soletrar isso para mim? – Can you spell that for me?

Some of the names I'm given come out a bit wonky, others are easier: Ewan Msrixar, Tilda Swinton, Tony Blair.

In the Italian class we are given the Italian alphabet in the same way – repeating the sounds the letters make after the teacher. And we are also given a spelling task.

Come si scrive il tuo nome? 'This isn't fair,' protests the first person picked, 'I'm just a beginner and I've probably got the longest name.' The tutor writes the names on the blackboard as we spell them out for her. 'Have I spelled my name wrong?' asks one of the learners in horror as the results of her labours go up for all to see. And everyone laughs.

Being able to pronounce the sounds and being able to spell are key foci in the tourist language learning classes. For all the classes I joined the desire to pronounce words and to be able to spell out words orally and correctly were strong. Much time is spent early on, on pronunciation and drilling the sounds. 'Its relaxed though,' says the Portuguese teacher, 'they'll be glad if you just try.' She pronounces the funny letters for us again. 'Just repeat,' she says. 'Watch my lips.'

In both these examples we see a move from highly structured, concentrated, rule-bound fixity in the language, to its opposite, to the anti-structure of relaxation, laughter and a flow in English for commentary on either the aesthetic properties of the new language, or on the errors made in pronunciation and spelling and on the delight at the feel of a different word, its aesthetic qualities and strangeness. The move from structure to anti-structure, as Turner terms it, is a constant throughout the class (Turner, 1982; Turner, 1995) The class like the strange feel of the sounds in their mouths, but they also concentrate on acquiring the discipline, the rigidity of structure, through repetition, that will help them make the strangeness their own, make it fit in their mouths, make it find a way of being familiar, of being less strange, comfortable even.

The body is fully in play in the situation, not as a determined organism but as the whole person strains towards new expressions, strains to 'speak from the body' (Farnell, 2000) and to move around in the new ways suggested by the sounds. As with Mcfague's metaphorical thinking, which I discussed in the previous chapter, there is no speaking without the body. It is not helpful to talk in dualisms of mind and body here but rather to think in the terms of Merleau-Ponty's considerable thesis on the *Phenomenology of Perception*, which sees the person, or agent, as a being-in-the-world, as an embodied presence:

> The analysis of speech and expression brings home to us the enigmatic nature of our own body [...]. It has been observed that speech or gesture transfigure the body, but no more was said on the subject than that they develop or disclose another power, that of thought or soul. The fact was overlooked that, in order to express it, the body must in the last analysis become the thought or intention that it signifies for us. It is the body which points out, and speaks (Merleau-Ponty, 2002: 229–30).

When the tourist language learning body 'points out, and speaks' there is considerable effort expended. It is often hot work, concentrating and trying to make the right sounds emerge from within the body. It is conscious, unpractised speaking. As such it reverses the situation of relative ease which accompanies the speaking of one's native language. For tourist language learners here, in the lessons on the alphabet and on the pronunciation of letters we see a further inversion at work. Writing, in child language acquisition, succeeds the acquisition of speech, sound, mimicry of the patterns of language and sound. For these tourist learners, as for most adult learners coming to a new language, writing has already been acquired, literacy is largely in place and the structures of writing, the letters and shapes we recognise as the alphabet, the written signifiers – in Saussurian terms – are used as a basis from which to develop the new language. This is also true of languages that use characters and that are not based upon the Roman alphabet. In acquiring Greek, Hebrew, Arabic or Chinese, literate learners use their ability to create signs from these written signifiers as a point of departure, not as a point of arrival. There is an inversion here in patterns of learning.

This relationship between the shape and feel of a sound and the written shape of letters or characters is important here. What we see evolving, in these examples, is something of a hybrid form of speech/writing and a shifting between the modalities of the oral and the written. It is not of any real importance to these tourist language learners to be able to write the language correctly. No *linguistic capital* accrues to the written forms, for them. There is an acceptance of the necessity of grammatical rules, exercises in grammar and in the correct, comprehensible structuring of the language, but the communicative focus, in these classes, is oral and aural – listening and speaking with reading and a little writing. Rather than the focus being that of a written culture, it is as though the writing and reading elements – the alphabet – serves the production of speech and pronunciation.

In the communicative hierarchy of performance targets the production of good, well-pronounced, correct speech comes in first, understanding a close second, followed by reading and then writing. It would not be fair to say that we are dealing here with an oral culture as opposed to a written or literate one as literacy rates in the class are high and the dominant culture, in which the learning occurs, and in which the tourism takes place, is one which places a high premium on advanced literacy. The relationship between the production of sound and the production of written text is an important one when it comes to considering the development of languaging in tourists, as opposed to language learning. The point of the exercise for these tourists is that they will be able to actively produce speech that works and that enables survival in relation to lands where their language may be visited.

Structure and Anti-structure

It is through the structuring device of the alphabet and a growing relationship with its sounds and with the pronunciation of the language in the earlier stages, through 'full on' encounters with the strange nasally sounds of Portuguese or the felt lilt and perceived poetry of Italian that our tourist learners begin to develop a relationship to the language that moves between structure and anti-structure.

For Turner, working on the cusp of structuralist and post-structuralist anthropology, structure and anti-structure related to ritual processes (Turner, 1995). Much has been made, in the tourism literature, of his contribution and of the liminal dimensions, the transitional phases that are or that resemble a rite of passage, that may be found within tourism, together with the kinds of inversions that occur in tourism (Burns, 1999; Graburn, 1978; Smith, 1977; Urry, 1990). Indeed, in many ways, this would seem to be one of the main contributions to the study of tourism from anthropology. Within the study of tourism and of social behaviour more generally, anthropologists and other students of tourism have become adept at identifying the times that accord to the liminal, anti-structural dimensions Turner identified. Those that are more rule-bound and structured, largely, in the tourism literature, equate the liminal to the holiday, and the structured to everyday life.

At the end of his discussion of the ritual process and of structure and anti-structure Turner has this to say:

> Society (*societas*) seems to be a process rather than a thing – a dialectical process with successive phases of structure and communitas. There would seem to be – if one can use such a controversial terms – a human 'need' to participate in both modalities. Persons starved of one in their functional day-to-day activities seek it in ritual liminality. The structurally inferior aspire to symbolic structural superiority in ritual; the structurally superior aspire to symbolic communitas and undergo penance to achieve it (Turner, 1995: 203).

Tourism, under such a reading for those following Turner (Coleman & Crang, 2002; Urry, 1990), is accorded the status of a sacred journey with a ritual function. The analysis works at a macro level and with pre-existing social categories. To summarise, tourism is seen as a mode of being in which the rich seek asceticism, the poor seek to be king or queen for a day; the old seek rejuvenation, the young seek independence and responsibility (Graburn, 1978; Urry, 1990). The oppositional nature of these statements is somewhat problematic, as is the view of tourism as a sacred journey, and as somehow existing apart from everyday life, rather than richly imbued with the everydayness of life, just located in different places to those habitually dwelled in.

There is more to the learning of a tourist language than this. Such neatly categorised divisions, for all the theorising in tourism studies and beyond on the borders and boundaries between categories and cultures, bind time into relatively large chunks, into hours, days, weeks or even years of structure and anti-structure, rather than attending to the micro fluctuations in the qualities and experiences of structure and anti-structure in time at a micro level.

In the examples of learning the alphabet and using it to learn to pronounce the languages here, anti-structure and structure are in continual flux, shifting in and out of the modalities, between intense structured concentration and concentrated bursts of laughter and anti-structure. There are other identifiable layers of structure and anti-structure here too. The class is part of a formal educational structure, but it is also taking place in the liminal moments of the day, it is an evening class, a holiday class and as such both structured and anti-structured at one and the same time. And further still the class is seen as 'not work' and either as preparation for future language use or as 'leisured learning'. Finally, this is oral cultural work not written cultural work, but encountered in inverted, hybrid form. *Linguistic capital*, to return to the Bourdieusian framework examined in Chapter 3, accrues to the spoken language and any written competence is incidental and irrelevant to tourist learners. This is not, however, to deny that literacy practices abound and create their own ecologies within tourism, and tourist language learning. Indeed there is a growing body of research demonstrating the textual, discursive nature of literacy practices in tourism (Jaworski & Pritchard, 2005; Jaworski *et al.*, 2003; Thurlow *et al.*, 2005).

What I am led to argue here, then, is that when a relationship to a language is sought out and practised by tourist learners it necessitates intricate and often subtle flux between structure and anti-structure at various levels. In fact, notions of structure and anti-structure come to refer to such different phenomena – the time of day, the holiday, an instance of laughter – that they lead to something of a theoretical cul-de-sac for our purposes here. In short, the interplay of tourism and language, the encounter with strange new sounds and their sensations in a tourist language class demonstrate that there is no ready script, no set pattern or structure for imagined life. At the very same time there are pre-existing forms, rules, ways of speaking, of knowledge in the *bodily hexis* of the teacher and those who already possess the language that these learners desire.

In attempting to learn to speak differently, from the body, to embody the language and make it present, tourist language learners are also attempting to speak for others, on behalf of other members of their families, friends and even other tourists. But they are also speaking *for* others in a different sense and one which brings into view a certain moral sense of their social duty as linguistic guests, to use Ricoeur's term, as well as a projection of what Derrida terms the 'monolingualism of the other' (Derrida, 1996). Not only is there a bodily effort expended here in pursuit of the virtue of being able to speak with the host in *their* language but there are also certain assumptions and projections in play here that relate to the imagined presence of the destination. These aspects are as follows: (1) virtuous, courteous guests will not make assumptions about their hosts ability to speak English (or any other foreign language); (2) virtuous, courteous guests will make an effort with *the* language; and (3) the hosts become a single *monolingual* entity, assumed, even desired, to be monolingual Italian, monolingual Portuguese.

To understand how these tourist learners grow to possess, inhabit and dwell in new ways of speaking that are durable, and enact their moral sense of linguistic guesting, we need to look beyond the analyses that the conceptualisations of structure and anti-structure afford and to move beyond the potentially oppositional notions of oral and written culture. These may be adequate descriptors but they do not show how it is that new speech is engaged as a phenomenon or created in new tourist bodies out of a new and unfamiliar soundscape. Nor do they explain why it is that tourist language learners in particular – those who only require their language for short-term stays – might engage in the long and arduous work of learning to speak another language and embodying a different range of sounds and syntaxes to those in which they flow and make meaning more readily and easily.

Tongue Twisting

There is more to this than just a shift between concentration and the laughter at error, however. This is the beginning, one of the first moments of encounter with the structuring of the sounds and with the strangeness of adopting this way of speaking and pronouncing. This is where the enormity of the task makes itself manifest. These learners may be able to read the letters before them, but making them sound 'right' is a whole other ball game. Some, of course, give up at this stage. There are many who enroll in language classes with great intentions and find it all too daunting, too tiresome, too long term a project where the rewards seem entirely unattainable. In the classes I came to about a third fell by the wayside early on. It was hard going, through the dark winter nights, week in week out, with all the other competing claims of friends, home, leisure and work to negotiate and resist.

But the majority of us stuck with it, turning up week by week to get our dose of language-work, and to practise saying the words. Gradually pronunciation became easier, less amusing, less of a perceived oddity in our worlds, and more integrated into our ways of being and speaking. In the early classes, however, our reactions to new words and to the shapes they seemed to form within us provoked clear reactions – of joy, desire, repulsion, curiosity.

> We have come to the section of the course where we learn to buy and to order food. 'La lattuga' – lettuce says the tutor. 'It sounds like a dance,' whispers my partner to me. 'La fragola – with the emphasis on fra.' We begin to repeat words listed on the board. 'Olio d'oliva' – 'Oooo doesn't it sound lovely, it feels liquid in your mouth,' says my partner. 'Maiale' – 'that's a nasty word,' she whispers, 'not like olive oil.' We break into groups and begin discussing holidays we have had, food we have eaten, things we love to taste when on holiday.

At one level, following Saussure, all that is occurring here is that a chunk of sound is being united with a concept – the sound *lattuga*, with the fresh leafy, green summer salad vegetable. Practised sufficiently and this union will come 'naturally', will become durable and fluent. But there is more going on here than this. The classroom, occupied as it is for these two hours every week, is inhabited by a range of new sounds, expertly and inexpertly pronounced. It is not just a classroom for learning a tourist language, it is also a soundscape, a place in which a set of distinctive sounds come and go, arrest us, move into us, change us or leave us cold. It may be in the heart of a big, post-industrial British city but it is trying to mimic the sounds of tourist Italy:

> A place owes its character to the experiences it affords to those who spend time there – to the sights, sounds and indeed smells that constitute its specific ambience. And these in turn, depend on the kinds of activities in which its inhabitants engage. It is from this relational context of people's engagement with the world [...] that its place draws its unique significance. Thus whereas with space meanings are *attached* to the world, with the landscape they are *gathered from it* (Ingold, 2000: 192).

In the lessons in pronunciation we see both an *attaching* and a *gathering* process at work – both a sticking of meaning into place and a collecting of things with which to create, to make meaning. This process works in the interstices of written and oral language, it is both structural and antistructural. It is the work of making sense that literally makes sense – in that it twists tongues and bodies into different ways of touching meaning – and it also makes very little sense under the dominant paradigms of efficiency. To repeat an earlier but nonetheless important point, these learners are not here because they are going to 'get better jobs' or 'have better prospects' or serve the travel industry or any of the functionalist, technicist reasons that we may generate as reasons for learning another language. Tourist learners and the bodily effort and time they expend are peculiar, nonsensical creatures. By any of the normal measures of argumentation used to justify the place of subjects in the curriculum today, or to respond to the needs of a hungry agenda for employability, these actions and approaches do not make sense, they do not add up.

So, if this odd work, this labour in leisure time, for leisure time, does not respond to the imposition of analyses relating to oral or written cultural frames, or those of structure and anti-structure, how might we come to understand this aspect of human behaviour? How might we interpret the phenomenon of the tourist language learner's language learning and in particular, in this context, the particularly astonishing action of being rendered mute, being utterly silenced and incompetent in the face of symbols and the new sets of sounds that their enunciation brings into the world? And how might we engage with the phenomenon of the soundscape, produced in a context where it has nothing to attach to, nothing with which to readily produced full linguistic signs, save that of the tourist experience and the tourist imagination?

It is difficult to attach new meanings to a world to which a different set of systems, structures and linguistic formulations usually and 'naturally' attach. To create a different world is, if we follow the popular interpretation of the Babel myth, to be voluntarily cursed by the punishment that is linguistic diversity. Steiner and Mühlhäusler both see the story of Babel, independently, as one which tells of the punishment of linguistic diversity, as a second Fall, one which frustrates human desires to enable communication (Mühlhäusler, 2003; Steiner, 1998). However, it would be equally possible, in this strange context of tourist language learners, for learners to imagine relations to other people and other places, relations that see Babel, not so much as a curse, as a human story of relatedness (van Wolde, 2000).

The Paradox of the Tourist Language Learner

We have a paradox here. The paradox of the tourist language learner. The paradox of the person who lavishes huge amount of time, care and attention – time which is symbolic and significant, time which is highly prized and cherished leisure time – on the long arduous process of learning to relate to other people and places in their language. For this takes us to the heart of the matter. Learning to enunciate the strange sounds, to build up a soundscape, fleeting and momentary and bounded as it may be by class activities, will require the vicissitudes of the hour-long allocations of time for formal learning.

The kind of 'waste' of time that is implicated here does not fit easily with notions of work or of leisure as it is both of these, and neither. The work going on here is the work of relating, the will to relate, the desire to make meaning. But it is also already touristic work. It is already the experience of the unfamiliar, it is already touching the fragments – material, embodied, linguistic – which open up new worlds of meaning and of being in a tourist world. For all the ridiculousness of the learning, the soundscapes transport us in our imagination.

This activity does not involve quietly studying knowledges and curricula that can be reproduced in the examination hall or in assessment form and then are over, learned and graded. It is not even about an engagement with a subject where there may be a genuine interest and passion for the subject – an open and rigorous engagement in the adult classroom with the materials and ideas in play. It is about all of these things, for they are all part and parcel of the language learning process, but it is also about more than this. Tourist language learning, is about doing all of these from a place where the means of expression and the ability to communicate in and through language are removed, absent and where the engagement requires a formidable act of will. This act of will and engagement is the will to suspend the ability to speak, to understand, to *be* an articulate being. It is the will to try, to play, to feel the touch of new sounds and to do so for little obvious reward.

The paradox of the tourist language learner – of this engagement and this stepping out of one's habitual ways of speaking and ones habitual safety zones – a stepping out that relates to risk in important ways (see Chapter 3) indexes aspects of human life. It points to ways of being human in an age of mass tourist dystopias, cosmopolitan ideals and mass relatedness, which are not amenable to standard interpretative frameworks for either languages or for tourism. Persisting in regarding these activities as liminal or *liminoid* – Turner's term for transitional practices in advanced, modern societies – does not help address this paradox. Nor do views of languages as serving functional ends. And nor do they respond well to the kinds of exhortations to citizenship we find clustering around languages at a macro level, on the part of UNESCO or the European Union, for example, though they are, in their own way, one of the answers to the problems such agencies put before us.

Tourist language learning engages in this activity on behalf of others, as well as the self. It does not do so because some languages are endangered, or because it will help the East Nottinghamshire tourist industry, or because the European Union believes all citizens should speak three community languages. It speaks for others and it imagines the others in often quite homogeneous, even stereotypical ways – ways which are much maligned in the intercultural literature and which intercultural education, perhaps rightly, seeks to eradicate (Coleman, 1999; Guilherme, 2000). And it does so, as mentioned earlier in the chapter, by imagining others in the tourist context as more or less homogeneous, but as nonetheless human and worthy of respect and relation. As such, the practice of tourist language learning bucks the trends well documented in the tourism literature, of the alienation felt by hosts from guests and guests from hosts (Pi-Sunyer, 1978; Smith, 1977).

We might even go so far as to say that tourist language learning desires the other to be monolingual and homogeneously so. The heterogeneity and attendant cosmopolitan dimensions of tourism confuse otherwise unsullied ideas about the destination and the intensity of the relationships that may be had as tourists, with hosts, much more so than with other, linguistically diverse tourists. The simple device of sounding out the alphabet gives us ways of imagining ourselves on holiday, in a place that is not home, and with imagined others. This imagined place is a place where the soundscape is perhaps a little like the one we are creating, where there is a difference that is refreshing, and also, ultimately, one that makes these words and sounds stick in patterns that work for us. The repetition of the sounds week on week allow us to make meaning in ways that bring other rewards and, importantly, reveals aspects about being human in an age of mass mobilities, globalisation and cosmopolitanism.

Pronouncing Respect

Tourist language learning and the struggles to pronounce words well point beyond this activity to wider aspects of human life, and suggest that other things are pronounced as well as words in these efforts. This is the labour of languages for intercultural being. These tourist language learners become *languagers as they become tourists*. They are engaging with the world in ways that the term tourist language *learners* does not adequately grasp. They are in the 'quick' of human relatedness – in the thick of things, where meanings get mimicked, made *and pronounced*.

> The wonder of mimesis lies in the copy drawing on the character and power of the original, to the point whereby the representation may even assume that character and that power. In an older language, this is 'sympathetic magic' and I believe it is as necessary to the very process of knowing as it is to the construction and subsequent naturalization of identities (Taussig, 1993: xiii–xiv).

Performance – as pronunciation – is part of a mimetic process, which makes things stick. It doesn't just make the words that need remembering or the sounds that through rehearsal and repetition come to mean stick.

But why pronounce meaning in a new language and in one which is not your own? Why do this in the 'quick' of human relatedness, in the midst of things, and in speech, when writing may be easier, less embarrassing and exposing? And even, more to the point, following the moves of linguistic theory over the last 30 years that have dominated scholarship in the arts and humanities, why bother when language is something of a prison house, full of slippery meanings that conceals as much as ever it can reveal. If the one language, the one we may indeed have to some degree of fluency, cannot do the work of making meaning and of communicating for us, then why tackle another one when we are bound, surely, to fail even more than before as we stumble around in a minefield of arbitary signs?

An answer may be found in these first attempts at pronunciation. What, we might ask, is it that is actually being pronounced? Is it the letters, the signifiers, *just* the rustle of breathe on tongue and larynx and palate to make the noise that may come to join with others and may create some sense of meaning? Is this all that is occurring here?

The responses of the tourist language learners to the sensation of new speech and the pronunciation of letters, the mimicking of sounds and the production of new words are illuminated, here, by Merleau-Ponty in the *Phenomenology of Perception*: 'The phenomenological world is not pure being, but the *sense* [my emphasis] which is revealed where the paths of my various experiences intersect, and also where my own and other people's intersect and engage each other like gears' (Merleau-Ponty, 2002: xxii). What Merleau-Ponty is arguing here is that we come into being in the world through our perception. There is nothing else behind the perceptions we make than those perceptions themselves and these disclose the world to us. Under such a view, he argues, 'words leads one to expect sensations just as evening leads one to expect night' (Merleau-Ponty, 2002: 17).

Let us imagine the typical, monolingual tourist experience, in a shopping street for instance. Although there are other sounds of other languages and even one's own here, the dominant sound is the one of the language in which life, in this place, is lived. Some of this living, an aspect of it, may include the need to work with an accented English – one which is more or less fluent – but one which serves the purpose of the work of the tourist industry. Predominantly, however, life is lived, say for our purposes, in Portuguese or in Italian. These are the sounds of language in which the everyday life of the place, and of the hosting part of the tourism equation, are most at ease.

This is the experience of the world that has triggered sensations, that has come, rather like the Proustian Madeleine, to lodge in the perceptions of the tourist, now back home, in the memory of these times, as ones that evoke something of the leisure and pleasure and distanciation of the tourist's experience.

Now it is fair to say that, particularly for wealthy tourists and business travellers, hosts put much effort in to *managing* the aspects of difference and distance, and of *performing* a cleaned up version of everyday life, its colours and the sensations that give aesthetic pleasure. This kind of tidying up for tourists may take the form of floral displays for the season through to all manner of heritage and culture displays, which emerge again in the tourism studies literature under the rubric of authenticity (MacCannell, 1973; Waller & Lea, 1999). There is a thickening of potential sensation, a drawing out of the sense potential from the backdrop of everyday life against which they may merge into normality. And there is a thinning down of other senses, of the familiar, an easing of the habitual routines through a variety of devices from the turning down of the hotel bedcovers by a chamber maid, to the handling of utensils in a restaurant that otherwise one would touch and use oneself.

This thickening and thinning also occurs within the soundscape. Translation devices are brought in to help ease the process, to thin down the difficulty, to create a linguistic milieu that is easier, managed, familiar, helped in the same way as a lift that carries the luggage. But for our tourist language learners the thickness, the impenetrability of the languages spoken habitually, the languages lived in by those who dwell in the destination, is an aspect of the backdrop, one which evokes sensations. The experience for the majority of the tourist language learners in the classes has been one in which 'I couldn't understand a word', 'I couldn't catch anything', 'It was all so foreign', 'I couldn't speak it at all', 'I couldn't get my tongue round it'. Sensations of bodily distortion, of impenetrability, of all words merging into a vague sense of sounds that do not mean anything.

The encounters with lessons in pronunciation, with the sounds of the alphabet, and the practising of pronunciation of words, like 'lattuga', 'olio d'oliva', 'maiale', in Italian, of the nasally sounds of *sim, cafezinho, tudo bem* and *o pequeno-almoço* are times, following Merleau-Ponty, when the sounds which merged into an impenertable soup of meaninglessness, begin to be detachable, begin to be laid down with meaning, when they become something, then the language begins to be revealed in and through these intersections. This mode of learning is a mode of reflection, one which, in Merleau-Ponty's terms:

> [...] steps back to watch the forms of transcendence fly up like sparks from a fire; it slackens the intentional threads which attach us to the world and thus brings them to our notice; it alone is consciousness of the world because it reveals that world as strange and paradoxical (Merleau-Ponty, 2002: xv).

The words, the sounds, become phenomena that stand alone, in these moments of learning, they emerge as sensations from the field of perception and, as they detach, through the conscious action of all engaged in this task of education, from the impenetrable morass of sounds, they are accompanied by the kinds of cries of astonishment, laughter, recognition that Merleau-Ponty, quoting Husserl's assistant Eugen Fink, speaks of as 'wonder in the face of the world' (Merleau-Ponty, 2002: xv).

This brings us back to the question we posed earlier in this chapter, in attempting to make sense of the act of tourist language learning – an act which is both 'strange and paradoxical' – as to why invest so much in this act? The answer that is beginning to emerge here, at this juncture in the book, is one that suggests that this strange and paradoxical relationship between tourism and languages is one that indexes aspects of human life that relate to respect, imagination, desire, fear, mess, relationship and humility. Tourist language learning is an effort to pronounce respect. It is a virtue (MacIntyre, 1985). Such aspects of life are ones that structural and anti-structural arguments, and economic or psychological modelling, or even attention to the language (as opposed to languages) of tourism (Dann, 1996; Jaworski & Pritchard, 2005; Pearce, 2005) cannot help us to access. As Freire maintains, in *Pedagogy of the Oppressed* 'to exist, humanely, is to name the world, to change it' (Freire, 1970: 69). The original Portuguese used by Freire for 'naming' is *pronunciar* – to pronounce – the action of pronunciation being at the heart of humane attempts at living.

The questions and phenomena I am concerned with here are not ones that respond well to scientific method. They are the kinds of empiricism which, in Law's terms, are 'complex, diffuse and messy' and are 'textured' in ways that cannot be made 'clear and definite' (Law, 2004: 2). These acts of learning are ones which, phenomenologically speaking, help us to sense wonder, expressed in gasps, from out of the 'quick' of human relatedness. They make the familiar strange, letting us watch as something impenetrable becomes our own, to enter into the languaging of others with our own effort and interrelatedness. As such, they are messy. They point, again, to the 'quick', the sparks from the fire. They also point to a fascination with the incommensurability of life, tourism and language. Such aspects of life require metaphor, description, deliberation and an 'ontological methodology' (Law, 2004: 154), which relates the 'quick' of being and relating: 'We may speak several languages, but one always remains the one in which we live. In order completely to assimilate a language, it would be necessary to make the world which it expresses one's own, and one never does belong to two worlds at once' (Merleau-Ponty, 2002: 218).

To answer the question posed at the head of this final section, what is being pronounced, amongst other things, in the lesson in pronunciation, is respect. Tourist language learners, I would argue, embody aspects of global citizenship and intercultural communication agendas discussed in Chapter 1, through their very grasping after language and speaking from the body in new ways.

Conclusions

Pronunciation is a bodily phenomenon involving the whole person. In making the effort to pronounce, to utter the right sounds in the right way, the tourist language learner moves in and through speech, and imagines others in new ways. Pronunciation is also a relational activity involving the imagination of others, monolingual hosts, and of encounters with such beings within tourism. Pronunciation evokes clear emotions and reactions, laughter, curiosity, love of new sounds, and even repulsion. Finally, pronunciation, as the first stage in detaching from one language and understanding another, points to a desire, connected to the specific language, to be able to live, fully, 'humanely' – in Freire's terms (Freire, 1970) – in the tourist world and the world of the destination. It indexes something of the respect and the connection that may be felt by tourists, as well as the aspects of capital and control I examined in Chapter 3.

Much has been made of the distinction between the tourist and the sojourner, and yet, under this reading, the difference is one of degree. Both are on a continuum of learning to language as a way of dwelling in another world. The paradox of the effort to do this is complex, but the fact of its existence as a labour of leisure will entertain me in the chapters to follow. It is an effort that suggests that the relationship of the tourist to the tourist language is one which is incarnational, which points to the word as made flesh and lived in and through. As such, it reverses ideas of tourism as a sacred journey and points to the 'quick' and to the everydayness of human movement and human relationships. This effort also tells us of the tourist imagination, the encounters and sensations that are in the world as we encounter it as tourists, and it suggests important, yet complex, diffuse and messy dimensions of tourist life, which habitual frameworks in tourism studies and in the anthropology of tourism fail to penetrate.

Chapter 6
Conversations

Tourist Orality and Literacy

The multilingual, intercultural soundscapes of tourism are created out of everyday practices and concerns. Tourists may attempt to order food in the language of the destination; they may write the name of their home country in the language of the destination on postcards, they may equally hope that someone they are with will make the attempt for them. There is a rigorous market in tourist phrase books. Textually, tourist destinations are multilingual sites, full of multilingual signage, as are the spaces through which tourists pass when in transit. The commentary and stories that accompany tourist experiences are crafted in and through languages, picking up words and accents from the destination, to describe the place and to craft it into stories.

> *My first visit to Prague was with a German school trip. We experienced Prague with our German friends and with a German-speaking tour guide. Those serving us in the bars and cafés spoke tourist German. I never left the German bubble, even though my mother tongue was English. When I describe Prague it is with German words... Karlsbrücke...Charles Bridge...Wenselsplatz... Wenceslas Square.*

The shifts between structure and anti-structure, in the encounters with the sounds of a language, as they are detached from the messiness and incomprehensible noise of being a language that is not known, are both subtle and micro scale. The *attaching* and *gathering* process at work in the pronunciation of sounds is peculiar to the language – in the case here, of Portuguese, or Italian. This occurs in the 'quick' of human relatedness, in the thick of things, through mimesis and repetition. These particular moments of experiential intersection reveal something of how the *thickness*, indeed the opacity of a language, may be *thinned* down, through this *gathering* and *attaching* process that does not require some separate mode of thought but *is in itself the process of thinking* (Ingold, 2000; Mcfague, 1975).

Through these observations I address the central question, for the purposes of this book, namely, why might it be that such a terrific expenditure of time and energy might be found so commonly in tourist language classes where the actual opportunities on the ground for use of the language or for further interaction are at best limited and at worst non-existent?

This line of questioning opens up a field of possibilities that shows the strange and paradoxical relationship between languages and tourism to be one which indexes something of what it means to communicate interculturally and to be human in the contemporary world. Tourism is arguably the phenomenon that enables the most intercultural encounter for the most number of people in the world today. As we have already noted this encounter is highly partial and fraught with inequalities of power, but, in the situation under scrutiny here, we have tourists who are prepared to work, actively, against the dominant flow of language, insulation and anonymity in the western world. Tourist language learners, through languaging, open themselves up, in risky ways, ways that impact on their very sense of themselves and their understandings of the world. They attempt, in short, to use a strange language to engage in intercultural conversation.

Conversation comes as tourists move from mimicking the sounds of a language and pronouncing new words, to looking to make sense of the new language and beginning to talk sense, with others, themselves. This is the aspect of language learning which is usually discussed under the rubric of comprehension – written comprehension and listening comprehension. In the literature on both second language acquisition and on orality and literacy the divide between these modes of comprehension of production remains largely in tact. Ong, for instance, in his now seminal study on orality and literacy maintains that:

> Wherever human beings exist they have a language, and in every instance a language that exists basically as spoken and heard, in the world of sound. [...] Indeed, language is so overwhelmingly oral that of all the many thousands of languages – possibly tens of thousands – spoken in the course of human history only around 106 have every been committed to writing to a degree sufficient to have produced literature, and most have never been written at all (Ong, 1982: 7).

As such, following Ong's analysis, oral and written comprehension are different things with different effects and a fundamental contrast is set up between the literate west, and the 'primitive' – or in Ong's replacement term – 'oral' rest. Ong's work helpfully demonstrates the written logocentricism of much of the study of language in recent decades, and makes a case for the primacy of orality and oral modes of learning to relate to the environment, but his work also sets up a clear divide and an opposition between these different modes that is rather more complex than his account would initially suggest.

As mentioned earlier (Chapter 2) the *curriculum-as-desired* by tourist language learners is one which pulls hard in the direction of orality practices. Comprehension that is desired is oral and aural, as opposed to written. The existing literacy of western tourists, however, is used as a foundational structure from which to move into more oral modes, rather than the impulse being the other way around. As such, this direction bucks the trends identified by Ong, suggesting more of a dialectical process than his thesis appears to entertain:

> Orality is not an ideal, and never was. To approach it positively is not to advocate it as a permanent state for any culture. Literacy opens possibilities to the word and to human existence unimaginable without writing. Oral cultures today value their oral traditions and agonize over the loss of these traditions, but I have never encountered or heard of an oral culture that does not want to achieve literacy as soon as possible (Ong, 1982: 172).

I would follow Ong's statement here with my own statement regarding tourist orality: *I have never encountered or heard of a tourist language learner who does not want to achieve orality as soon as possible.* The literacy that is already intact is a means to an end. A by product of the learning may well be literacy in the language, an ability to read newspapers, literature, as well as adverts, opening times, guide books and shop signs. This is an act of intercomprehension – of understanding words in other languages without having knowingly been exposed to them or to their learning (Blanche-Benveniste & Valli, 1997). The effort, in learning to speak, is one focused powerfully on producing the right sounds, and of *talking sense* – of what Byram develops into the idea of the intercultural speaking, and to which must also be added the idea of intercultural listening (Byram, 1997; Phipps & Gonzalez, 2004).

From Comprehension to Conversation

It's week nine. We've learned some pronouns, regular and irregular verbs and some prepositions so far. We've some grammar to work with and some vocabulary in our lists. It's been freezing in the classroom and is freezing cold outside. We are all moaning about the ice, journeys home, defrosting. We learn how to say we are cold in the first minutes of the class – tenho frigo – and the class finishes a few minutes early because we all say we are too cold to think. We are learning to ask to buy tickets so we can travel by train or bus to certain tourist destinations. We talk together about Portugal fondly, dreaming of beaches, clean trains, punctuality, warmth, holidays – indulging in the commonplace stereotyping that goes with the tourist imagination of Portugal. We catch up with each other's knowledge of names of cities, phrases already successfully used to get around. As we pronounce the names of destinations in Portuguese we stop feeling the cold quite so intensely and enjoy the sensation that the naming brings and in learning to say we'd like a single ticket to Cascais:

Queria um bilhete para Lisboa, Cascais, Faro, Évora, Estoril
Queria reservar um bilhete para Sintra na 6a. Feira, 12 de dezembro
Simples ou de ida e volta?
Parte às 6h ou às 14 h
Quero ir às 6 h. A que hora chega?
Vai chegar às 9 h
Qual é a linha
É a linha 4
Quanto é
São 5 euros
Queria ir mais tarde.

Every now and then we use up the words we have. We aren't doing badly. We are sitting back to back so that we can't see each other and we are now trying to order tickets. We both have our books on our laps and we keep having to pause to check phrases and look at our notes, but we are managing to speak to each other as if we are on the phone, trying to book rail tickets to these lovely, warming places. But every now and then our words just run out. We just don't have the words we need to say the things to each other that will make it feel as though this is an exchange which is smooth, socially smooth, that makes it OK for us to be communicating as human beings. I want to say to my partner – 'its your turn now' – she wants to say the same to me. We get frustrated eventually and ask the teacher. Just using the one small phrase gives us a sense of relief.

In academic contexts the learning of another language primarily serves the purpose of literacy – to be able to read the learned language, and even write it, to be able to use it to create a written record. In tourist language learning contexts writing is a common activity. Learners constantly jot down words of vocabulary, make notes from phrases on the board, write out their own exercises and use the written text as an aide-memoire. However, the end goal is not the reading of a poem by Pessoa or a story by Calvino. The goal, both for the classroom contexts and for the destination, is *comprehension-for-conversation*. In tourist language classes, on the contrary, it may well be that the movement into another language leads to other moves, turns towards music, poetry, magazines, literature, but the aim is to underpin the conversation. In the extract above we see the relief that comes from being able to sustain something approaching a conversation, to find the right turns of phrase. Whatever we may think about the rigidity of an 'oral–literate' divide, Ong makes an important contribution in distinguishing between some fundamental qualities that pertain to sound and to speech, and that do not, in his view, pertain to writing.

Is the use of writing the same as operating technology? Ong says yes. Ingold disagrees. He argues that writing is not merely added on as a cultural supplement but that writing is a *graphism* and as such it is inscriptive not transcriptive. Texts, he maintains, following Carrithers' reflection on the root of Latin *textere* – to weave (Carrithers, 1992: 403) are *woven* not made. Writing is a graphic counterpart to speech. Both work with the warp and the weft of language, pulling against each other to form a whole.

Vocabulary list	
Demais	Too much
O dever de casa	Homework
Para	For
O restaurante	–
Barato	Cheap
O auditório	Auditorium
O coração	Heart
Em geral	In general
Agora	Now
Generoso	Generous
Urgente	–
Falador	Talkative
Professor	–
Pessimista	–
O jornalista	Journalist
O substantive	Noun
Boa remuneração	Good pay
A ambição	Ambition
Dynamiso	Dynamism
O vendedor	Seller

Sound, says Ong, cannot be stopped, or held, or paused (Ong, 1982: 32) in the way the box above, a random page from my vocabulary notes from my Portuguese class, holds, records and even pauses the language in writing. Whilst photography, that iconic touristic activity, may fix and freeze and frame and record for posterity, spoken language, the sounds of words spoken totally resists being held. Sound is of and in the moment – more like the 'quick' of theatre, than the replay of film – and as such 'the spoken word forms human beings into close knit groups' (Ong, 1982: 73). Thus, we might argue, that the questing for orality from out of literacy, by tourist language learners, works against the fixing tendencies, the homogenising, stereotypical tendencies so well documented in the tourism literature, and works instead in that 'quick' of human relatedness.

A list of words in a vocabularly book does not make any immediate sense. It serves as a foundation for the move, yes, in to more complex written language, but, for tourist language learners these notes are part of the building blocks for conversation, they help serve the weaving of conversation and speech. The learning, for tourist language learners, or, to use the term adopted in the previous chapter, the *fixing, gathering and attaching* of words in the memory, for the purpose of speech, serves the ephemeral, the insubstantial, that which cannot be captured, held down or recorded.

As such, it once again points to a counter-direction for tourist language learning as an activity working against the conventional grain of a pull to literacy, and to the fixing, materialising, recording gesture so well documented in tourism studies in the domains of postcard writing, souvenirs and photography (Jaworski & Pritchard, 2005; Love & Kohn, 2001; Thurlow *et al.*, 2005). Further, in the context of postcard writing, that most literate of tourist forms, communication is not with the destination, it is a gesture back into literacy, with durable relationships and the everyday modes of literate life, rather than one which steps away from this mode and into new, often fleeting, ephemeral and intangible relationships with people and places.

What, then, is occurring when tourist language learners begin to speak, *understand* and listen to each other, in the classroom context, and with others, in the destination? What happens when language moves from being a odd, amusing collections of sounds to be mimicked and worked at, to being a proto-conversation? Or in other words, what does this pull to orality tell us about the paradoxical relationship between languages and tourism that are unfolding here?

> To speak, you have to address another or others. People in their right minds do not stray through the woods talking at random to nobody. Even to talk to yourself you have to pretend you are two people. [...] To speak, I have to be somehow *already in communication* [my emphasis] with the mind I am to address before I start speaking. I can be in touch perhaps through past relationships, by an exchange of glances, by an understanding with a third person who has brought me and my interlocutor together, or in any of countless other ways. (Words are modifications of a more-than-verbal-situation.) I have to sense something in the other's mind to which my own utterance can relate.

Human communication is never one-way. Always, it not only calls for response *but is shaped in its very form and content by anticipated response* [my emphasis] (Ong, 1982: 173).

Tourist language learning, then, and its pull into orality, from literacy, is a mode of speech which is shaped by the response imagined, and anticipated, from the place, the culture and the respondents. As practised in the tourist language classroom this form and content differs, and acts as a dress rehearsal for the kinds of interactions and responses that may be anticipated on holiday, in the destination. The language classroom is the place where this relationship is initially made manifest and takes structured, practised communicative form; where the relationship that is already in place, through the mode of intercultural communication that is tourism, begins to come to life in language. More than this, however, the pull into orality from literacy indexes the pull into conversation. Tourist listening, tourist speaking and oral comprehension is not comprehension for its own sake, or for the sake of literacy, it is comprehension for the sake of conversation, widely conceived.

Ong maintains:

A sound-dominated verbal economy is consonant with aggregative (harmonizing) tendencies rather than with analytic, dissecting tendencies (which would come with the inscribed, visualised world vision is a dissecting sense). It is consonant also with the conservative holism (the homeostatic present that must be kept intact, the formulary expressions that must be kept intact), with situational thinking (again holistic, with human action at the centre) rather than abstract thinking, with a certain humanistic organisation of knowledge around the actions of human and anthropomorphic beings, interiorised persons, rather than around impersonal things (Ong, 1982: 73).

These are qualities which resonate with the modes of being that Turner identifies as those pertaining in situations of communitas and in the 'quick' of human relatedness (Turner, 1995). In this reading there is something in oral mode, or, for my purposes, in the impulse towards orality out of literacy, which is potentially holistic, situational, humanistic and harmonising. An answer to the question as to why on earth tourists might bother to learn the language, however partially, may, under this reading, take on a positive, even romanticised light as a desire for conversation and relationship, however limited, which requires comprehension to stand a chance. Although Turner's theories of communitas have been widely used in the anthropology of tourism they do not easily serve my purposes when attempting to understand this desire for conversation, and the movement into conversation. For this we need to turn to theories of relationship, and in particular, I would suggest, to the work Rowan Williams on the 'social miracle' of conversation and on the need for a common language.

The Social Miracle

Tonight something changed. We had almost all arrived before our teacher. As each of us walked into the classroom we said 'Olá' before we said 'Hello'. It had become natural to do this. We started chatting together easily, often about the fact we hadn't really done our homework, or about the traffic, the weather, the dark nights. Jonnie had brought along a bag of jelly babies to share out. He handed them round even before the teacher arrived and as soon as she walked in he offered her one too. We got started on the work, but the bag of jelly babies went up and down the rows. Sometimes we would deliberately pop one into our mouths, in an obvious gesture, to avoid having to answer pointed and difficult questions. And of course this would be funny. It was a bit of a game.

After this, food, became a weekly ritual. One of us would always bring a bag of sweets and share them out.

In *Lost Icons: Reflections on Cultural Bereavement* Rowan Williams reflects on the meanings of the old idea of 'charity'. Charity, rather like 'quick' is an old and resonant word. Drawing on the considerable scholarship of historian John Bossy (Bossy, 1984), Williams shows how 'charity' in the Middle Ages, in the time of the great pilgrimages, which are so often held as parallels for our reflections on tourism, involved the 'opportunity for suspending relationships characterised by competition, rivalry' (Williams, 2000a: 68–9).

The civilities of the fraternity – greeting, meeting and eating, as Bossy nicely puts it – direct energy away from competition and towards the maintenance of friendly exchange; or, in other words, the way to 'succeed' in the context of the fraternity is to become proficient at receiving and at initiating acts that embody mutual recognition and thus mutual honour or respect. [...] an agreement to speak the same language and listen to the other as an equal. [...] Charity is very like a *game* (Williams 2000a: 68–9).

Considerable effort is being made in the tourist language classroom to make meaning nicely, to make meaning in ways which are fun, inclusive, which allow for a greeting, a meeting and an eating: the biscuits or sweets brought along to class, the pausing to celebrate the ends of terms at Christmas or Easter, and to do so with wine and with food – wine and food from Portugal, or Brazil or from Italy. It is this social bondedness of the class the *meeting*, the *greeting* in the new language, and the *eating* that

Williams mentions here quoting Bossy. There is a charitable aspect to the class, and there is, I would also argue, a charitable aspect to the tourist language learning – a gratuity, a wastefulness, a lack of self-interest, a stepping out of own's own comfort zones for the sake of conversing with another. Here, I would argue, are more answers to the question, more ways of understanding the paradox, 'why bother?'.

The gratuitous nature of the language learning, in terms of its enjoyability and social nature, was reinforced by jelly babies, and by the games, the role playing. It fostered conversation and reinforced the rigour required to sustain the imagined tourist conversations of the future. Sometimes these role plays would be as described above – the play of being on the telephone booking tickets or rooms. At other times we invented the games ourselves, out of jelly babies or our own imagination and desire to push ourselves to say more and more outrageous things, because of the sheer joyful possibility of being able to do this. Both these aspects of game playing and role playing are further manifestations of the game like nature that emerges in the fundamental impulse to conversation in the gratuitous learning of a language as a tourist. 'Games' to cite Williams again, 'are unproductive' (Williams, 2000a: 69).

To return for a moment to the question of the integrity of the normative, functionalist discourses on the language learning in general. We might argue here, and with the resources of the jelly babies and the 'waste of time' that what we can say about language learning for tourist purposes is precisely not that it is useful, precisely not that there are 700 uses of the language, but rather that it is fundamentally *useless* and that that is the whole point. For what it serves is conversation – the 'quick' of human relatedness – and there is nothing more to conversation than the social bond, the common language, the social miracle (Dunbar, 1996).

Conversation is made in mouths, in speech, produced *from* the body (Farnell, 2000). It is primarily an oral form, though the scripts to be rehearsed in these classes are written up on the black board for us to use as an aide-memoire, in ways identical to the rehearsal processes for the staging of drama (Chapter 8). The physicality of the production of language *for* conversation is significant here. The language is one which has the immediacy of conversation. It occurs in real time. It is direct, even if it is focused on role playing for imagined future tourist conversations. Ong's insights into the distinctions between orality and literacy are useful to us again here: 'Because in its physical constitution as sound, the spoken word proceeds from the human interior and manifests human beings to one another as conscious interiors, as persons, the spoken word forms human beings into close-knit groups' (Ong, 1982: 73).

Speaking, in Ong's view, differs fundamentally from reading as it is focused on sociality as opposed to interiority or individuality. And in the examples drawn from our tourist language classes we see this aspect enacted in the mix of English and Portuguese chat occurring to smooth the passage to social bondedness in the group of tourist language learners and also for the imagined social bonds of the tourist destination, in the future tense. The role playing and game playing is a crucial aspect to this development and one to which I shall return. For now, however, the important point to be made is that there is a movement enacted here, supported by the social rituals of the class and by the desire for conversation as an expression of and maintenance for the social bond, at home, in the class and crucially, with others in tourist settings. Comprehension serves conversation and does so in ways that are demanding.

Gratuitous Speech

According to Williams (2000a) conversation, the speaking of sensible words to others in ways that form 'human beings into close knit groups' is fundamentally gratuitous. It cannot be analysed functionally. It does not serve the social bond so much as constitute the social bond. It is itself, to use Williams' term – a 'social miracle'. 'At the most basic level no one *decides* to start talking. In a crucially important sense, language is not an *invention*, a way of solving a problem. The very idea of a problem to be solved *assumes* language' (p. 72). So although we have seen ways in which tourist language learners see and imagine risks and problems to be solved using their tourist language, the actual talking, the flow of words that constitutes the conversations around such problem solving is more gratuitous.

Williams acknowledges the existence of speech acts (Austin, 1975) – the fact that conversations can also exchange information and be *for* social purposes, can help the functioning of social life (Williams, 2000a: 100). But fundamentally what interests him – his point, so to speak – relates to the gratuity and the *unnecessary* nature of conversation. In this he maintains that the gratuitous nature of 'starting a conversation' breaks with the structures of the world, which Ong would term 'literate' – the structures that are founded on rivalry, competition, on the idea of scarcity, limited material goods. Conversation, and this also includes the work of comprehension, does not play by these rules. Conversation and role play of the kinds we see at work here are aimed at developing a fluency, not just in the language but in conversing, with an activity that need not be based on scarcity. There *are* enough words to go around, which 'presupposes mutual recognition, an activity in which "success" is measured simply by the maintenance of the activity itself' (pp. 71–2). 'What we have in common is simply the conversation itself' (p. 99). In touristic situations, where the social bonds are often fleeting, the conversational aspects become all the more remarkable.

Languages are inalienable goods. They do not detach well for the market. They have suffered as a consequence of the shift to marketisation. There are scarcities in languages – diminishments that indicate the way in which languages are killed off under consumerist paradigms – but we do not pay to converse. As such they have built into them the idea of the common good, they are not scarce until endangered, and, ironically, unlike many rare and therefore highly prized goods, the endangered species of languages do not attract high prices in the linguistic markets. 'Conversation thus represents [...] the break-through into a recognition of common goods, things we can only value or enjoy together' (Williams, 2000a: 93).

Conversations

In embarking on a discussion of the impulse to conversation drawn from the work of theology I feel the need to offer a note of caution or even defence. A scholar of tourism from the arts, social sciences or humanities does not easily and readily read theology unless she is either employed and trained as a theologian or unless she possesses an interest in such reading that is drawn from the exercise of a particular rule or understanding of life. My own formal training is not in theology but I would understand myself to be theologising in as much as 'a person shaping their life in a specific way, seeking discipline and consistency in relation to God, is theologizing, forming a reflectively consistent speech for God' (Williams, 2000b: xii).

Of course such a position within the critical, sceptical and atheistic milieu of academic theorising outside of theology (and even within theology) in Europe today is highly problematic. It raises questions about the possibility, in the writer, of objectivity, of impartiality and, perhaps most of all, of reasoned and even reasonable argument. Theology, worked out in the church and the practice of faith through many centuries, bears the burden of both a violent and an inspiring legacy for its work. It goes without saying that, in using theology here, and in theologising on the subject of the strange and paradoxical relationship between languages and tourism that I have such difficulties in mind, and that I do not proceed lightly. I could, for safety's sake, perhaps hide the references, bury them in a bibliography, pretend that the Williams in question was a Raymond not a Rowan, and Raymond too, figures in the overall architectural argument of this book. But that would be disrespectful of a readership in whose critical engagement I trust.

Our urge to theory, as critical scholars of tourism and of languages is not usually an urge that takes us into theology. Indeed, when our pet theorists begin to show 'worrying' signs of engaging with the big metaphysical questions of faith and belief and 'God', then we use this turn of theirs in often dismissive ways, retreating into the safeties of agnosticism, at the very least. I could turn here, of course, to Foucault, or Derrida, or Zizek, of even Bourdieu, and where appropriate and helpful, even compelling, this is what I would wish to do as a scholar. But the questions I am raising here are not satisfactorily answered for me by understandings of power and discursive control, by the slippages in language or by the inequitable distribution of forms of capital. Although these frameworks help considerably, they do not aid me in the gnawing question of the paradoxical relationship – the question as to why such time might be wasted, for so little obvious reward. The question, for me, is, in its most extreme or most profound form, a theological one, not a philosophical one. It is a question of the 'third term' – the sense that between or beyond myself and the other there is a meaning to be discovered that is more than the sum of the whole. It poses questions as to how a community of human beings comes to relate beyond themselves, it is more than the question of why it is that some human beings do good, when to do ill would be a much easier option.

My own understanding of God or belief is not important here. What is significant is that the kinds of questions I am raising are ones which, I believe, are at the heart of the most interesting lines of enquiry in tourism, hospitality and in modern language studies – questions about the necessity of rest, the pursuit of happiness, the reinvention of community, the embodiment of other languages, the 'waste' of time, the reinvention of work. These are questions that are about the practice of common life and language, life lived out beyond the self and for the self. In the midst of great, grave and also entirely legitimate misunderstandings of the task of theology and its potential to illuminate our broader academic understanding 'theology can remind the world [...] that it offers not a total meaning but the possibility of a perception simplified and unified in and through the contingencies of human biography: not the conquest but the *transformation* of mortal vision' (Williams, 2000b: 13–14).

The learning of another language for tourist purposes is one of the contingencies of human biography. 'I can speak a bit of Portuguese. I did an evening class. I can get by, order food, have a simple conversation.' The *perception* that theology can offer accords with the sense of transformation that the 'being able to' ('I can...') aspects of these tourist language learning statements offer. Here, the aspect *of being able* to *comprehend* another's language, a stranger's language, in such a way as *to be able* to hold a conversation takes the tourist into *languaging*, beyond the supports and socialities of a classroom community of practice and into relations beyond the self, posing an ontological risk and destabilisation at the same time as re-enacting aspects of 'charity' through the gratuity – the particularly acute gratuity – of tourist conversation.

The theological perspective, helpful as it may be, is not the only one which may be brought to bear in this context, however. There are many potential answers to the questions: Why bother? – Why put so much effort into a relationship for the sake of fleeting conversations with ephemeral others? Why, in a context of rapacious technological, consumer capitalism, a context when everything that moves has to be counted, accounted and *for* some tangible, profitable gain, would anyone waste their time learning a language *for their holidays*? How is it that the desire for conversation can have such motivational power, such transformational, counter-culture, counter-intuitive effects? Modern linguists in particular have, has noted earlier, spent much energy engaging in finding reasons for the continuation of formal language learning as an important intellectual and civic duty.

700 Reasons to Bother

The modern languages teaching profession has worked long and hard to justify the learning of another language, in the face of the rise of global English alongside global capitalism, and the constant erosion of its place in the academy as a discipline with something to be *for* that is functional and can play on these terms. There are now 700 reasons for studying a language. (www.llas.soton.ac.uk) all carefully collected from language learners who are themselves inhabited by the functionalist discourse, and from the fun they have had with learning another language. Some of those reasons are tourist reasons, they relate to travel, mobility, connection. But the problem with such initiatives is that ultimately, even though done with great integrity, they are not about the 'quick' and the conversations between people, they are about a desperate search for attractive numbers, operating at two levels:

A two level discourse is one which steps back from the risks of *conversation* – above all from those two essential features of conversation, the recognition of an 'unfinished' quality in what has been said on either side, and the possibility of correction. [...] To make what is said invulnerable by displacing its real subject matter is a strategy for the retention of power. It can operate at either end of the social scale: in the language of those in control, which will be essentially *about* the right to control, and in the language of the powerless in the presence of the powerful, which takes on the images and definitions offered by the latter as the only possible means of access to their world, their resources (Williams, 2000b: 4).

To have 700 reasons to learn a language is admirable. But it also closes down the possibility of debate, discussion. If there are 700 reasons then there can be no answer. The weight of numbers, in a world that counts, is enough. Of course for modern linguists, under the analysis above, this is the response of the (relatively) powerless to the oppressive effects, real and painful, of the application of a model of market forces and competition to the 'good', the 'social good' that is languages. A response that reaches beyond the weight of statistics into the 'quick' of the stories, and which did not react out of powerlessness, would be the response I am uncovering here in tourist language learners; the response that bothers in ways that appear to be gratuitous and are about the desire for conversation with others.

Conclusions

So what is unfolding here is a scenario in which the learning of languages for tourist purposes is seen as both a pull into orality and a strange manifestation, perhaps even a surprising manifestation, of the gratuity of conversation as social miracle. This 'miraculous' aspect is perhaps even more noteworthy as it is not the miracle of regular contact with neighbours, with those thrown regularly into one's path, but with unknown peoples, strangers. Of course these are people, strangers, who, like any potential stranger, may be called upon to host and with whom the languaging relations will be relations that follow cultural rules for hospitality. In the desire for conversation in the tourist language the learners here are demonstrating all these aspects, and more, for they are already role playing and enacting the very structures they imagine to be significant – the meeting, greeting and eating – that will foster conversation.

The desire for conversation is a desire for orality. But the rigidity of divisions set up by Ong do not serve us well in this context, as we shall see in the chapter to follow. There are aspects in play that rely on literacy and a scripting of potential conversations. As such there are parallels to the phrase book – that ubiquitous artefact of foreign travel. It would therefore perhaps be fairer to say that in this process of comprehension-for-conversation, and of conversation as the social bond, we find an *oralising literacy* at work, as opposed to a *literacising orality*. Further, I would argue that conversation is born of the very tensions in play in this pull to orality for literate tourist learners. These tensions, to return to my earlier point, may be compared, analogously to those of those involved the weaving of cloth, in texture, textile and, consequently, text.

Ingold is careful in his reception of Ong's important work on orality literacy to point out the dangers of such rigid divisions. He demonstrates the many different culs-de-sac of linguistic theory that have arisen as a result of an insistence on the primary differences between orality and literacy. Instead he prefers to see both as gestures, as emanating *from* the body, one using technological means but both being, he says following Mauss, 'techniques of the body' (Ingold, 2000: 403). All speakers are 'wholly immersed [...] in the relational context of dwelling in a world' (Ingold, 2000: 409):

> For such a being, this world is already laden with significance: meaning inheres in the *relations* between the dweller and the constituents of the dwelt-in-world. And to the extent that people dwell in the same world and are caught up together in the same currents of activity, they can share in the same meanings,. Such communion of experience, the awareness of living in a common world of meaningful relations, establishes a foundational level of sociality which exists – in Pierre Bourdieu's (1977: 2) phrase – 'on the hither side of words and concepts' (Ingold, 2000: 409).

To the extent that, under conditions of liquid modernity and the democratisation of tourism and travel, tourists are caught up together, for often quite fleeting moments in the same currents of activities and in distant destinations we see new forms of social worlds emerging. However thin and fragile, tourists are coming into being in and through conversation. And this is the point at which Williams, Ingold and Bourdieu meet – 'on the hither side of words and concepts' – in an ontological world where the rules of the intercultural game are written anew, through common struggles for meaning, to make meaning, to comprehend, to converse and to dwell.

This is not to say for a moment that this place and process – 'on the hither side' – will be a unified, easy place, free of tension. If we know anything from theology, sociology, anthropology and the study of tourism, we know that this is a highly contested milieu. It is messy. It is always messy in the 'quick' of human relatedness. Fundamental tensions between modes are important – intercultural communication cannot be intercultural communication if it erases differences and rests on harmony. The pull to orality is a pull into actual 'quick' conversation with others who we do not know.

Chapter 7
Games

Games for Guests

Much communicative language learning develops through the use of games. These games may be both oral and written – crosswords, acrostics, puzzles, story telling, quizzes. Language teachers are well versed in a wide repertoire of games and activities that can help draw learners out of themselves and into communicative interaction. These games take myriad forms in the tourist language classroom and aim at repeating vocabulary and syntax structures so that gradually the language can be learned, embodied and reproduced with ease, fluently, and with attention being paid as much to the process of the game as to the grammatical structures. Just as in theatrical rehearsal processes games may be used to induce role play, characterisation, concentration and development of muscle memory to embody scripts, so in the tourist language classroom contexts are developed in which there can be a rehearsal of phrases, words and imagined contexts in which the language may be used in conversation, allowing sociality to flow.

I didn't have chance to do my homework this week. I thought I might get a few moments coming in on the train to review the perfect tense but then I met a friend at the station and that plan was scuppered. By now the class has bonded, so those few moments to check over my notes in the relative anonymity of the new group have evaporated. I walk into the room, Scott, and Ana and Tony are already there and we are straight into the usual routines of talking about holidays. Our tutor arrives 'Olá' she says and we all chorus our now practised and correct replies in Portuguese. 'OK' she says 'Come and stand round in a circle.' She takes a piece of scrap paper, screws it up into a ball and then asks the question, in her Brazilian Portuguese: 'Que és que voce fez no fim de semana'. 'Oh help' anxiety rises, we all giggle, gulp, I am now completely rumbled – I haven't even got my notebook to hand. She throws the ball straight at Beryl. 'No sábado' she says – she has done her homework, the retired folk in the class usually have, its a rather wonderful moment of revenge on the youth, of the time-poor professionals amongst us. The same goes for the students and the unemployed. 'Fui à igreja, à missa.' 'OK' – it's coming back – 'fui', I think, 'fui', 'please don't pick on me next' I think. Beryl throws the ball to Gabriella – 'phew'. 'No fim da semana passado eu fui ao cinema ver um filme'…It's coming back to me, in fragments of memory from last week's introduction to the perfect tense.'No fim de semana passada fui com meu marido a Lisboa' lies Jean, boasting. Of course we all laugh – 'if only…' someone mutters. The ball hits me on the nose and I drop it. 'No sábado fui ao teatro' I lie 'e no domingo eu também fui à igreja. 'I'm so pleased to get the sentence out in one piece and without dropping the ball that I then forget to throw the damn thing on again.

It is clear, to any language teacher, from the buzz in a language classroom in which games are played, from the heightened sense of action embodied, and from the developing confidence of language students, that games work. They have the desired effect of creating relaxed students who use the language they are learning to play the games. It would be possible to argue that games *work* here because they introduce elements of competition, because they enable a focus on something beyond the language – on playing the game rather than getting the grammar right, or that games reinforce the aspect of leisure that accompanies both evening classes and language holidays. Games, it could be argued, are what are played when we are not working. As such, they mark a mode of being that is separate from that of daily work and routine. And there is something to this line of argument. It is different, fun, it *feels* gratuitous even though it is in the service of learning a language, and of doing so with tourist purposes firmly in mind. It also opens a space – rather as narrative opens a space, in Ricoeur's terms (Ricoeur, 1984) for something new to happen and it gives the learning time a different character and texture.

There is something socially and thus also personally refreshing about playing games. How this playful dimension of tourist language learning intersects with wider questions as to why tourists bother with the language, is the question that will detain us here. Further, I am concerned to examine the ways in which the pull is into more oral modes of being and, importantly, how *conversing* with others is sustained by games. What is it about being a tourist, and therefore also a guest, about linguistic guesting, that attracts playful modes of being? To answer this question I will now turn to social and theoretical work on games, play and language in order to see how these relate to the discussions of the previous chapters. What place do games have in maintaining the social bond and in helping the awkwardness and hard work involved in learning a new language?

Language Games

Talk of games and language invokes Wittgenstein and his concept of language games (Wittgenstein, 1953). Wittgenstein's notion of language games refers to the irreducible variety and plurality of contexts that make up the language(s) in which we dwell. He illustrates the ways in which gesture, pointing, words, interruptions, repetitions, etc. mean that human beings inhabit language as they learn it and as they point it out to others.

Physical gestures do not fix meaning, rather they should be seen as 'organs of language'. There is no connection to be made between the world 'out there' and language: 'Here the term 'language game' is meant to bring into prominence the fact that the 'speaking' of language is part of an activity, or form of life' (Wittgenstein, 1953: 23).

This view of language has proved productive for reflection on language. Without conflating these authors it is worth noting that the idea of language games is often paralleled to Derridean conceptions of 'writing games' and the slippery nature of meaning, and it is also traced into the symbolic systems of meanings elaborated by Lévi-Strauss and by Saussure. It may also be read in the direction that our theoretical framing has taken us thus far – into the world of perception and phenomena. Wittgenstein appears to argue that the world of everyday life and phenomena, the world of the social bond and of practical activities is, what we might term here, a language-world:

> 'Without language we could not communicate with one another' – but for sure: without language we cannot influence other people in such-and-such ways; cannot build roads and machines, etc. And also: without the use of speech and writing people could not communicate' (Wittgenstein, 1953: 491).

It is a world brought into being by a wide variety and plurality of concepts produced by persons as they *'inhabit* language'. Our tourist learners are certainly engaged in different language games watching as slowly – rather like Wittgenstein's examples of 'primitive language' or 'children's language' – games are played, objects are pointed out with the hand, stress is laid on words and patterns are repeated so that the language is learned, as self-contained.

There is, however, more to the games played in the tourist language classes than the development of language games, or the application of tried and tested pedagogical devices. The key here is more the idea of *inhabiting* than necessarily of language. Yes, these tourists are learning to inhabit a different language, but whereas Wittgestein argues that the world is language and the language is world – that it is self-contained – Merleau-Ponty would argue that the world of perception is greater than that of language. Indeed, to equate language and the world is to miss out on the different modes of relation that develop out of a sensing perception of the environment, of the human world of language but also of non-human worlds.

The tourist language learners, as we have seen thus far, are trying to inhabit a language, but are also attuned to the environment and the material world in different ways, through language games, but also through modes of perception. We learn, in embodied ways, from where we dwell, from the locus of the inhabiting that Wittgenstein speaks of. As noted in Chapter 2, learning occurs as a result of what Ingold terms 'hands-on' training in everyday tasks and through an 'education of attention' (Ingold, 2000: 167):

> [...] the world becomes a meaningful place for people through being *lived in*, rather than through having been constructed along the lines of some formal design. Meanings are not attached by the mind to objects in the world, rather these objects take on their significance [...] by virtue of their incorporation into a characteristic pattern of day-to-day activities (Ingold, 2000: 168).

And so it is that a ball of paper may be bricolaged into becoming an item in a game with a new tourist language; that it may act as the prompt, as the game is lived and played for what has been learned in order to be *languaged*. One of the moves made and enacted by tourist language learners in these games is into the simulation of live performance. This is indeed a live game for the relatively small private audience of those in a language class, but it also acts as a bridge into languaging from language learning. Through being a live game in and of itself it points beyond itself to the real contexts of travelling, ordering food, asking for directions, meeting people that are the imagined presence in the tourist language class.

The *learning* dimension returns here. How is it that role playing and language games serve the gratuity of conversation? What is it about the conjunction of tourism and language learning that creates situations where we can remember that there are enough words to go around, that rivalry may be suspended, or playfully evoked, and the life rules of learned cultural games may be re-written? How is it that games help give social confidence for actually using the language, for languaging? In short, what is it about these conjunctions that makes aspects of learned behaviour and taken-for-grantedness *deconstructable* through tourist learning?

Cock Fights

Clifford Geertz writes of the considerable energy, excitement, acceptance and exchange that grew out of his headlong escape from arrest by the Balinese police when the cock fight he was attending as part of his fieldwork studies was suddenly busted, and everyone fled – him and his wife, as he writes, included. His feeling led him, he writes, to be instantly defended and accepted:

We were suddenly the object of great outpouring of warmth, interest, and most especially, amusement. Everyone in the village knew we had fled like everyone else. They asked us about it again and again (I must have told the story, small detail by small detail, fifty times by the end of the day), gently, affectionately, but quite insistently teasing us: 'Why didn't you just stand there and tell the police who you were?' 'Why didn't you just say you were only watching and not betting?' 'Were you really afraid of those little guns?' [...] In Bali, to be teased is to be accepted (Geertz, 1973: 416).

This event and the switch it facilitated for Geertz in his fieldwork led him to reflect upon the meaning of gaming, betting, cock fights and status in Balinese society. It took him away, in the 1970s, from structural function-alism, or social mechanics as he terms it, and into questions of social semantics, ushering in the interpretative turn in anthropology. Culture, and 'deep play' – a term he takes from Bentham – contains symbolic mean-ings that may show us dimensions of our own subjectivities – be these through the cock fight for the Balinese, or through Macbeth. By 'deep play' Bentham is referring to play where the stakes are so high that it appears, from Bentham's own utilitarian standpoint, to be irrational to engage in it. Indeed Bentham's own view was that men (*sic*) should be protected from 'deep play' for it is immoral to pursue either pain or pleasure in this way.

For Geertz, the notion of 'deep play' gives him a way of explaining the symbolic dimensions of status and money as embedded into the struc-tures of the Balinese cock fight. The play is deep because much money, status, honour and display is risked. Money and status are played with, according to Geertz, in ways in which the stakes are very high indeed, in *irrational* ways, because both matter so much. Geertz's own irrational headlong dash from the cock fight when the police arrived to join his hosts rather than protecting his 'Distinguished Visitor' status (Geertz, 1973: 416) took him to the heart of the things revealed in the risks around deep play. Consequently, he tells us, he demonstrated to his hosts, through his sudden half-conscious choice in the thick of things, that he too was able to engage in 'deep play' with the things of status in his own life – namely his papers.

This risky behaviour, the awkwardness of his graceless running, the amusement of his stories for his hosts also led him into direct conversa-tion, the gratuity of language games where his hosts drop in all manner of questions and possibilities for the telling and re-telling of the story. It opens up the floodgates of words – not just in his own context but for many ensuing anthropological conversation in the context of interpreta-tive, symbolic anthropology. What Geertz reports as the sign that he had been accepted, that his hosts welcomed him, was their teasing, and this was made manifest in the conversations, and in the gestural mocking, in the language games, and in the re-enactments of his story that they developed in response. In other words Geertz knew he was accepted as a guest because of the linguistic hosting of fluent, passionate, teasing, eager conversation.

Geertz's observations are often taken as indexing the interpretive turn in anthropology, and have been criticised too for their textualism, for 'imputing to the object the manner of the looking' (Bourdieu, 2000: 53). I do not wish to rehearse the arguments for and against these views here, but wish to focus on the dimensions in the description rather than in the line of argument that Geertz takes, legitimately in his struggles against certain dominating paradigms at his time of writing. Indeed, my own struggles here point to the intersections and domination of other paradigms and their development – 30 years on from the Balinese cock fight narrative.

The dimensions that interest me here are those that grow out of the conversation, the 'quick' and the narratives Geertz reports as indictating his acceptance, and out of the gratuity and *irrational* nature of deep play: '[...] despite the logical force of Bentham's analysis men [*sic*] do engage in such play, both passionately and often, and even in the face of law's revenge' (Geertz, 1973: 433). I believe there is a parallel to be drawn here between the levelled out gratuity of conversation and intense playing out of alternative rivalries in deep play. These are apparent in Geertz's text, but are also apparent in the games played with language in the tourist language classroom.

The 'communitas', as Turner describes it (Turner, 1995), of the hosting which Geertz experienced in conversation and through inhabiting the flow of language games, flowed out of the deep play – not of the cock fight, but of his own risking of his 'Distinguished Visitor' status. Turner uses the Latin deliberately to make a distinction between the place of common living – community – and the modality of a social relationship – communitas. Communitas, he argues, is an inherently dialectical element of any functioning society. Turner makes it possible to identify certain common characteristics pertaining to communitas. 'Community is where community happens' he maintains, drawing on Buber (Buber, 1958; Turner, 1995: 127). It is 'of the now', as being 'with one another', as involving 'the whole man [*sic*] in relation to other whole men' (Turner, 1995: 113) and as enacting potentiality.

We've all been given a drinks menu in Italian. It is for a restaurant with a suitably authentic sounding name, and it is printed out in a suitably menuesque font. It is a photopcopy from a text book we assume. Everything on the menu is priced up in

Euros. This causes some consternation as we aren't very familiar with this new currency 'The lira was easy' says one seasoned tourist. Our tutor writes up useful phrases on the board:

mi dispiace – I'm sorry
mi dispiace ma il caffè non c'è – 'I'm sorry but' ('literally', says our tutor) 'the coffee, there is none'. Everyone laughs at the idea of there being no coffee.
vuole qualcos' altro? – anything else?
in tutto – in total
il resto a ley – keep the change
va bene così – that's fine
basta così – that's enough.

We are put into pairs and we play the 'there is no coffee' game. It is hilarious. Firstly, we are imagining being in Italy – Land of Coffee – when there is none, a game in itself. Secondly, my partner is just downright mean. I'm being the waitress and she is refusing to tip and asking only for a glass of tap water. If I'm lucky I'll make 0.30c from her. 'Basta così' – she says, giving me absolutely nothing. I come back with a pretend glass, plonk it down and say 'mi dispiace ma l'acqua non c'è'.

In this example we are involved in playing out risks to status, in the 'now' of the language class, where communitas happens in the game. We also have an eye to the future and to the structured interactions between the respective statuses of tourist and waitress. We play games in the present, with the imagined tourist future, and with our own sense of justice and fairness. We are taking the tourist–host relationship into its extremes using our very limited grasp of tourist Italian. The status of both tourist and waitress is in play, as is the language. We know full well that we would be beaten by more complex exchange, but here we can show some of the worst of what we hear tourists and hosts do, we can enact the archetypes, and so demonstrate to ourselves that, in learning the language and in role playing as we are doing together, we are somehow above this.

Status and play are also at work in the language classroom and in the role plays and games that accompany the learning. As we noted in Chapter 4 there are forms of capital at stake – *linguistic capital*, the ability to do things with words, to perform socially and successfully, the status one usually occupies in society. But there are also other forms of status in play here. Our own status as good guests is up for grabs in this exchange. In putting our language and our ability to be good citizens, as tourists or as hosts, on the line here, through the language game, we are showing something of what is important to us, in this social context. Much may be at stake, even erased, when learning to inhabit a different language and this dimension is heightened when game playing with the language. But more than this, the irrational, countercultural dimension of bothering to learn a language for tourism, which is at the heart of my questions and concerns in this book, also indicates dimensions of deep play.

Pain and pleasure both may accrue to the tourist who attempts to speak the language in context – the pain of humiliation, misunderstanding, difficulty, grammatical error, of not being heard, of being accorded the status of stupid – these are some of the status anxieties at play. But equally there may be considerable acceptance, generosity, intercultural listening, a reaching out that brings pleasure – the pleasure of conversation, connection, social bonding in the face of extraordinary odds.

Geertz's observations on the Balinese cock fight, and on the irrational need to raise the stakes and for human beings to engage in deep play – in its deep pain and its pleasure – gives us some tentative ways into understanding the dimensions of role play that accompany tourist language learning; its gratuity and its irrationality. And we may, unlike Geertz, turn not so much to the symbolic dimensions – though these are not irrelevant, even though they may appear to be more obvious – but to the ethical questions raised by Bentham and dismissed by Geertz: 'Bentham's conclusion [about deep play] was, therefore, that deep play was immoral from first principles and, a typical step for him, should be prevented legally' (Geertz, 1973: 433).

For it strikes me, in these reflections on the 'why bother?' of tourist language learning and the role of deep play in the tourist language classroom, that the moral dimension is what is actually 'in play' – even more than questions of symbol and of status. *Learning is kinship*, we might say, developing Ingold's point that geography is kinship. Turning back to Bentham's sense of this moral dimension – though not, in this case so much to its dubiety as to the dimensions that work *irrationally and gratuitously* towards social bonding despite the gracelessness, awkwardness and clumsiness of conversation – may enable us to explore the role of deep play in the context of tourism and languages.

The Pain and Pleasure of Deep Language Play

The context of tourist language learning and of languaging is one of dwelling as movement – not just of *linguistic capital* but of *linguistic currency* – of being able to inhabit other languages, other worlds, with hoped for ease. So far I have described some of the pleasure and fun with languages that I experienced as a tourist language learner. However, the process of arriving in a place where we may indeed speak with ease is not always easy, not every tutor is always and consistently a 'good intercultural listener'. And I was far from a good, model student. Sometimes, the process of deep play is genuinely difficult.

I am now completely out of my depth. The class has moved on, everything is being taught in the language and I just don't understand anything: what I'm supposed to do, what the homework is, what the exercise is in front of us that we've just been given and how on earth I'm going to participate in the role play exercise when I don't know what the rules are. The rule in this class is that we only speak Portuguese. I try and speak to the teacher but I still don't really understand her answer and I'm convinced she doesn't understand my question. I feel she speaks quickly, that I'm not accommodated. I ask her to speak more slowly. My sense is that she doesn't. I go red with embarrassment and then just pretend I have understood, when actually I haven't, and I shut up, hoping that all will become clear from the context and the others in the group. We go round the class in turn.

I listen hard to what Susie says, and then to Kirsten as, in turn, they act out a situation. We've been going round the table taking turns. I'm third up, but so I've been able to jump ahead to my bit and work it out something to say. I've written down 4 verbs that I know I can use in the first person and I make things up that I know I can say and get through my turn. Everyone else seems to realise I'm struggling. They wink at me and mouth words across the table. But I'm slow and find the new game, using verbs in the imperfect tense, too hard for instant production. Thankfully the others jump in to either cover my mistakes, or spare me, or make things speed up. But I feel bad.

I'm relieved when the end of the class comes. I feel both motivated and humiliated at one and the same time. I also feel a social responsibility to the rest of the class not to slow things down too much. It's not been a comfortable session.

The pain and the pleasure of humiliation and social acceptance are all at work in this context, in this language holiday class. On the one hand, the stakes are now too high for me as a language learner, on the other, I find my classmates are entirely accepting of me as I struggle, out of my depth, to engage. The situation here is very different to that of the earlier example, but it still depends on others – I am helped along by the language those learning with me have learned themselves. Here I am the halt and the lame, but I am included in the group by my efforts to engage in the games that are being played out, even though I find these particularly difficult and potentially humiliating.

This is 'deep play' in the sense that Bentham and Geertz describe it – the kind that leads to learning – social, linguistic and also moral. It is not moral in any grand, universal sense, but more in the context of fairness and justice in this small group. This is moral in the sense of being concerned with the virtues of the group that are in formation as we bond socially. A virtue is defined by MacIntryre as 'an acquired human quality the possession of and exercise of which tends to enable us to achieve those goods which are internal to practices and the lack of which effectively prevents us from achieving any such goods' (MacIntyre, 1985: 191).

Without the virtues of patience, generosity, sharing, help and even resistance shown by my classmates I'd have struggled even more. As such the goods of the language were being shared out. There was no sense that there was not enough language to go round. Moral questions, for MacIntyre, are not grand universal principles, such as those we find in the discourses of endangered languages and intercultural understanding. They are particular and as such are about precisely this kind of fleeting, local, small scale interaction: '[T]he construction of local forms of community within which civility and the intellectual and moral life can be sustained' (MacIntyre, 1985: 191).

I hit up against a whole range and variety of issues of power and resistence, in this moment in the language class, rather like those suddenly thrown into relief for Geertz through the cock fight – villagers, police, families, the teasing. I find myself winked at, words being coaxed and teased out of me in order to define the sudden and – from our point of view – unreasonable demands being made by our teacher at this juncture. The moral dimension is fully in play, in that it relates to our ability to incorporate each other as included social beings, to make sure that all are able to join in the conversation – regardless of where they are in the language being learned.

What this example of pain demonstrates is the converse of our earlier examples of pleasure – with regard to deep play. In the very first example, where we throw the paper ball around the group, the sense of moral obligation was on my own part and the sense of failing was very much with me as my own responsibility, my own social failing both as a language learner, a classmate and ultimately as a potential languaging tourist. In this example the reverse is true. Now it is our common sense that the moral structures of the class are failing, that I am being excluded from the opportunities to play at being a *languager*, that my relatively weak position vis-à-vis sets of knowledge and grammatical structures that I have not encountered before is being systematically frustrated as we assert our *curriculum-as-desired*, and it clashes with the tutor's own *curriculum-as-designed*.

Our response here is to instigate our own 'deep play'. In the first example the role play was introduced by the tutor and I leaned, nervously, on others. Here I lean again, only this time everyone is aware that I am leaning and is happy for me to do so – in fact, we are all leaning on each other in order to enable a common conversation to be possible and to be maintainable. It is awkward, clumsy, frustrating – *painful* – but the social dimension we establish in the face of what Freire (1970) would term here an oppressive pedagogy, enables us to find pleasure in its overthrow and in the maintenance of the social bond and the conversation. We have a sense of having succeeded somehow, in something important. We joke together about it in the break after class, by the water cooler, despite the barriers. Again, this is rather like the discovery of Geertz and his wife, suddenly sitting at table – genuinely meeting, greeting and eating in the context of the cock fight and to the delight of all others.

What is clear both from Geertz's example and from the context I am describing here, is that 'deep play' occurs in time set aside for leisure. There may be considerable effort expended, but it is not being expended for daily routine work – even if capital or currency, in varying forms, are in play. Effort may be expended under in the modalities of tourism, indeed the effort expended may be greater than as part of daily routine work, but it occurs in different spaces and places and temporalities. It is also clear that these are spaces and temporalities that allow a certain awkwardness and clumsiness, that accept 'quickness' of life, its inherent struggles, failings and dilemmas, and find ways of incorporating them into the wider social bond and conversation.

We are a very long way here from the 'skills' discourses that so dominate the learning of languages inside formal educational structures of the mainstream curriculum for languages in universities and in schools. Indeed here we find ourselves much closer to Williams' sense of a flourishing educational institution, which would be 'one in which conversation flourished – that is, one where activities were fostered that drew students away from competition as the norm' (Williams, 2000a: 108). The learning of languages in these more marginal, unusual contexts of tourism takes place in an atmosphere where 'deep play' can flourish and conversations can be forged out of its structures, where the social bond as an intercultural, interlingual bond can be reimagined. It is also clear that the routines of everyday life need to be suspended, and other disciplines and tasks created outside of the usual routines, for 'deep play' to be able to flourish. These too are found in the leisured interstices of tourist language learning and, as I have argued previously, in the suspension of routines and the break with habits that comes when on holiday (Jack & Phipps, 2005). The focus is not on skills acquisition – critiqued vigorously by Williams (2000a), Barnett (1994) and by Ingold (2000) – in these instances of deep play, but on enskillment, on skillful learning (Phipps & Gonzalez, 2004), on how it might be that the language moved into and towards may be more fluently embodied.

Learning and Lassoing

When it comes to considering how it is we come to learn and to be skill-ful in different practices of life, Ingold takes the example from his own fieldwork of both learning another language and of learning to lasso. He argues that:

> Contrary to the axioms of cognitive anthropology the communion of experi-ence that lies at the heart of sociality does not depend upon the organization of sensory data, initially private to each perceiver, in terms of an objective system of collective representations. Rather, sociality is given from the start, *prior* to the objectification of experience in cultural categories, in the direct, perceptual involvement of fellow participants in a shared environment (Ingold, 2000: 167; cf. Ingold, 1993: 222–3).

Building on the work of Merleau-Ponty, Ingold is keen to argue against Geertz's culturism and textualism and to demonstrate that learning occurs in the world of direct, sensory perception, not in neat cultural categories. 'Deep play' and games in the language learning environ-ment for these tourist learners are direct, they are part of the 'quick' and at the same time there is something irrational, deeply playful and some-thing that raises questions of morality and utility at work. The sociality of the classroom activities, and their position outside the mainstream assessment and curricula regimes of dominant language learning, allows deep play to flourish and to flourish as the social bond and as stumbling conversation. Through this process much is learned, includ-ing language.

Ingold compares two different learning activities: that of learning to play a musical instrument and that of learning to throw a lasso. In the former, his example is one that 'does not achieve any direct, practical effect beyond the rapidly fading tapestry of sound' (Ingold, 2000: 414) and as such may be comparable to our own example and to the orality, the gratuity and the ephemeral nature of tourist language learning. It is clear that some practical effect may follow from learning a tourist language. Contrary to the argument of the dominant discourse of utilitarian lan-guage skills, however, the actual contexts in which the language is used are more akin to those of music than of direct practical use. As such lan-guage learning may be compared again to Merleau-Ponty's view of speech as a 'way of singing' (Merleau-Ponty, 2002: 217).

In the latter example, the example of the lasso, the learning is in the context of a tool and a skill that has direct practical use. Ingold compares the kind of 'attentive action', the 'feeling' and the 'absorption of play' (Ingold, 2000: 414) to that of the playing of a musical instrument:

When not in use it [the lasso] hangs limply in a coil from the hand, or trails loose on the ground. Yet in the moment of being cast, it assumes the lively form of a flying noose, a form which never stands still even for a single instant. Like the musical phrase shaped in sound, the form hangs suspended in the current of action. Thus, working the lasso, like playing a musical instrument, is pure movement or flow [...] it involves an embodied skill, a skill acquired through much practice (Ingold, 2000: 414).

To *play* a lasso, an instrument, or a language well, fluently, successfully, is to have a feel for the flow of embodied action. In each of these three examples playing becomes a key element. And it is here, following Ingold, that I shift to speak of *playing a language*, alongside the preceding discussions of learning a language. For learning is also part of the game, punctuated by much laughter and clumsiness. Ingold describes the novice learning to the throw the lasso as follows:

[...] the lasso can miss its mark, ropes can become entangled, the efforts of other herdsmen working in the enclosure may be disrupted, animals can even be injured. The frustrated herdsman then becomes an object of embarrassed self-regard, not to mention abuse from his fellows (I speak here from experience). The flow is broken, and one has to begin all over again (Ingold, 2000: 414).

And this is all too obvious in *learning to play another language*, a point Ingold also acknowledges: 'The clumsiness of the novice in handling unfamiliar tools is matched, as every anthropologist knows, only by his incomprehension of spoken words' (Ingold, 2000: 146–7). I do not know if learning to throw a lasso involves games, I do know that musical instrument exercises will sometimes bring in such elements of play – but in learning to play another language the situation is somewhat different to the two cases Ingold describes. The lasso and the instrument both come between the human body and the intended prey, or audience, they *mediate* the human body, they draw attention away from the body outwards, to the sound or the rhythm of the action. This is also true of writing, the production of the words is mediated by paper, pen, keyboard, screen – by specific tools.

In the speaking of another language, or the singing of a song, this situation is different. The effect is unmediated, the body is in direct play, not mediating breath or muscle through material objects. The context is consequently more intense and there is more at stake in the social game – not just wounded pride, for which one may indeed blame ones tools, the faulty reed, the thickness of the rope, the sticky keyboard, but a wounded body – a language wound and a language lack. Derrida refers to this wound as follows:

I feel lost outside the French language. The other languages which, more or less clumsily, I read, decode, or sometimes speak, are languages I shall never inhabit. Where 'inhabiting' begins to mean something to me. And dwelling [*demeurer*]. Not only am I lost, fallen, and condemned outside the French language, I have the feeling of honoring or serving all idioms, in a word, of writing the 'most' and the 'best' when I sharpen the resistance of *my* French (Derrida, 1996: 56).

There is much to this passage but the important point here is the sense of inadequacy, the clumsiness refered to which echoes Ingold's attempts with the lasso. Fluency, the sense of being 'at home' in a language serves to heighten the difficulty – for Derrida the real impossibility – of ever dwelling in another language.

Conclusions

It is no accident, then, I would argue, that 'deep play' accompanies the learning of languages for tourist purposes, in more marginal and touristic contexts. One finds aspects of play in the structured and mainstream language learning contexts of university degree programmes, but in the contexts already understood as part of leisure, there is more freedom to play, and thus to laugh off some of the difficulties of the pursuit. For the languages do stick, they are clumsy, one gets it wrong – often hilariously so. But in the social, leisured contexts of the tourist language class the wound and the lack are taken up in play, and in a way that does not assume that these language wounds or this language lack are related to the individual, but are a social concern. They point to a wound in conversation but one which laughter and practise can help make flow. Without the element of the game the language may be learned but never played, never unmediated and connected to others for whom the sounds of the words, the hanging phrases, are intended. It can have neither practical, nor beautiful consequences.

Williams discusses the role of the game in the maintenance of the social bond and in such a way as to lead us here to consider whether the irrational peculiarity of language learning in a world of global English and tourist encounters is actually not possible unless deep play occurs. And when deep play is frustrated, as in my example above, it will come back into being as resistance, regardless (Scott, 1990). Playing languages needs audiences. The practice audience is that of the classroom conversation, the real audience is the world out there. The deep play that occurs points to the social ethics into which the learning of a language, *the learning to play a different tune on the body* takes place:

[...] no project is *just* mine, wholly unique to me. I have learned from others how to think and speak my desires; I need to be heard – but that means that I must speak into, not across, the flow another's thought and speech. And, in all this, in the thinking of what it is for me to think at all, I may gradually understand the sense in which the robust, primitive, individual self, seeking its fortune in a hostile world and fighting off its competitors, is a naïve fiction (Williams, 2000a: 113).

In other contexts there is no play, there is winning and losing. In learning to converse, *to language*, there is no winning and losing – there is flow and fluency, yes, and there is embarrassment, clumsiness and awkwardness, there is generous listening and there is an ethics of conversation. 'We "learn" each other, we cope with each other, in the trials and errors, the contests and treaties of speech; which takes time' (Williams, 2000a: 86). This is true in our mother tongues, where conversation and learning also take time, but it is even more the case in the context of learning another language, and doing so as a tourist. For in tourism we do take time for other things that are not normally accorded so much time in daily life – washing, eating, sleeping, conversing...learning other tunes, other languages – all of which reinforce the social and kinship bonds (Bausinger, 1991).

The games, the deep play, we have discussed here point to the fact that 'games are unproductive' (Williams, 2000a: 71). The social ethic at stake in deep play with languages, with the unmediated, speaking, singing body is one that affirms that languages, despite all and afterall, are inalienable goods. 'The point is not to make anything concrete out of the common activities agreed, but to perform the activities themselves' (Williams, 2000a: 69). The play is the thing.

Chapter 8
Rehearsing Speech

And the learning process must be co-ordinated so that the actor learns as the other
actors are learning and develops his [sic] character as they are developing theirs. For
the smallest social unit is not the single person but two people. In life too we develop
on another
(Brecht in Willett, 1964: 197)

Tourism, to repeat, happens in languages and does so as an extension of everyday life. Tourism concentrates the multilingual, intercultural and material experiences of people, significantly. It does so at times of great symbolic significance to tourists, times that are anticipated and that are associated, culturally and often personally, with happiness. Such times are often, following Turner, characterised as both liminal and liminoid, as discussed earlier. They regularly involve an inversion from fluent speaker to a 'foolish' gesticulation in a variety of contexts of communication, as translation fails. What might happen when tourists begin to learn set scripts from phrase books, or elaborate scripts from tourist survival language courses? What is the relationship between mimesis, tourism and language learning and what forms and modalities does this relationship take?

In this chapter I develop the focus on play by examining the place of role play, of script and of performance in the context of tourist language learning. In previous chapters I have shown how there is a shift from literacy to orality in the tourist language classroom and in the *curriculum-as-desired* by tourist learners. The motivation is for good conversation to occur and the phrase book, the black board, the vocabulary books and notes to become redundant artefacts, with their contents being carried in the body and not in the bag. The processes I focus on in this chapter relate to the way in which this occurs as phrases, grammatical rules, elements of phonetics and of wider vocabulary begin to form into fluency. Tourist language classes are significant rehearsal times involving role play and enactment of tourist scripts for tourists as language learners.

There is a considerable literature in tourism studies on tourism as a 'staged' phenomenon. 'Staged authenticity', a coinage of MacCannell's (1973), has proved a fruitful concept for examining the events put on for tourists which aim to be in some socially imagined sense 'authentic' to a culture or way of life. The response of host communities to the demand on the part of tourists for staged, colourful, authentic behaviours has led many anthropologists, often rightly, to see tourism as contributing to cultural change in damaging ways (Greenwood, 1978; Nuñez, 1977; Pfaffenberger, 1983; Russell & Wallace, 2004; Wiley, 2005) However, it is possible to argue that far from eroding cultural diversity tourism has actually served to provide a context for the continued life of certain aesthetically pleasing or desirable cultural forms. Indeed, Yamashita argues that tourism is one of the main sites of cultural innovation (Yamashita, 2003) and Daniel Boorstin (1961) sees touristic dance in particular as a continually creative form. What we can say is that the situation in these stagings, scriptings and performances is complex as Kirschenblatt-Gimblett (1998) and Schechner (1985; 2002) admirably describe in their separate descriptions of tourists encoutering staged authenticity at The Pilgrim Village of Plimoth Plantation.

What is missing from all these excellent accounts of staged authenticity, performance and tourism is the notion of rehearsal, of *practising for the practice*. This is a key feature of the movements from tourist language learning to languaging.

It is week three of the tourist Italian class. The first 10 minutes are spent going over the work on directions we began at the end of last week's class. Everyone feels comfortable with the revision. Words are written on the board that feel familiar, some of us have even been practising this between the classes this week. The answers to our tutor's questions come readily. And then suddenly she wraps this part of the revision up and asks one of the class: 'Como ti chiami?'

The is audible hesitation and a sense of disorientation envelops the whole class. The poor unsuspecting tourist language learner repeats the question out loud once or twice and then gives the correct answer. She is immediately asked: 'Di dov'è sei?' The class holds its breath and the concentration levels and tension rises. I begin flicking through the pages of my notebook to find the work from week one – the work I and everyone else in the class has suddenly realised they have forgotten. 'Qual e il tuo numero di telefono?' Now it's me – oh boy – I need to remember both the phrase and the numbers – numbers! They are always impossible. I feel foolish, a bit stupid. I'm torn between mild panic, annoyance at my memory and the fact that I'm already rusty on the simplest of phrases, and admiration for my tutor and her excellent pedagogic technique. She is smiling at us with a glint of humour and knowing mischief in her eyes. I know, we know and she certainly knows that we will all be well and truly caught out by this sudden change of question out of nowhere. I find the right page in my notebook with some relief. I manage the sentence; she repeats it for me so I can hear the difference in pronunciation. I repeat the word I've stumbled over 'telefono...' and then, in the intervening period, realise I've managed to drag the right words for the numbers in to my mind and I give her my telephone number. The relief! The next learner does a little better as the repetition of the questions and the phrases allows us all to rehearse together. Gradually the foolish feelings subside, the rustle of papers and the sounds of reading and murmured phrases being repeated give way, in these few phrases, to fluency.

Rehearsal

The tourist language class acts as a space in which the life lived in that language, as it may be encountered by tourists, is practised. Tourist language classes are, I would argue, a rehearsal space for tourism and for speaking the language in tourist contexts. The tourist language class is, as I have already argued, part of the imagined structure and actual structure of tourism itself, but it is in a different mode – it is not the real performance, not even when students are required to perform in tests – it does not involve face-to-face speaking with fluent speakers of Portuguese, people encountered in holiday mode and with all the considerations of such face-to-face encounters and exchanges in an intercultural mode of being. Even when classes contain a mix of students from different linguistic, ethnic and social backgrounds, as did my own tourist language classes, these spaces are much more akin to the rehearsal spaces for a play, than to the performance of the play itself.

The aspect of language rehearsal described above takes us into the process of how it is that the language comes to be embedded and embodied and reveals something of the pedagogic and theatrical process at work in the learning of the language. There are a number of aspects to be noted here:

(1) *Expectation*: The initial elements being revised are the things we are atuned to as learners. We've been given plenty of cues to suggest that directions are one of the things we will have to be ready for in this particular class. It comes as no surprise when the class begins by going over these elements.

(2) *Surprise*: The surprise of the return of work from an earlier class, the surprise at the ropey nature of our memories, our note taking, our revision practices – the equivalent of learning our lines for the play – are suddenly exposed. We are not ready or prepared, we don't even know which page we are on in the script. Surprise exposes all of these aspects and shines a light on the work still to be done in order to embed the language into a reflex action that means we will be released to engage, exchange, speak.

(3) *Memory*: The question jogs our memories, we reach for our aide-memoires, we try and find the written scripts that will help us to

speak. We are still, at this point, dependent on the script, on the text and on literacy – the oral mode of interaction has not yet been reached.

(4) *Improvisation*: Like all good rehearsal and drama workshop the finding of the right words is improvised – half-known phrases, gestures, ideas – nothing practised, polished, clean-cut, predictable. The words are a bit sticky, as with improvised action.

(5) *Foolish feelings*: The fact we can't do this easily makes us feel a bit foolish, not only because it is such an easy thing to do, to say your name, but also because it is intensely difficult at this stage. The distance from what we can do as fluent speakers in the one language is thrown into awkward, foolish relief by what we cannot do in the other. The enormity of the task of learning is felt, is palpable in these moments of foolishness.

(6) *Social learning*: Even though it may feel as if, under the spotlight, you are the one who is letting everyone down and who has 'forgotten' the lines, lost the place of the script, the repetition of questions, the developing, though difficult talk that emerges in this activity does eventually lead to something resembling – for these scraps of language – fluency, embodying and embedding of language and possibility. The process is a social one – as all language learning inevitably has to be – one in which the individual can never completely possess the language, though they can be possessed by it.

(7) *Possession*: The feeling of being possessed, being overwhelmed by the force and the power of the words, the attention to the action required, is magical – it creates the same kinds of transformations in tourist language learners as reported by shamans when rituals that entrance are performed.

The seven elements described are part of the rehearsal process that occurs in the learning of languages and in this case in the learning of languages for tourist purposes. They index something of the effects of the transformation that occurs and is embodied when new skills and dispositions for actions interact. I hesitate to call this process learning – not because this is not what is occurring but because this word is now so freighted with technocratic meaning that it fails to encompass the quasi metaphysical dimensions in play in this process. People are being unmade and remade in this moment; there is conflict, difficulty, ache, struggle, laughter, insecurity, humiliation and intense concentration in play in these instances. We are a long way here from the discourses of knowledge transfer, autonomous learning, effective teaching and other such watchwords of the contemporary education landscape. Such discourses seek to tidy up the mess of learning and languaging and, working within the dominant performative paradigms (Lyotard, 1984), they render the complexity, struggle and subtley of learning and of pedagogy as technologisable, rather than as interhuman, and interagentic. There is a straining towards something new, something that needs to take possession and be welcomed, for all its difficulty and, at this juncture, social discomfort. In this instance of surprise and revision we see the way in which what is not known is, to paraphrase T.S. Eliot, 'all we know' and 'where we are is where we are not'.

It would be possible to argue that this is an element in play in most good learning contexts and that tourist language learning is no exception to this rule. I would concur to a certain degree and certainly language learning is unusual in the way it makes demands on the whole body, it requires physical embodying in a way few other subjects of do – however practical or however intellectual their orientation. But, as I have argued earlier, tourist language learning is particularly unusual in that it is a countercultural procedure, whereby the tourists, not the hosts choose to do the intercultural speaking, and at some personal cost in terms of time and leisure. It is an effort focused towards the times in life when rest is legitimated; it is unproductive effort that encompasses the whole human being. It is not 'just' physical activity, such as sport, or dexterity, such as a craft, or academic training, such as the study of local history, or film classes in lifelong learning programmes. It requires the whole person to body-forth the results, unmediated by racket, or paintbrush, or essay, or artefact. In this respect the analogy to rehearsal processes in acting – where the actor is also, ultimately required to body-forth language in and as action – is a good one and worth more detailed consideration here.

Restored Behaviour

Richard Schechner, the theatre anthropologist who worked alongside Victor Turner for some years, writes of the process of rehearsal as a process of *restored behaviour*. It is worth quoting his definition of restored behaviour here at some length:

> Restored behavior is used in all kinds of performances from shamanism and exorcism to trance, from ritual to aesthetic dance and theater, from initiation rites to social dramas, from psychoanalysis to psychodrama and transactional analysis. In fact, restored behavior is the main characteristic of performance. The practitioners of all these arts, rites, healings assume that some behaviors – organized sequences of events, scripted actions, known texts, scored movements – exist separate from the performers who 'do' these behaviors. Because

the behavior is separate from those who are behaving the behavior can be stored, transmitted manipulated, transformed. The performers get in touch with, recover, remember or even invent these strips of behavior and then rebehave according to these strips, either by being absorbed into them (playing the role, going into trance) or by existing side by side with them (Brecht's *Verfremdungseffekt)*. The work of restoration is carried on in rehearsals and/or in the transmission of behavior from master to novice (Schechner, 1985: 36).

Schechner applies his notion of restored behaviour to all embodied performance actions – ritual or aesthetic. Although he does not explicitly apply the idea of restored behaviour to the process of learning a language, there are striking parallels that are worth further exploration here. *Firstly*, it may be argued that the varied activities, the moments of attentive action in the language classroom, as well as those moments of rest, watching others perform from the sidelines, are ways in which tourist language learners 'get in touch with, recover, remember or even invent strips of behaviour'.

On the one hand, the strips of behaviour are those relating directly to the language – in my case Italian or Portuguese. Be it engaging directly with what begins to come back to me as I remember back, and refer to my notes – my script – from early lessons so that I can answer the questions posed by the tutor, or be it listening attentively to others responses so that I can practise and contribute my own strip of behaviour in turn. On the other hand, there are other touristic strips of behaviour at work in these contexts that refer to the expected and already experienced aspects of social behaviour in touristic contexts. For instance, when learning to order food in a restaurant the strips of behaviour are not purely a linguistic game but also body-forth other experiences of similar social practices, often those which are remembered out of existing holiday experiences, but equally those learned from other touristic performances, encountered across a range of aesthetic media – film, theatre, literature and even other experiences of language education.

The language classroom becomes a workshop in which this work of restoration can be undertaken, a work that is at one and the same time a work of transformation. This is particularly true in the context of our question as to why it is that tourists might bother learning the local language. Why might they put themselves through the difficult process of transformation? It is here that the imagination is at play, according to Schechner, in the *process* of restored behaviour because 'restored behavior offers to both individuals and groups the chance to become what they once were – or even, and most often, to rebecome what they never were but wish to have been or wish to become' (Schechner, 1985: 38).

We stand together outside a bar selling drinks. It is our first lunch break and we need to buy some water. It is a hot afternoon. We are all a bit lost for words having moved from the classroom to the streets. We go in to the bar together, checking out with each other, in German – for it is our common language of easy communication, what we should say. Susie goes first. She has a bit more Portuguese than the rest of us who are pretty much absolute beginners. She greets the man behind the bar. He smiles and nods. She asks for water and a sandwich. We follow suit, repeating her words, modifying them, making them our own. I ask for orange juice and mess up the pronunciation. He helps me, carefully, patiently. I repeat the right word and everyone smiles. He asks us where we are from and wishes us a good holiday. We are tourists here, clearly, but somehow we feel, for a moment, like we have stepped over the language barrier with a stranger, for the first time.

Tourist languaging is a multilayered process of rebecoming, of rebecoming a person who can operate socially and interculturally in another language, of rebecoming a certain type of tourist, of fulfilling a certain role that has been once imagined as a transformation of the self and is, in the rehearsal space of the tourist language classroom, being made, unmade and remade. The example above attempts to capture something of the sense of reciprocity that can come when *diagonal* moves are made through language, across language stages and in everyday, yet particular places.

Secondly, what is also clear from Schechner's description of restored behaviour and from both the first example cited above from the tourist language classroom, and the second one from the bar, is that, as rehearsal, language learning and languaging involve repetition. It is not possible to learn a language by hearing a word once, by hearing a phrase once, by saying it once. The mimetic work requires words and phrases to be repeated many times over. To speak another language, much speaking of that language has to occur and many errors have to be made. As my Portuguese tutor insisted at the start of our course: 'A word about mistakes. Mistakes are good. I want to hear lots of them.' Or in Schechner's words: 'Performance means: never for the first time. It means: for the second to the nth time. Performance is "twice-behaved behavior"' (Schechner, 1985: 36).

In order to *play* a language well involves, to use Brecht's terms, working with words, gestures and meanings in the body until what emerges in performance is the 'least rejected object', the phrase that is believed to be most efficacious in encounters and exchanges with others. And this is the case at any stage in the process of learning, from the beginner to the fluent speaker. For the rehearsals in the language classroom to reach any kind of fulfillment in 'real' tourist situations and in face-to-face speaking and listening encounters with hosts, as guests, then the tourist language learners have to rehearse, restore and be transformed to such an extent that what they utter ultimately becomes 'second nature' – or 'twice-behaved behavior' as Schechner puts it.

Furthermore, they have to also be able to be possessed by the language. The right words and phrases are sought after and tested out. For the language to be fully embodied, to be *played* – and this is true, I believe, of any language learning process – then it has to take possession of the speaking subject. As I argued in the previous chapter, we are dealing, in these rehearsal-like classroom processes of tourist language learning with the knowledge of a wound, a lack, a language and a languaging wound. In face-to-face encounters with others we will be helpless *with* their words and unable to meet if we do not possess and are not possessed *by* their words. We will be entirely thrown on the generosity of their readiness to be languagers themselves, to offer some form of linguistic hosting for us as guests in their language. And we know this profoundly and it makes us anxious and dependent.

In language learning of any kind, but particularly acutely and symbolically in tourist language learning, there is no such thing as learner autonomy or autonomous language. As Young argues:

> We do not experience ourselves as free meaning creators, but as involved in a struggle for the capacity for meaning. While we make meaning, we do not always make our own meaning. [...] Autonomy in the old liberal sense is impossible. A fully autonomous person would have no language to speak and no way of life to live (Young, 1996: 88).

Schechner makes the same point about performance:

> All performances [...] share at least one underlying quality. Performance behavior isn't free and easy. Performance behavior is known and/or practiced behavior – or 'twice-behaved behavior,' 'restored behavior' – either rehearsed, previously known, learned by osmosis since early childhood, revealed during the performance by masters, guides, gurus or elders, or generated by rules that govern the outcomes, as in improvisatory theater or sports. [...] Because performance behavior isn't free and easy it never wholly 'belongs to' the performer (Schechner, 1985: 118)

In Chapter 3 I discussed the potential of the tourist language to act as a charm, as magic, protecting against harm and ill. Here the magical, shamanistic element of language learning as a process, rather than as an object, returns. The language needs to possess and be possessed at one and the same time. The repertoire of words needs to be picked up and practised and played before it can actually be invested *with* magic and *work* its magic. The practice of a language is like the rehearsals of music, it is rough, ropey, fumbled, halting, tough, it makes demands on the body.

It is a long way from being 'spell binding', 'captivating', 'efficacious', or even 'beautiful'. The stance of the tourist language learner, like that of the practising musician is a reflexive one, thinking out loud with the body, concentrating, trying to make words flow, trying to find what feels like magic when the words take hold and begin to work.

Languagers and Magic Metaphors

And when words begin to take hold and to work their magic – be it the simple practical 'magic' that does eventuate in the arrival of a cup of coffee, or complex magic that leads to a long, even patient, conversation with a stranger who is prepared to do the arduous work of intercultural listening – we enter the realm of shamanism and performance. Abram, in his investigation into the connections between perception and language sees magicians, be they modern entertainers or tribal sorcerers as having in common 'the fact that they work with the malleable texture of perception' (Abram, 1997: 5).

> *Um café se faz favor – I've practised the phrase may times over. The waiter at the bar smiles and goes to the coffee maker and returns, with another smile and with my coffee. 'Muito obrigada' I say – the smile returning. 'Não falo bem Portugues, é uma lingua muito difícil.' The women at the bar next to me shakes her head and in chorus they contradict me. 'Sim, fala' they say and I am encouraged into conversation – halting, highly partial but nonetheless working limited magic as together we speak a little about life.*

Here, I'm working, with the limited resources of my tourist Portuguese at the margins of perception. A tourist who speaks and is encouraged to do so. A surprising tourist perhaps, one who changes the perception of what is possible and how the world of tourist–host interaction normally is. I don't possess the language nor is my speech magical to others, flowing freely and readily and creating ready exchanges between language worlds with ease. It is clearly wounded, marked, struggling but able to progress and possess nonetheless.

Abram describes his reception by the shamans and sorcerers he encountered during his field work in Indonesia. They discovered he was a magician and capable of the kind of alteration of perception, of what we might term mischief, with the given world and its expectations, that they too were capable of performing:

> When the local sorcerers gleaned that I had at least some rudimentary skill in altering the common field of perception, I was invited into their homes, asked to share secrets with them, and eventually encouraged, even urged, to partici-pate in various rituals and ceremonies (Abram, 1997: 5).

My halting attempts at speaking Portuguese to strangers encountered as part of my travels to Portugal had a similar effect. My rudimentary skill and their generous attention and intercultural listening opened homes, turned sour mouths into smiles, it turned encounters from functional to habitable relationships. It had transforming, magic effects.

It may well be possible that I am extending the metaphor of magic too far at this juncture, and in my earlier use of it in Chapter 3. Theatre and performance, however, have long been associated with magic, as ritual spaces for the staging of expressions of human social drama (Turner, 1982) that work at the malleable textures of perception. Stagecraft is a form of magic. Furthermore, Law argues, the study of complex social practices requires magical metaphors such as the metaphor of enchantment (Law, 2004: 154). It requires the enchantment metaphor *as* a method with which to undo the dualist Euro-American approaches to the 'enchanting complexities' of real-life research. Without it, and other such metaphors, Law argues, we will be unable to 'gather and generate' a rich plethora for action of all kinds (Law, 2004: 133):

> Localities. Specificities. Enactments. Multiplicities. Fractionalities. Goods. Resonances. Gatherings. Dorms of craftings. Processes of weaving. Spirals. Vortices. Indefiniteness. Condensates. Dances. Imaginaries. Passions. Interferences. These are some of the metaphors for imagining method […]. Metaphors for the stutter and the stop. Metaphors for quiet and generous versions of method (Law, 2004: 156).

I worked on my vocabulary on the plane and then got into conversation with the man next to me – clearly a Portuguese man – who had asked to read my Portuguese newspaper.

We then talked for an hour…it was so motivating. I was terribly slow, searching for words, stuttering lots. He was patient, kind, gentle with my words, complimentary, impressed by what I had learned. By this stage I was impressed with what I was able to produce one to one and without all the subjection of the classroom earlier. There was a flow to some of my sentences, I could ask questions, find words, try things out, I had a stab at the imperfect, I could understand what he was saying…he kept checking out with me that I was understanding. My travelling companion asked questions. I could respond and I did follow at least half of what was coming at me. We spoke of our work. We talked about languages. He wanted to know which languages I spoke. I told him where I had been, what I'd done with my colleagues, what food I'd enjoyed, about Belem, the museum, the monastery, the beauty, about Sintra. He asked me if I'd been to a beach…beaches are clearly high in tourist consciousness, in fact the beach is the default discourse or metonym for tourism here. And then he asked about my family, my home, my job, whether I like Lisbon and comparing it to London, how long it would take me to get to Scotland and I was able to say how long it would take, that I was flying not taking the train, that the flights were cheaper….

He then gave me his phone number and told me to call him...if I was in Lisbon again and he would show me where he lived and help me learn more Portuguese. I should meet his daughters – they were my age. We also talked about cakes and how they make you fat...and that I was writing about languages and tourism and was returning to Coimbra, Viseu and Averio in September. He told me they were beautiful places.

I was wary of the invitation – for women travelling alone there is a common understanding that such invitations are to be viewed with suspicion. Histories of gender relations mess with the magic. Methods used to understand these gender relations have often been too clear, to quick to answer difficult questions about the 'quick' of human relatedness, the magic in meetings, the flux of performance and languages in flow. But the encounter happened nonetheless. It was warm, encouraging, human and without threat – in my view – and it was the language and the listening that that 'worked with the malleable texture of perception' to enable something to happen beyond the functional or the hostile or the impossible.

Modes of Language Performance

In both examples of my attempts to use my Portuguese with those I encounter in tourist situations – in the bar ordering coffee and on the plane travelling home – the strips of behaviour I have practised in the language class are turned into live performance. The notebooks, phrase books, dictionaries and other 'scripts' upon which I can rely as a tourist language learner are out of sight in bags, packed away and my body is at work in the encounter, without the aide-memoire. The situation, as with others I have described earlier, has shifted from being enabled through literacy to being predominantly oral. Similar feelings of nerves come to the fore as the strips of behaviour are rebehaved and words and phrases are chosen out of the stock of those that rise and suggest themselves in this encounter and in this instance. Schechner maintains that '[r]estored behavior can be put on the way a mask or costume is. Its shape can be seen from the outside and changed' (Schechner, 1985: 37). Those I meet work with the language I'm playing, seeking to hear it and adjust it so that it becomes more tuneful, more pleasing to the ear, less difficult to cope with in social interaction. My own mode, in these halting performance situations, points to the partiality of the language, excusing my lack, trying to show some awareness of the awkward nature of such listening and speaking and such hard work, on both sides, at understanding. 'Put in personal terms, restored behavior is "me behaving as if I am someone else" or as if I am "beside myself", or "not myself"' (Schechner, 1985: 37).

In this respect the mode of interaction contains elements of what Brecht terms *Verfremdung* – or distanciation. It works to point to its own partiality, its own inadequacy, its own constructed, restored nature. It draws out the need in others – as Brecht wishes such techniques to work on his audiences – of action, help, attention, change. My audiences – those Portuguese folk I encounter as a real tourist – respond to me not with sympathy but with action, with encouragement, with didacticism, coming to my aid with words and subtle corrections and careful repetition, and helpful pronunciation. And I work with what they give me, trying to repeat what they say, laughing at my own ready mistakes, feeling more than a little foolish, with a sense that the show, messy and broken up and awkward as it may be, must go on.

Tourist language performances, as I am terming them here, also reflect other aspects of Brechtian acting theory. 'At no moment' says Brecht in *A Short Organum for the Theatre* 'must he [the actor] go so far as to be wholly transformed into the character played' (Brecht, in Willett, 1964: 193). In the dominant forms of western acting – Stanislavskian theatre – action appears natural and realistic, a seamless flow. Brecht works to inject what Benjamin terms a 'halt' – a pause in the flow of any performance so as to reveal its constructed nature and to allow space for reflection, restoration, transformation and for citation, for the drawing of a strip of behaviour from the context of its formation into the context of performance. The tourist languager cannot *be* the Portuguese host, the context relies on the tourist not going native or being a native speaker. Indeed the much maligned goal of reaching native speaker status in foreign language education literature is not present as a possibility in tourist language performances (Byram & Fleming, 1998; Kramsch, 1993).

The linguistic guest cannot become the linguistic host. Brechtian theatre interrupts the flow of action by speaking about the character, by allowing in a space for reflection. Tourist–native interactions in the language are punctuated with reflection on origin, on home, on difference, on the nature of experiences, on the things that are expected of each other in the given roles. These aspects are a continual source of comment as is the artificiality of the language being spoken. The tourist languager enables the host to see the arbitrary, constructed, difficult nature of their language, through actual performances of the language. The host is enabled to listen and see their own language, what they take for granted, in new, inflected ways… cakes, beaches, the construction of the imperfect tense, the accents, the heat, the vegetation, the food.

From Ritual to Theatre

In Chapter 5 I discussed some of the subtleties and limitations of Turner's model of liminality, structure and anti-structure, noticing how, in the learning of the alphabet, each letter and each instance of pronunciation could break through the structure of the class and the activity and create liminal laughter that would change the flow and punctuate the learning. Such moments of punctuation, in the learning and repetition of sounds, are common in the learning and teaching of languages. It is possible to see such interruptions as a distraction from the task in hand, but, as I have argued here, they appear to be vital to the process of rehearsal and practice and of embodying and of bodying-forth the language – of *learning to play the language*. They mark out the moments of difficulty, loading them with laughter and consternation and enabling them to make their mark on the memory.

Turner developed his theories of liminality in a late work *From Ritual to Theatre: The Human Seriousness of Play*. In this work he makes a key distinction between the kinds of deep, anti-structural play at work in ritual contexts and those of late modern societies that he sees as more fleeting, less ritualistic and that he terms liminoid.

Turner's work on the theatre and on the liminoid helps us focus on the aspects of 'performance' in tourist languaging. In focusing on rehearsal and performance it can also help us understand how it is that new speech is engaged as a phenomenon or created in new tourist bodies out of a new and unfamiliar soundscape. In addition, his understanding of the crucial role of performance in social structure helps explain why it is that tourist language learners in particular – those who only 'require' their language for short-term stays – might engage in the long and arduous work of learning to speak another language and embodying a different range of sounds and syntaxes to those in which they 'flow' and 'make meaning' more readily and easily:

> The growing complexity of the social and economic division of labor, giving specialization and professionalization their opportunity to escape from the embedment in the total ongoing social process, has also provided complex sociocultural systems with effective instruments for scrutinizing themselves. By means of such genres as theatre […] performances are presented which probe a community's weaknesses, call its leaders to account, desacralize its most cherished values and beliefs, portray its characteristic conflicts and suggest remedies for them, and generally take stock of its current situation in the known 'world' (Turner, 1982: 11).

Tourist language learning is not theatre, nor is it performance in any of the senses of the word as used by Turner or by Schechner or by Brecht. But it is part of social drama – it highlights a wound, a lack, a breach, a lack of connection. And the learning, taking place outside of the structures of everyday work life, in the leisure of the classroom and the tourist-time of holidays, allows the social actor both to rehearse and potentially also to perform the kinds of magic performed by shamans, healers and performers in mending that breach, covering over the lack by playing another language. Equally within the process of a tourist language performance, in the encounters between the linguistic host and the linguistic guest there is of necessity and out of the often halting nature of the performance a reflexive element that punctuates the performance and creates the potential for transformation. Languagers as intercultural speakers and listeners are both possessed by and caught up in the dramatic social action but they also, in struggling to remember the lines and to make sense of utterances, need to stop, reflect and consider their lack and their differences.

Considering tourist language learning and tourist languaging as both rehearsal and as performance, analogously, begins, then, to provide ways of understanding the effort and social necessity of the otherwise peculiar and seeming pointlessness of tourist language learning. What tourist language learning and tourist languaging allows, is entertainment, is *entretenir*, taken literally 'holding between' (Turner, 1982: 121). 'Entertainment is liminoid' says Turner (1982: 120) 'rather than liminal, it is suffused with freedom. It involves profoundly the power of play and play democratises.' As noted here and in earlier chapters there is a good deal of playfulness and mischief involved in the rehearsal processes of the language classroom, and the laughter that accompanies the learning and punctuates the seriousness reveals the work involved in holding oneself between two languages. The double nature of entertainment, finally, also allows both the magical possession of tourist speech as entertaining, leisured flow and it allows, through its reflexive modes, of *Verfremdung*, ways in which other worlds and ways of being may be entertained, bodied-forth, and considered.

Chapter 9
Breaking English

Do You Speak English?

We were never taught how to say 'Do you speak English?' The phrase book tells me this but in class, and with the tutor and classmates, this was never an option and we never asked how we might ask. In fact even more than this it never crossed our minds that English might be an option. Although English is widely spoken, we know it is widely taught, we know it forms part of the statutory training of service workers in the tourist destinations abroad, somehow all our classes and role plays had to make us act as if this were not the case, as if we, as the guest, could only offer the few halting words of Portuguese or Italian to those with whom we wished to communicate. As if – the subjunctive mood – is the dominant mood. Our interactions in the language class and on the language holiday take place as if we do not have the language of English in common. The mood is strong, it never hesitates, never falters, it does linguistic body swerves as we improve, doing everything it can to describe things in Portuguese or Italian words for which we do not know the accurate word. It requires patience in our classmates and in our tutor as we attempt to say the unsayable in words that are not ours. English is the absolute and unspoken – literally unspoken – last resort.

In the previous chapters I have attempted to answer the question why bother? Why bother learning a tourist language for a matter of moments on an annual basis? And what happens when people do bother? Thus far the answers emerging are answers that emphasise the social and aesthetic dimensions of human ways of being. However, this question is also a material question. It doesn't just relate to the tourist language classes of course, it also relates to the language industry of 'teach yourself' books, tapes, CDs and programmes, a thriving language business that provides the materials, that materialises language and locates it outside of the body. During car journeys and on trains, and at home over the washing up another language may be encountered and certain phrases, courtesies and necessities may be taken into the tourist body and *stored* as scripts for the eventuality when they may – to use Schechner's phrase again – be *restored*. In all of this work of collecting, repeating, rehearsing and then ultimately restoring, we are a long way from the commonplaces accorded to languages in the tourist industry – as an add on, functional extra in the training of those employed to serve, and from the commonplaces of various university language courses where the emphasis is on employability or on intellectual literacy. Here, as noted earlier, we are dealing with orality, not literacy, though with an orality that depends for its scripts on the way language has been recorded in a variety of texts.

This point about materials and recording is an important one in the context of this chapter, continuing the focus on the way in which some tourists do bother to learn the language of their hosts. For fluent speakers and native speakers of the world's dominant language to come to a point where they actively work at giving up the linguistic power with which this language is invested – its linguistic, symbolic, cultural, economic, consumerist and military power – a double break is required: a break with the dominant tongue and a break with its perceived power. This is not the same as when other speakers of minority languages come to learn the language of dominance or colonial power through necessity, imposition and the pervasive hold it comes to have on everyday life through the necessary bilingualism that comes with language inequalities (Canagarajah, 1999; Phillipson, 1992; Skutnabb-Kangas, 2000). Such inequalities are present in touristic relations as they are in other forms of social relations and are well documented (Nash, 1978; Nuñez, 1977).

Though some elements of choice operate in such cases, the move to learn the dominant language is less paradoxical than the move to learn a language other than English, particularly for tourists and travellers of all kinds. The economic, social and mainstream educational reasons for learning the dominant language are clear. For the worlds conditioned by liquid modernity (Bauman, 2000) and globalisation it is not difficult to find reason or motivation for the world's dominant language to be learned, or for the ever-widening social modes available for its rehearsal and its use in interaction as a lingua franca (Brutt-Griffler, 2002; Cronin, 2000; Cronin, 2003). 'Languages do not exist in ideal symmetrical relationships and the coefficient of power is higher for some languages than others. In contemporary circumstances, this power is generally related to economic preeminence. Money talks' (Cronin, 2000: 118–19).

This is not at all to celebrate the status quo or to revel in the possibilities of a language of common communication, as some scholars have done, in the inevitable and inexorable rise of world English as Babel is rebuilt (Crystal, 1997; Edwards, 1995). The dangers are real, well documented and have been covered by significant scholarship in recent years (Colomer, 1996; Crawford, 2000; Cronin, 2003; Di Napoli *et al.*, 2001; Fishman, 2001; Laver & Roukens, 1996; Skutnabb-Kangas, 2000). This is not my concern here – though it is undoubtedly concerning. Rather, my own interest in tourism and languages points to the counter-example, the counter-script, the work of unmaking the dominant language through tourism as a major and highly symbolic social form.

I do not wish to celebrate tourism here as the saviour of languages, though the arguments made about the way in which cultural forms evolve and are even preserved through tourism may also apply to languages. In the context of tourism to Scotland it is clear from empirical research that the Gaelic language is indeed partially sustained by its link to tourism (MacDonald, 1997; Sproull, 1996). Similar patterns may be found with Irish (Cronin & O'Connor, 2003). My views about tourism reflect my views on life. It can always be more just, more beautiful, more lovingly undertaken – we are, as Bauman points out 'hoping creatures' (Bauman, 2005: 151) questing after happiness as a way of living with and critiquing the status quo of the here and now (Bauman, 2002). If tourism is life lived temporarily in another place then it is as fraught with all the difficulties, political iniquities, complexities, joys and sadnesses as any other aspect of life. *That* tourism takes place as a phenomenon of dislocation from ordinary routine and pattern means that the patterns that emerge through tourism express something of the ways in which life is lived when rest, recuperation and happiness are sought.

A Material Break

When tourists learn other languages where English would do to 'get by with' something peculiar is occurring. These are social actors who articulate a sense, yes, of the practicality of this move, and yes, of the usefulness and insurance that may come with the language and that may render their travels more efficacious and socially smooth. But below the discourse of practicality and functionality – a discourse one would fully expect to find given its dominance as a discourse about languages – is a surprising discourse, hesitantly, often idealistically and slightly awkwardly expressed, though not without passion – on *courtesy*. To break English is to be a good guest, is to be *practically* courteous; it is to be *charitable* – in the best sense of the words. I shall return to both these concepts – courtesy and charity – in more detail in the final chapter of this book. For now, it is enough to suggest that, as a courteous and charitable action, breaking English, going against the grain, involves giving up *linguistic capital* and *trusting* other people and other materials that mediate and educate in the ways of that language (MacIntyre, 1985).

A key gesture in the breaking of the powerful hold of English – or any other dominant language for that matter – relies, in the modern world, on the work of recording. For there to be a language that can be learned for contemporary tourists, there has to have been a long-term project of collecting, recording and presenting the language in ways which accord to the modern life. For Williams, 'form always has an active material base' (Williams, 1977: 190) and the form of the packages of languages for tourist purposes – those to be bought as consumer products in airport lounges and stationary shops, and those to be used in tourist language classes – are examples of the kinds of textual forms that match the social patterns of everyday life. They fit into the kinds of technologies that accompany our lives when we are doing other things.

Adenjumobi offers a detailed commentary on the recording practices of African languages and the patterns of their usage in popular culture alongside the dominant colonial languages and the dominant global language – English (Adejunmobi, 2004). She shows how it is that the recording of languages renders them mobile, breaking their links with geography and rendering them useful and portable for other purposes: mission, trade, aid and entertainment. This is also the thesis articulated powerfully by Abram in *The Spell of the Sensuous* when he considers the impact of writing technologies on the links between geography and language, and by Ingold as he considers speaking and writing as different manifestations of technologies (Abram, 1997; Ingold, 2000).

The link between geography, community and language is invariably broken, in the modern world. When language is seen as a mobile good, fetishised like any other, it is in tourism and in the opportunities afforded by touristic modes of being, that we see – mixed in with the mobilities and paradoxical modes of postmodern being – a potential for a renewal of the connection between language and geography. However migrated, diasporic and mobile the languages may be in the people they inhabit and who inhabit them, in tourism the dynamic relates once again to an acting out of the belief in the language of a place. In point of fact many of the encounters made by tourists when they are on holiday are often with speakers of other languages, with other tourists who may also share the language of the destination in common, or, as in my own case in Lisbon, who speak French and German or Spanish or Italian from previous language forays. These other languages are activated and encountered as much as those of the actual destination. But the language learned, always, by learners of languages for tourist purposes, is the language of the place and associated with what is understood as a specific culture.

Tourism then, becomes a way of reimagining a connection between language and place despite and alongside the palpable mobility of tourists and the multilingual nature of tourism. I do not wish to make huge claims for this connection – though the symbolic nature of tourism to which I have alluded earlier does not render it insignificant – but when the trends, according to sociolinguistic and anthropological research, appear to be in the opposite direction, it is interesting that in tourism the links between languages and geography are renewed.

Again we may turn to Abram here and his assessment of the connection between orality and geography. Language lives in places. They are attached to the sensuous, material features of a place. The last things to change their names, Abram maintains, are often the physical features of the land, long after cities have renamed buildings or street names. 'If names can get lost in translation', says Cronin 'they can also be seen as "typical" in their untranslatability, their referential uniqueness' (Cronin, 2000: 31).

> *In the language class we move in and out of place name translations ourselves. Places, somehow represent a certain need for a doubling of names. When speaking to each other in English about trips we have made we accentuate the names of places by repeating them in the tourist language, as if to highlight their presence in our memories, our imaginations and on our language itineraries. Lisbon – Lisboa, Naples – Napoli, we say.*

The sensuous aspects of tourism are those that dominate the language classes – the pronunciation, the food, the music, the modes of transport that will move the body along so that it knows that it is travelling, the different ways of greeting. To these we might also add the sensuous connections that are felt and enacted and embodied in the language, to particular places where the language is imagined to predominantly dwell, to be most at home. Place names act here as 'a currency of desire' (Cronin, 2000: 60), bringing the sense of the life of place – its 'quick' – into sharp relief. When social life is recorded textually – becoming a graphic, inscribed counterpart to speech (Ingold, 2000: 404) – then the connection of language to place is easily broken. Mobility breaks the relations between language and place, and records that which originated in one place in modes that will allow it to move to others.

Tourist language learners are in the business of living without reliance on these portable records. They are attempting to put what is in the books and on the tapes into their bodies so that it moves in them and *as* them, *not* as an accessory (Kelly-Holmes, 2005; Pourhashemi, 2005). In short, what this does, for all its clear dependence of the recorded texts and records, is break the connection between languages, language learning and texts, and render them in the oral mode. This accords with others aspects of touristic everyday living that I discussed together with Gavin Jack in *Tourism and Intercultural Exchange* (Jack & Phipps, 2005). The move is away from a dependence on guide books and towards a reading of the land and a reliance on speaking with those encountered – both other tourists and local hosts, for information on where to go and what to see. The guide books, though picked up occasionally when on holiday are quickly discarded again in favour of orality. Tourism, then, in moving people to *do* everyday life in other places breaks habitual ways of doing things in a wide range of different ways. Tourist language learning and languaging break habits of monolingual speech, for all its impossiblity (Derrida, 1996).

Breaking

To break English, in the ways made manifest by the social effort of tourist language learners and tourist languagers is, then, firstly a move from literate to oral modes of being and knowing (Young, 1996: 109). The knowledge is displayed not in written text but in the body and through the whole person as they search for expression. The first stage in breaking English, as identified here, is that of recording. To this we may then add the subjunctive mood – the *as if* – of the language class described earlier. Always the action in the role plays and in discussions was as if there was no alternative. In this there was a willing suspension of reality and of the opportunities for an easier life, in an easier language. The effort in the classroom was palpable – the relief, as we lapsed into the easiest social languages in the break times – sometimes German, sometimes French, sometimes English, was equally palpable. The effort of breaking English, of living as if there were no alternative, was such that it required moments of linguistic rest in the intertestices of learning.

On the language holidays these restful interstices were sometimes multilingual – not necessarily English.

> *It was my last evening at the end of the language holiday. I went to the café to meet my two Portuguese friends from the North. We had a short conversation in Portuguese and stopped and switched to English to exchange news. It was just easier. I was desperate for a rest and for some space out to digest the lessons and the buzzing in my head. Gradually the buzzing died down and my head felt less sore as the evening progressed. We would sometimes interrupt the flow of English with only occasional Portuguese words, questions from myself and snatches of conversation.*

To break English, to speak in broken language – as a non-native's attempts are rendered as broken English – is do more than just be a courteous, linguistic guest. It is to dwell in another language, to take that language as the point of departure, and in such a way as to live out the full knowledge and reality of the disconnection and unbreachability of the linguistic wounds between speakers. It is to attempt to live with Babel but without its tower. Again, in tourist languaging practices – and not just my own, though these are indeed my own point of departure – we see a glimpse of other ways of being enacted against the odds. And these come to the fore – complex, partial, hopelessly bound into all kinds of difficulties of power and domination as they are – through activity, a political activity, with languages.

The Broken Middle

These actions, on the part of tourist languagers, rooted in the intentions of the tourist language learners, are political, not in the sense of grand statements and policies, but political because they mediate the power and hegemony of languages, people and places.

In her extraordinary work of rethinking the modern philosophical tradition, *The Broken Middle*, Gillian Rose (1992) expounds what she terms 'the phenomenology of the diremption of law and ethics'. 'Diremption' she sees as the forcible or even violent separation of law from ethics. She is concerned, against the grain of some aspects of postmodernist and post-structuralist thinking, to resist attempts to tidy up the mess of relating social structures and institutions to everyday life. She sees at every turn in post-structuralist and post-Holocaust thinking a determination to elevate death and justice and to imbue these with the power to 'mend the broken middle, to create a holy middle' (Rose, 1992: 57). Through force and fantasy, what she believes is being created through separation and dualistic thinking is what Williams' terms 'communities of the perfect' (Williams, 2000b).

In the literature on English as a 'world', 'imperialist', 'global' language we find the tropes she critiques so powerfully repeated. The holy middle is the call to all to communicate in one language. In Philipsson, Canagarajah and Skuttknabb Kangas (Canagarajah, 1999; Phillipson, 1992; Skutnabb-Kangas, 2000) we hear the cry of death, imperialism, genocide and a raging against the institutions of the state and law as ethics and calls to bring justice and to save the dead and the dying languages. Likewise in the grand performative narratives of tourism literature we see a clutching at the saviour of economics or the ethics of tourism concern, of fair trade and sustainability. As our common institutions and political action crumble under the pressures of neoliberalism and globalisation, as the nation state comes to make less sense to us as citizens then law and ethics are dirempted, to use Rose's terms. Morality becomes a fluid, personal business and law is the work of the state:

It has become easy to describe trade unions, local government, civil service, the learned professions: the arts, law, education, the universities, architecture and medicine as 'powers'. And then renouncing knowledge as power, too, to demand total expiation from domination, without investigation into the dynamics of configuration, of the triune relation which is our predicament – and which, either resolutely or unwittingly, we fix in some form, or with which we struggle, to know, and still to misknow and yet to grow...Because the middle is broken – because these institutions are systematically flawed – does not mean they should be eliminated or mended (Rose, 1992: 285).

Here, in this difficult passage, Rose is pointing to the way in which, by demanding the end to all domination and by refusing to associate with the institutions of society and of political power, we try and cover over the mess of life rather than working together to find ways of living together which will include, even embrace the brokenness and the impossibilities. In the context that detains me here it has, equally, become easy to describe the institutions of English and the institutions of tourism as 'powers' and either to disengage or to call, idealistically, for their end. To assert the broken middle, if I am understanding Rose at all correctly here, in the context of languages and tourism, is to try, working against the grain, to learn the language of other places and peoples, for that reason. These are not learners who maintain that they can break the domination of English as a world language or that they will simply refuse to 'be tourists' in the contemporary world. Instead these are people seeking out relation in the midst of things, and doing so in ways which work with the brokenness and in the face of paradox.

In the Middle of Things

Such action is to begin 'in the middle of things' as Williams says (2000b: xii). It is to begin by acknowledging that 'there is a practice of common life already there, a practice that defines a specific shared way of interpreting human life lived in relation' (p. xii). To use Young's terms, it is to acknowledge that:

[...] [t]he language, and the wider meaning-repertoire of the culture existed before us, lives around us (in others) and will go on after we depart the scene [...] Life and language are moving things. They are not static. Nor are they monolithic, they are flawed and ambiguous [...] The real political question is how do we relate to others in the inter-making of this reality (Young, 1996: 88).

It would be possible, at this juncture, to conclude that the learning of languages for tourist purposes is an attempt to overcome and mend the broken middle, to minimise risk, to cover the messiness and awkwardness of encounters that are so clearly flawed, to make up for the wounds, the sheer embarrassment *of knowing we do not even know* how to ask for bread or for water. It would be equally possible to point to the hopelessness of the tourist learners enterprise, a hopelessness that asserts itself in my question 'why bother?' when the gains and rewards appear so futile and temporally insignificant. This would be to commit to mourning the impossibility of all communication, the partiality and arbitrary nature of language, the incommensurability of differences and to mourn endlessly the impossibility of life in Babel and without its tower.

Further still it would be possible – and I acknowledge fully the risk I run here in my own biases – to construct tourist language learners as 'holy' social actors, a community in which all our hope for our linguistic futures and for the peaceful resolution of the tensions in tourism – horrific, violent and objectifying as they so often are – are resolved by their own – my own – ethical resolve in the face of a language and intercultural crisis. There would be a rhetorical satisfaction and perhaps even some intellectual reward in pursuing such lines of argument, in loading the balance one way or the other. As a believer in languages and in multilingual worlds, as a champion of translation, my own desire is clear and unashamed, but I too accept that such a conclusion would be forced and fantastic. And if such a conclusion, or such conclusions, are ultimately unsatisfactory then the breaking and creating of English – through recording, rehearsing and languaging performance, in that most unlikely of contexts: tourism – becomes a non-dualistic way of living in and with the broken middle; with others and with the world: 'All dualistic relations to 'the other, to 'the world' are attempts to quieten and deny the broken middle, the third term which arises out of misrecognition of desire, of work, of my and your self-relation mediated by the self-relation of the other' (Rose, 1992: 75).

Rose (1992: 122) is impatient with discourse on an ethics that refuses to entertain 'activity beyond activity. [...] For power is not necessarily tyranny, but that can only be discovered by taking the risk of coming to learn it – by acting, reflecting on the outcome, and then initiating further action' (p. 121). This is the combination of the celebratory, communicative and critical modes, which Williams regards as meaning that 'the self is free to grow ethically (that is to assimilate what is strange, to be formed into intelligibility) only when it is not under obligation to defend itself above all else – or to *create* itself, to carve out its place in a potentially hostile environment' (p. 250).

Tourist language learners are rather improbable and largely – in the intellectual literature at least – invisible social actors who come into a kind of power. This power is certainly not necessarily tyrannical. There is no sense, for a minute, in the tourist language learners subjunctive mode of operation in the language classroom, and even less so in the halting attempts at communication in touristic actuality, that their 'as if' is either powerful or complete. The tourist language learner is never setting out to become one with the other, to reach some communion through language and action but rather to act in the midst of things, in a courteous and chari-table manner, as they are given day by day. Nor is the tourist learner seeking to mend the middle, to find a way of denying that through auton-omous action the difficulties of communication may be overcome by their action, and their particularity, or by a universal programme of other similar actions. High ideals of mending and perfection, or of loss and incommensurable differences, are far removed from the ways in which tourist language learners proceed.

These are not language activists in any conscious sense, setting out to act as God and tear down the Tower of Babel, but people engaged and invested in the middle of things, in the 'quick' of human relations – in what Buber terms 'das Zwischenmenschliche', or what Young refers to as the 'inter-making of this reality' (Young, 1996: 88). They are absorbed by the *task of the translator,* in its impossibility and at one and the same time, in its desirability, in the need to try anyway, and not by the larger ques-tions that attend to translation.

Broken Fragments

If we consider the languaging attempts of tourists, and their learning attempts at making meaning in the face of considerable odds of time, space and resources as practical ways of beginning in the middle of things, we might observe the ways in which, following the recording, the break-ing and the subjunctive mood, a tourist language practice emerges that breaks English as the dominant language resource.

In the literature on globalisation, transnationalism and transcultural-ism, in the celebrations of the 'transcultural' mode of being that is ushered in by the flow of languages, goods and workers bodies in the service of capital and growth, there is a tendency to view the opportunities for inter-cultural encounter, for cosmopolitanism, as uneven and unequal. According to Hannerz (1996: 103), for instance, cosmopolitans are those who are outraged when thought of as tourists; they should be understood as, in contradistinction, those who display a willingness to engage with

the other. For Balibar, equally, in positing translation as the 'language of
Europe', as the medium of communication upon which all others depend
and which may allow us 'to conceive of a practice that would be a means
of cultural resistance and a countervailing power' (Balibar, 2003: 178) we
find extremes. The language of Europe, as translation, for Balibar belongs
either to cosmopolitans or to migrants. Thus, argues Balibar, rushing
hastily to a conclusion,

> we must reduce – and not surpass – the gap and work to normalize it, which
> also means rediscovering on another level the spirit of the great 'cultural rev-
> olutions' of learning: the generalization of literacy of schooling. The task is no
> less gigantic. It will be more than enough to occupy several generations of
> artists, teachers and technicians, and to reestablish the true aims of a 'postna-
> tional' historical transformation' (p. 178).

Maybe. But at one and the same time there are our tourist languagers, in
that gap, not surpressing it but already reducing it. They are neither necessarily intellectuals nor migrants – though both may be implicated and
were in the classes I attended, but they are certainly engaged in the *tasks of
translation and of tourism*. Furthermore, they are normalising the languaging practices, breaking the hold in partial ways, working away in the
broken middle as it presents itself to them and with the fragments of
scripts with which they may act to restore social behaviour for a moment,
fleetingly, in social encounter. Of course for Balibar and Hannerz, the tradition of not seeing the normal, of only seeing what is at the centre or the
margin, continues apace. Heaven forbid that the 'great cultural revolution' should be occurring right under our noses, in the 'marginal-yet-
normal' evening classes of our university institutions, in the places where
the teachers are the least well paid and most ignored, amongst the tourists
and out of broken fragments that do indeed create a medium of communication that re-establish, however fleetingly, the 'post-national historical
transformation'.

The fragmentary speech, in lengthening strips of behaviour, which form
part of the tourist's mode of translation, of the first step into languaging,
are those we highlighted early on. They happen to be the fragments that,
like tourists for cultural critics and anthropologists, are the most maligned,
because of their touristic potential by those in the business of teaching
languages to intellectuals or to migrants. They are the fragments that, to
return to Williams, involve meeting, greeting and eating. We are back,
here, in the place where we learn to ask for a cup of coffee.

> *I found a stand to buy coffee and stood talking for ages with someone from Brazil and
> someone who speaks German – Marcelo both of them. They were struck by my use of*

'uma bica' – it clearly marked me as a foreigner who know something about the language and who cared about the language. I managed to tell them lots about the languages I speak – languages are really the constant subject of conversation…words flow between us all the time. Much of my conversation was oriented towards home and their questions were about where I was from not about where I was going or even so much why I was here. It was a real boost to have such attentive listeners and helpers with the language.

Of course it is possible to ask for coffee and other regularly required beverages in English. The language of beer, wine, water, tea, orange juice and coffee is indeed almost universally understood. This makes the instance of this as the worst and as the first of learning tasks, alongside the please, the thank you, the hello and the goodbye, all the more puzzling if languages are only functional resources for tourists and for tourism. But if, as I have persistently argued here, language learning and languaging oil the wheels of social, if not cultural, interaction, then meeting, eating and greeting are the cornerstones of civility and are consequently the first indicators that the intention in the tourist is to attempt to overcome the objectifying relations, so dominant in touristic practice and understanding, of the quick and easy interaction that includes no sense of commitment.

For to ask for a coffee in Portuguese, when English would always do, is to signal that one knows one is a guest *in* the language, to a guest *of* the language (Derrida, 1996). It is to begin to change the dominant mode of the relations between people. Asking for a cup of coffee is a material sign of the social bondedness that comes, to return to Williams' point, through 'eating meeting and greeting', which 'directs energy away from competition towards the maintentance of friendly exchange' (Williams, 2000a: 68). During times of tourism, as an everyday activity, we spend more time attending to the body, argues Bausinger (1991), to eating, sleeping, washing, than we do in workaday life. Asking for a coffee, then, affirms the social bond around food, in tourist-time.

To take time over a coffee when on holiday, to linger over the drinking is one thing, but to linger, to stutter, to take time over the asking, by using the tourist langauge is to create a mess and a melée in human relations. It is, to return to Rose, to make the middle a broken place – not mourned and not mended, but tearing at the fabric of the person. Twisting the body into different sound shapes, gesturing in language, with, in and through the body, thus demonstrates that other worlds are possible, that one's own comfortable words are not comfortable for others and that human interaction depends on the ordinary risks of translation.

A Perspective on Dwelling

And then we went off to have Pastel in the Pastelaria de Belém, the one in the guide books that all of us had read about, and we had the traditional coffee and cakes, bonding, writing out happy birthday, learning to use the safer option of thumbs rather than the harder option of fingers to count with and then finally drinking the right kinds of drinks with the warm cakes. Our guide was just naturally showing us how it all worked.

Eating, meeting and greeting was one of the things we practised and enjoyed doing together as a bonded language class on our language holiday. Just as jelly babies formed something of a social glue in the classes at home, just as we always said *olá*, not hello at the start of every class, so the multilingual, multicultural class of mixed ability Portuguese learners in Lisbon met in Portuguese, and rested together over food and drink – in touristic places, places in the guide books, places one had to experience, in Portuguese.

It is tempting to interpret this as a form of cultural learning but the focus is first social. We learn what the right kinds of coffee are to order, how to eat the cakes, how to use the serviettes, how to count with ones fingers and thumbs. There is much space for reflection on the many and varied differences in our approaches to such simple ways of dwelling in the world. If, as Ingold argues, the culture concept must go for translation not to be created as a problem (Ingold, 1993) then the rethinking of intercultural communication, as being more than the learning of detached facts about how ideal or model others behave, is perhaps best exemplified here.

Dwelling together in the tourist world, dwelling together with a focus on languaging, in a subjunctive mood, breaks the possibility of English being the dominant way of interacting and replaces interculturality with the 'quick' of interagentivity. It keeps the misunderstanding and stumbling in the relationships rather than working towards an intercultural communicative nirvana in which awareness has erased all difficulty in communication. This is the kind of intercultural technologising that Douglas Adams writes of in *A Hitch-Hiker's Guide to the Galaxy* when he describes the 'Babel fish':

If you stick a Babel fish in your ear you can instantly understand anything said to you in any form of language. The speech patterns you actually hear decode the brainwave matrix which has been fed into your mind by your Babel fish […] the poor Babel fish, by effectively removing all barriers to communication between different races and cultures, has caused more and bloodier wars than anything else in the history of creation (Adams, 1979: 50).

In other words, it is not the cultural difficulties that are the focus in the dwelling perspective, but the attention to the social taste – of right language, and of social flow. Indeed the surprise and playful responses to the right Portuguese way of doing things – expressed in Portuguese – mock intercultural and cultural awareness training models. Cultural learning is easy – it is easy to gather from a guide book that the Pastelaria de Belém is the place to go for coffee and cakes. To go, consume and leave, in English – even if asking for the 'right' things, will not do any more than display cultural knowledge as fetish, acquired through literacy.

To dwell in the language, with the objects, in the tourist places, is to develop and to enact new perspectives on dwelling. It is also rhizomic, it is matted, untraceable, full of dense connections, some impossibly difficult and untraceable, some broken and in the middle of things. To bring in English is like taking a knife to the knot. It is to cease to dwell in the world of complex connections, it is to refuse to see the world as continuous. Of course this is one of the violent ways in which diremption occurs – the easy solution, the mended middle.

Breaking the hold of a powerful language is to bring in new perspectives on dwelling, to engage the body in new tasks of translation and it occurs in the often maligned touristic yet ordinary places. It is in and through these acts of languaging that dwelling occurs and continues in fresh ways with new constellations of people. There is nothing permanent about these moments in language, over food. There is nothing that is detachable and transferable about tourist language learners.

Chapter 10
Tourist Language Learners

'So why are you learning Portuguese?' This followed our first greeting, after saying a cautious hello before the first class began. It actually took a couple of weeks for us to gather. It was a bit of an enrolment shambles and no one quite knew where we were to go or when and how the whole thing would really start. With only 6 folk in the first class but with 10 enrolled for Portuguese we thought we'd be in luck. 'So why are you learning Portuguese' was a mode of greeting, of breaking the ice and finding a way of making sure we began to form a connection. 'I want to go to the football this summer'; 'I go there every year, to the Algarve, to the same place. I know the people, I just feel I should know their language too.' 'I'm going travelling for six months and I want to travel through Brazil. I can speak Spanish but I'll need Portuguese'; 'I'm studying Spanish and I like the work of Paulo Coelho – I want to be able to read him in the original'; 'My daughter lives in Rio – I go there every year on holiday'; 'I go to Portugal a lot with business. I love it there, the people are so nice.'

Who Bothers?

Tourist language learners is the term I have used throughout to refer to those people who I worked alongside to learn Portuguese and Italian in the various language classes I attended. There are a variety of other, more indigenous terms that I could have used here. The way we talked, in everyday terms, about what we were doing included phrases such as 'I'm doing a Portuguese class', 'I'm learning Italian, for tourists', 'I'm taking the survival course'. To my knowledge the term 'tourist language learner' is not one which any of us chose to use to refer to what we were doing. It is a slightly clumsy phrase, like the term languaging, but as with that term, I believe it can open up a space for thinking beyond what is suggested by the normal, easier terminology.

People generally want to go on holiday but, as the anti-tourist literature amply demonstrates, there is little social distinction accruing to being a tourist. 'Tourist' is something of a pejorative term (Hennig, 1997). Yet everyone on my courses was learning language either as a tourist already – for those on the language holidays – or was intending to go on holiday and to use the language they were learning. Even those whose main purpose for travel was business travel or to be with friends during holidays knew that a large chunk of their time would be spent being entertained in the destination as tourists. Hospitality for visitors, whatever may bring them to a place in first place, at some point becomes a form of tourism. Both language holidays and survival classes at home contained repeated opportunities either to be a tourist, in the former case, with visits organised to a variety of tourist sites in Lisbon, or to view tourist sites from a distance, with books, videos, television programmes, audio-tapes and personal narratives constantly being used to evoke the culture – the tourist culture – of the destination.

By referring to language learners as tourist language learners I'm attempting to make present the degree to which tourism was a place of dwelling, from which, and for which and through which the language was learned. Cronin makes the point that language learning turns people into travellers, that at some point it requires a period of residence abroad, or at the very least prolonged engagement with other speakers. As such language learning may be understood as a cosmopolitanising process, having, in Beck's words (2002) 'both roots and wings':

> In the process of translation, the translator engages in a form of dual tran-
> scendence. On the one hand, there is the journey out into the source language.
> On the other, there is the return to the target language. [...] Translators have
> been justly celebrated over the centuries for the journeyings to other cultures
> and the manner in which they have broadened the horizons of their own.
> Conversely, translators have also been ignored, disregarded and viewed with
> deep suspicion (Cronin, 2000: 64).

The same, of course, could be said of tourists – they journey out and they return home, their trips are both celebrated and are viewed with suspicion. So in speaking of tourist language learners we are doubling the stakes: of celebration at the physical and linguistic lands attained; and of suspicion at the dubiety of the enterprise and the treachery of the practices. For, to repeat what is a fundamental point, in a globalising world where much of what might count as travel is also at one and the same time tourism, and where tourism is the number one industry, language learning also turns people into tourists. Language learning is a practice through which people become tourists and are marked out as such.

As such, tourist language learners might be understood to be cosmopolitans, only to suggest this raises the spectres of many of the rather grand statements relating to cosmopolitanism as an elite, distinguished aspiration or, on the contrary, as an irresponsible, parasitic dabbling in cultures:

> For some, the term holds out the prospect of global democratization along
> with the hope that cosmopolitan groups will be in the forefront of establishing
> values, institutions and lifestyles which are less directly embedded within

nation-state societies. For others, the cosmopolitan is a figure to be reviled as it has become associated with 'the revolt of the elites', the inability of upper and middle class groups to sustain a sense of responsibility towards the growing numbers of the excluded around the world. These mobile elites, who enjoy the freedom of physical movement and communication, stand in stark contrast to those who are confined to place, whose fate is to remain located (Featherstone, 2002: 1).

The tourist language learners I joined are 'ordinary' people – a levelled out group from a wide and improbable range of social and cultural and ethnic backgrounds. They are bound by what they know they do not know – the particular language; by a love of things they believe to be found through that language but which they do not have in any tangible way; by their different yet paradoxical common sets of imaginings that prompt them to bother to learn a language. Some of the motivation, as we have seen, is practical, if not directly functional, but always the move to *learn* and then *to language*, is a particular one – it involves a particular language, a particular, relational commitment, and a commitment of time and of the body.

Some may indeed at times, through their actions, be called cosmopolitans in the elite sense of the word and also cosmopolitans in the rootless, parasitic sense: 'This view of the cosmopolitan as voyeur, parasitic or some sort of cultural tourist again emphasizes this incapacity to form lasting attachments and commitments to place and others, the inability to participate in a community for which one feels obliged to make sacrifices' (Featherstone, 2002: 1). For identity, as we know, is not a fixed thing, nor may it be spoken of in the singular (Hall & du Gay, 1996). But mostly, through a focus on the in-betweenness and the 'quick' of tourist language learning, I am interested in the dynamism and fracturing of changes, social and ontological and epistemological, that occur over time, in place and in space, when people move into another language and its worlds.

I am concerned to hold onto the betwixt and betweenness of tourist language learning. To continue the metaphor from Beck (2002), I am concerned with the processes of 'uprooting' and of 'learning to fly'. I do not wish to celebrate this as a liminal mode of being or heightened moment of experience, following Turner's distinctions, but I do point to the fact that the modes of dwelling encompassed by the practices of tourist language learning take people travelling, materially, culturally, imaginatively, whilst also leaving them at home.

The in-betweeness, the 'quick' of human relatedness, is not a 'quick' thing. In focusing on the *learning* process and on languaging I see the actual time it takes to make slow, arduous progress in another language as an adult learner:

Learning a language takes time. Translation often involves the investment of many hours, days, weeks, months and, in some cases, even years. In both instances, we have what we might term *kinetic resistance*. The profound engagement with language and culture that is implied by in-depth language learning and attentive translation represents a substantial commitment of time. It is the acknowledgement of the extent of the *entre-deux* [of human relatedness], of the time necessary to chart differences and find points of contact (Cronin, 2000: 116).

This is the real time that we experience and measure off each other in a class and through our attempts to language whilst on holiday. We measure it out in weekly classes, homework, exercises, semester breaks and holidays to the destination, coming back to each with a 'field report' on progress made.

I feel very rusty and unsure of myself, as if my tongue has been glued to the roof of my mouth and nothing will come out. It's the first class back after the Christmas break. It's really hard getting back in to it, 'I've not touched my books over the break', we say to each other, by way of greeting. I'm disorganised, I need to go back and sort out the mess of my notes, vocab lists and sheets of grammar points. Gradually I warm up, unstick my tongue and, through the group work of just saying what we did over Christmas, we all end up thawing out and having fun with the vocabulary that accrues and with the things we know we are able to say. We end up cheating a lot in order to make the conversation work. One of the class claimed to have had a goose. I ended up having had turkey for Christmas dinner after all.

All the classes were places of conversation, in the particular language we had gathered to learn, but also in other tongues. We switched in and out of each other's languages, often resting most fully in English, but not always, in the breaks and pauses between activities, in the corridors and lifts where we congregated after class. There was a constant tension between the clearly defined, circumscribed focus of our having come together, as strangers to one another – though occasionally people came in pairs, with friends or partners – and the disclosure of ourselves as people bound together by a significant lack – that of the particular language. We were addressing this lack with the resource of money, and most particularly of time. The ways in which we disclosed our lives to one another were careful, humorous and always oriented towards the task in hand and what we might term the haunting presence of Portuguese and Italian as tourist places we knew or imagined and could share as a common stock of knowledge and experience, and as language. Indeed the way in which we came to know each other, through the task in hand, was as tourist language learners, with a new language, a course, a city and a classroom of dwelling in common.

What then, might we say is occurring in this in-between, ordinary yet equally cosmopolitan activity of tourist language learning, when people come together in loose communities of interest, around a particular language and its touristic potential? What paths are tourist language learners tracing and what are the dynamics of their languaging?

Grand Tourists and Guides

In the distinctly multilingual phenomenon of tourism, some of the linguistic phenomena to be encountered are predictable. In France we expect to speak and hear French. When travelling the globe we expect to be able to 'get by' with English. In fact 'everyone speaks English' has become a common narrative trope in tourist accounts. Anxiety, prior to a trip, is often linguistic: 'Could you make yourself understood?'; 'Did they speak English?'; 'Did you use Italian?' Sometimes, however, the phenomena are not predictable. Popular tourist destinations attract speakers of many different world languages. As people encounter one another in the often confined and highly circumscribed spaces of tourist sites, the languages intermingle and meetings between tourists may occur in a variety of different tongues. Increasingly, today, this will be in English as a common language of communication, but we may not assume that this is always the case.

In the past, being a good traveller involved fluency in other languages. The elite travellers, the diplomats, explorers, missionaries and their spouses and children, could learn certain languages as part of their general education. Governesses taught French. A measure of distinction accrued to those who were able to speak in foreign tongues and with the kinds of fluency that pointed to the kinds of leisure required to develop a passable ease with another language. But not everyone learned another language and those embarking on the Grand Tour would also hire guides to translate for them as they made their journey, for their knowledge of local culture and, importantly, of the local language.

The situation, in many ways, is not much changed today, beyond the fact that travel is now also tourism, and a massified social activity. For today some take it upon themselves to become linguistically 'autonomous', to use Cronin's terms, and others rely on tour guides to act as translators for them (Cronin, 2000). In between these two states – of language autonomy and language dependency – resides a range of literacy and languaging practices. These are some of the markers of the in-betweenness of tourist language learning. This is where we see clumsy attempts to fly, to use Beck's terms (2002). Some tourists use phrase books, guide books, dictionaries – all of which are mobile translation tools for use in a prescribed variety of social, touristic situations, containers of travel knowledge especially prepared to enable a degree of autonomy. Others use other languages than their own, trying to find a temporary third space (Bhabha, 1994), a lingua franca, which may indeed often be English, or French or Spanish, but sometimes, depending on the social and cultural nature of the situation, may be Latin, or indeed another chance common tongue all together. However, as Cronin notes: 'The more countries the traveller goes to, the less languages s/he knows' (Cronin, 2000: 85).

Guide books, according to Cronin, enable a degree of language autonomy, based upon literacy practices, not upon orality:

> The guide book *translated* the foreign culture into the mother tongue of the traveller, The traveller no longer had to rely on the oral translation of the guide/interpreter as the guide book provided the written translation. The Murray and Baedecker guides thus facilitated the transition from heteronymous dependency on the oral interpreter to an autonomous mode of travelling grounded in literacy (Cronin, 2000: 86).

Barton maintains that 'in going about their ordinary daily life, people today are constantly encountering literacy' (Barton, 1994: 3). When it comes to both the practice and the study of tourism we find a curious and paradoxical situation. In order *to speak* a tourist language a wide variety of literacy practices are mobilised. In order to learn a language and to learn *to language*, in order to become a tourist, a wide variety of texts are encountered.

I began by logging on to the website and scrolling through the different language courses until, at last, I found the one I wanted:

Survival Italian

The aim of this class will be to provide survival level Italian for the everyday situation encountered by travellers and tourists – sightseeing, banks, hotels, bars, restaurants etc. The class is also suitable for those who wish to gain an introductory knowledge of Italian language and the culture of Italy. The class will concentrate on speaking but will also include discussion of Italian life and society.

I registered, received email confirmation, followed by a formal letter, a note of the timetable, the location, the tutor's name. I was advised to buy a dictionary, a note book. In the first class we were given handouts and spent much time taking notes from the blackboard. When I listened to tapes these were voices of people reading out texts, the videos accompanying the course were carefully scripted, staged, dramatised. Literacy was everywhere straining towards oral autonomy.

And so it was that I entered into the community of practice (Wenger, 1999) of tourist language learners, and entered a wide network of language, translation and literacy practices that went beyond this network (Barton & Tusting, 2005). Literacy practices, here, act as a bridge but also act as a technology (Ong, 1982). Texts, written texts or texts read out onto tape or filmed for video purposes, for tourist language learners, enable the inalienable good that is a language, possessed and embodied by the human being, to detach, to become mobile as well. It is consequently no surprise that the in-between nature of tourist language learning, as opposed to languaging, should be a textured, literate experience.

Horizontal, Vertical or Diagonal Travel

The literacy and languaging practices of tourist language learners also help with what Keating terms 'the negotiation of self', based on her own ethnography of Portuguese migrant women in London (Keating, 2005). Through engaging in a variety of literacy and language activities Keating's subject was able to 'create her own sense of self and her basis for understanding, deeply situated in the contexts and in the materials that she had at her reach' (p. 126). In the same way, through an engagement with the activity of learning a language for the purpose of surviving as a tourist, I found myself, alongside others, in a community of learners who became 'tourist language learners', and 'learners of Italian' and of Portuguese. Our shared, common materials, deeply situated in the contexts of tourism and of language learning, as well as of everyday life – brochures and maps, text books and dictionaries, music and magazines – helped our sense of identities emerge, but with its critical temporal and spatial dimensions.

'Not only do we keep negotiating our identities, but they place our engagement in practice in this temporal context' (Wenger, 1999: 155). As such, our tourist language learning and languaging placed us in a rich temporal and spatial context. We were engaged in the *kinetic resistances* of language learning, that Cronin speaks of. We were also – to follow Wenger – *living* our newly found identities, *becoming* tourist languagers, *building* a social bond and community membership, both in the classroom and the new networks that opened beyond it. In addition we were *learning* through new attunements to the world, *playing* new languages, situated at a nexus of multiple practices and forms of life, and involved in a constant interplay of the local and the global, within the classroom, through the travels taken by the materials we encountered, and through our tourist imaginations (Wenger, 1999: 163).

This is not neutral activity. Giroux is careful to point out that critical literacy practice is the medium and constructive force for human agency and political action: 'The ideology of a given form of literacy is inextricably linked to the way it addresses the possibility of people becoming actors in the process of social change' (Giroux, 2001: 227). Out of the ordinariness of holidaymaking and of immediate social relationships, actions that promote dialogue – practical, critical, humane and resistant – in a new language unmake olds patterns and distinctions and unsettle the way things are.

Cronin makes a distinction between two different types of travel:

> The level of awareness of the finer detail of language use is related to the tension between what might be termed *horizontal travel* and *vertical travel.* Horizontal travel is the more conventional understanding of travel as a linear progression from place to place. Vertical travel is temporary dwelling in a location for a period of time where the traveller begins to travel down into the particulars of place either in space (botany, studies of micro-climate, exhaustive exploration of local landscape) or in time (local history, archaeology, folklore) (Cronin, 2000: 19).

On the surface of it, it would appear that tourist language learners, those who take it upon themselves to learn the language of the destination and to do this translation work themselves, are horizontal travellers, just wishing to go from place to place. The 'asking for a cup of coffee' aspect of tourist language learning is an example of what might be considered a horizontal travel practice. However, the reasons given for wanting to engage with the language, and the different sets of effort involved in the actually doing this – the crockery, the words, the taste, the sociality, the cultural context, the intercultural desire, the effort of will – contain within them many of the characteristics of those engaged also in vertical travel: a wish to deepen the relationship with a place, with a people, with a way of life, with a literature. When dealing with tourist language learners then, the distinction between horizontal and vertical travel – one which is, on the face of it, self-evident – begins to break down. The practices and activities of learning and languaging, the encounter and engagement with a variety of texts, the sounds and ways of being make the travels, and the identities in play, more complex.

Limits to Language Knowledge

> We've started learning about food and drink, particularly about ordering drinks. 'What do you know how to say?' asks our tutor. Even though we profess to be beginners and this is only our third class, she assumes a certain common knowledge, and she is right:

Vino rosso.

Una birra.

Aqua minerale.

Un tè.

Espresso – *My neighbour turns to me conspiratorily and whispers, 'Oh my goodness, I remember having my first ever espresso, in Italy. You had to scrape me off the ceiling.' We giggle. I remember my first too.*

Un caffè macciato – *'Oooh' says someone. The culprit turns round and says* – *'I had one in Costa the other day.' Laughter.*

Cappucino – *'And what's the plural? – not Cappucinos but...', 'due cappucini' – calls out someone.*

Latte – *Someone calls out. 'No' says the tutor. Suddenly the mood changes. We had been well into the swing of things, getting carried away by our Glaswegian coffee bar cosmopolitan knowledge. 'No, there is no such thing, it doesn't actually exist in Italian.' Our attention is caught. We've learned our Italian from coffee bars and Tesco. We thought we knew where we were when calling a 'panini' a 'panini', but here, as we worked through the list of food and drink our local knowledge met a different world and meanings unravelled.*

Tourist language learners unravel, constantly. The mistakes, such as the ones above, are ones we found ourselves making repeatedly in all the classes. They link us in to local, economic, literacy, social and cultural practices, as well as shaping us into tourist languagers. Sometimes they were the source of much hilarity, sometimes embarrassment. They weren't even mistakes of grammar or syntax. Gradually we discovered interlinguistic variations in accent, grammar, semantics, expressions that would pull us up sharp and invoke something approaching a sense of awe, as a linguistic penny dropped. Cronin describes how the voyage into one's own native tongue if full of language pitfalls, variations, dissonances and surprises. Our home languages can be a source of endless fascination to us. But tourist languages have the same mesmerising power, the same ability to unmake us, and to then carefully put the pieces back together in a different, satisfying way.

What we find in this example is neither horizontal nor vertical travel, or at least not in ways that enable us to bring a satisfactory understanding to the activity. Yes, the tourist language learners have moved their bodies from one place to arrive at this place and to learn, and yes, they might be characterised as deepening their knowledge of a destination. But the in-between nature of the tourist language learning situation is more complex than these terms suggest:

Distance here is not so much a terrain as a figure of movement. In other words, the pulsation, the oscillation of the entre-deux brings a subject near to and away from the Other. There is no absolute proximity but neither is there absolute distance. A dynamic conception of the in-between thus avoids a spatialization of contact that haunts reified notions distance (Cronin, 2000: 117).

Put another way, the changes, often infinitesimally small and of a frustrating pace for the stuttering, stumbling tourist language learner, are journeys made with the body into another language and all that that experience evokes. It is neither horizontal nor vertical but diagonal. It involves movement of the body, yes, but in the form of the embodied, concentrating movement of the mouth, the tongue, the lungs, the diaphragm, it involves absorption of the whole being. It involves being neither fish nor foul, neither up nor down, but in-between, *in the quick* – which is indeed slow – of learning new forms of human relatedness. And all of this, for those who actually bother, is hard work, and, in the wider contexts of the multilingual phenomenon of tourism, it makes bothering with languages an economic and political issue.

Labour with Languages

In tourism one of the many challenges of globalisation is that changing and expanding tourism markets and destinations, coupled with increased labour mobility, mean that those being welcomed and those doing the welcoming speak a host of different languages. Cronin has shown how translation, the work of languaging, has been placed upon different groups of people as a task throughout history (Cronin, 2000).

In Ireland today Cronin demonstrates how a migrant worker population now services the tourists in an English that is not the 'lilting Irish' that the tourists have come to expect. With English as the language of world tourism, those servicing this industry operate as often as not in conditions of language apartheid, with a diversely accented English spoken in the performance, commercial and service domains, on show to tourists who expect some 'authentic' local language colour, and with a multitude of different languages spoken below decks, or behind the scenes (Cronin & O'Connor, 2003). Under the complex conditions of globalisation the work of translation is now being placed on the hosts with the aim, as Cronin puts it, of arriving at a neo-Babelian future:

> [...] neo-Babelian scenarios in dominant languages perform a double sleight-of-hand. They seek to eliminate the costs of translation by moving the debt across to the translated who then become invisible in the linguistic accounts of the powerful. Language in a global monoglossic scenario becomes a process

without (resistant) subjects, whose agency is undermined buy the overwhelming fact of political, economic and cultural dominance. At best, the linguistically weak may be granted the consolation prize of a dissident heteroglossism and, at worst, they may end up being fully translated because there is nothing left to translate (their native language having been rendered extinct) (Cronin, 2000: 60).

Even in enlightened contexts, where Anglophone firms realise that they may be able to buy anything in English but they have great difficulty in selling (Cronin, 2003: 61) in English, we still find an emphasis on a training process in the service of the easy flow of capital and consequently as a technological tool aimed at either 'doing better or at expending less energy' – to return to Lytoard's definition of the performative discussed in Chapter 1 (Lyotard, 1984).

In host communities, wishing both to welcome more tourist dollars and also manage and preserve their cultural identity at one and the same time, language is a political issue. Refusing to the speak the language of the mass band of tourists is one strategy of resistance, another is managing tourists by language groups, through the medium of languages common to many and spoken by guides who, once again, do the translating and interpreting work, paid by in some cases by the host cultures, in others by those managing the tourists directly. What tourist language learners do, by bothering, is complicate the power dynamics of the resistance and the ordering of translation activity within tourism. When the labour of languages is taken up by the hosts, or by intermediary hosts – tour guides, for instance – on behalf of the guests then one way or another the tourist remains linguistically dependent but is given the illusion of autonomy, in the midst of the heteronomy of tourist multilingualism.

Tourist language learners will both slow things down – by asking questions *in the language* – and quicken things – by *languaging*, by stepping over the boundaries of language protection, or hostility, that may have been erected on the part of the guests. Tourist language learners confound the expectations because *they bother*. And as such they have the potential to change the nature of the touristic exchange.

Diagonal Practices: Global and Local

Encounters with people *as* tourists, then, are also encounters with languages in people *as* tourists. People speak languages. People are inhabited by languages. They dwell in languages. They speak from the body with languages. When people travel, *as* tourists, they meet other people who speak other languages and they may step outside of their habitual language, their mother tongue, to try out words and phrases in other languages. Languages act to mark out people in terms of their potential origin, nationality, history and education. When tourists meet and communicate they do so in and around a variety of language barriers. Sometimes tourists are also interpreters and translators. At other times they are lost, struggling to survive in a linguistically hostile world.

The diversity, complexity and connexity of human languages and world languages is not a new phenomenon. Nor is mobility. The two are linked in our human stories and myth. In the western tradition the story of the Tower of Babel (Genesis 11) or the tale of Pandora's box point to the curse of linguistic diversity and the way in which gods took their revenge on the willful desires of human beings by scattering and confusing the speech of humans. Linguistic diversity is not a positive story in our historical ad mythic imaginations, in the west. Modern languages offers itself, under the global paradigm, as both peace-monger and money-monger. In the dominant discourses on the fate of modern languages under conditions of globalisation, mass communication and the rise of English as a hegemonic language, we find both celebration and critique that mirror the wider debates around globalisation as in tourism debates.

Languages, we hear, are economic saviours, they are the ultimate, mobile, functional tools. Languages are doomed, they are being killed by globalisation, by the rise of English and with them, we learn, the environment dies too (Skutnabb-Kangas, 2000). For us to prosper, economically, we need to learn another language. But this misses the point: *languages dwell in people*. It is people, not the languages themselves that make the difference. It is people who learn and love and *language*. To continually objectify the technological power of languages, discussed in the previous chapter, means to miss the heart of the matter. *It is people who speak other languages.* And one of the most concentrated opportunities for people to do this is as tourists, in a globalising world. For us to live together in ways that prosper one another we need to be able to listen, and speak, interculturally and in ways that do not see language as a barrier. This takes us to the heart of the 'terrible paradox' of which Robert Young speaks:

> While we are clearly more involved in each other's lives than ever before, we appear no less deeply involved in brutal rejection of each other. While more people from more cultures are communicating and cooperating across differences, as many, it seems, are killing and maiming each other in the name of cultural and religious identity. [...] The dilemma of the global age is that, while we have finally discovered that we are one people who must share one precarious world, we are profoundly divided by race, culture and belief and we have yet to find a tongue in which we can speak our humanity to each other (Young, 1996: 2).

Finding a tongue, a metaphorical throw-away in Young's searching contemplation of intercultural communication, has been starting point for the take on tourism and globalisation that is the focus of this book. My concern however, is not so much with finding a tongue, but with *finding tongues* in common and with examining where it is, in the wider contexts of globalisation, that this kind of seeking for ways of communicating takes place and who it is that takes on this task of 'speak[ing] our humanity to each other' in the perhaps unlikely context of global tourism. For where the debates around globalisation, languages and tourism are so polarised into economic utopia or environmental dystopia, it is the bucking of the trends in unlikely places by unlikely people that is of particular interest.

Where Young is concerned with cultural difference and the divisions of race, culture and belief, my concern is with languages, tourism and with the labour of languages. How do we find, not a tongue, but tongues in which we can 'speak our humanity to each other'? How do we find ways of speaking and of listening that are not limited to the dominant modes of theorising offered by social and cultural theory, by economics or by psychoanalysis? Where are the places and the social possibilities for learning other languages and for learning to language? Who provides such opportunities? There has to be more to both tourism and to modern languages than a vague hope that awareness raising may bring peace, or to the inexorable belief in and equally inexorable critique of the neoliberal consumerist paradigm, which is the starting point for so much theorising about both tourism and languages today.

If world English, as a common language, is good for globalisation then the fact that globalisation is killing languages is merely an extension of the same process. The focus of the globalising activity is not important here, for this state affairs pertains in the domains of global business, global movements of resistance, education across borders, and tourism. World English is the pragmatic choice (Brutt-Griffler, 2002; Canagarajah, 1999) but with profound consequences for the speaking of humanity to one another.

Young's argument (1996: 212) is that a common tongue, a 'democratic dialogue among culturally diverse people relying on the role of communicative hope is the antidote to authoritarian poisons'. He proposes a critical-pragmatic theory of intercultural communication – one which focuses on cultural difference and the power of critique. But he is after 'a common tongue', he is working within a critical-pragmatic theoretical framework that does not manage to theorise its own medium of English – the common tongue of today – the one which causes the death of languages, under certain readings of globalisation.

His argument is a powerful and important theoretical grounding for intercultural thinking but his insistence on intercultural discourse preserving difference and enabling the finding of a common tongue is misplaced, as is his view that it is race, culture and belief that profoundly divide us. It is not cultural difference that causes enmity between peoples, it is injustice, exploitation and poverty. It is not knowing about differences in culture, race and religion that will bring an end to injustice. Awareness-raising, we know, does not change people, relationship does. Knowledge of the other 'out there' or at home is of little value in such a humanistic endeavour if it fails to transform people in to what Barnett terms 'critical beings' (Barnett, 1997). Similarly the ability to find appropriate cultural ways of speaking to the other is of little value when confined to the language of intercultural communication studies – English. The mess of life and injustice, of meeting, greeting and eating with others as we visit their place of dwelling, or they come to visit and dwell among us, as tourists, as well as in many other guises, will be little aided by knowing how things are done, or how life is lived in our destinations. Compare this to the changes and connections that may come if we speak with each, listen to and are able to hear something of each other's stories, with them and in their language.

For it has been my working hypothesis here that the answer to these huge issues of common speech and of just mobility in the globalised and globalising contexts of life in the world today are being worked out by those who do not insist on finding a common tongue – but those who work to find tongues in common. These are the people – the actors – who work with connexity and complexity at every turn, in the 'quick of human relatedness'. And so it is that the focus in this book has been on tourist language learners – language actors who take up a role every now and then on the global stage of tourism, who take on the work of finding and of using tongues in common, and ones which are not their own, which are messy and uncomfortable.

In this respect, with languages and tourism as the focus of this book, it has not been possible to remain with the binary reductions that personify, demonise, glorify or shun those who are tourists and linguists. For when the dominant perspectives available to us for considering globalisation are those of economics, sociology and psychology, when the speaking, listening human beings on holiday can only be viewed in terms of money, massification and motivation, then we have reached a pretty pass. For global man, is still hu-man, still does and *is* some of those things which pre-date econometrics, sociology and psychology and which, more particularly, are not easily revealed or understood from one dominant perspective. This is the arena in which some of the complexity is wrestled with and overcome, and connection is made real, tangible, is lived.

Tourists who language, who work hard over many months of attending evening classes, lunchtime sessions or even go on language learning holidays and study tours themselves are bucking the trend, making visible the long-term, relational work of translation and are finding ways to reach out to strangers, to the faceless workers who service their holidays and they are doing so because they see it as 'good'. In this respect their understanding of what is good is not the same as Lyotard's technological 'good'. They are not learning languages in this context in order to find ways of enhancing their touristic performance or expending less energy. The truth is quite the reverse. Languages are the anti-technology, they are the relational mode of address as a global tourist. Languaging betrays weaknesses in accent, in origin, in grammar, pronunciation – it requires a performance that is often an anti-performance or a bad performance. And languaging requires a great deal of energy – kinetic resistance – to be expended.

But what the personal, ordinary, everyday yet also extraordinary stories of tourist language learners begin to reveal, I would argue, is what happens when people bother with relationships, when they experiment with new forms of local community, when, often without having any sense of this at all, they become resisting actors in the craziness of the world as it is engaged today. To learn a language as a tourist is an odd thing to do in these 'dark ages' that MacIntyre speaks of (MacIntyre, 1985), it opens the tourist out onto new worlds of phenomena, it engages new relationships. It is the process of engaging with this world, the modes, directions and practices this may take, through those who may be encountered on the way, that has been the story in this book.

Chapter 11
Surviving

Throughout the course of this book I have been concerned to address the relationship between tourism and languages as it is made manifest in people doing tourism by learning tourist languages. I have asked the question: why bother? Why bother in a tourist world that speaks English and in a world where money talks? Why bother if you can speak English, whether as a native or a non-native speaker? Many don't. Some do. The question of why people do good is a perennial one in moral theory. The question of why people might not bother is easy to answer. So I have puzzled over the bothering. I have come at the issue from several directions, responding to the possibilities that the energy, time and will expended might suggest. I have found avoidance of risk, a desire for education, a broadening of the mind through travel and languages. I have identified the gains of *linguistic capital* and its currency in other languages.

I have shown the practice of tourist language learning and of languaging to be a complex process and have explored this, in a quest for some answers to the bothering question. I have done this by examining lessons in asking for directions and the practices of way finding, through discussions of the tourist imaginings, through the move into a language, through lessons in pronunciation. I found parabolic tales in the narrations that accompanied the language learning experiences. These led me to argue that the activity of speaking from the body as a tourist language learner and languager was an aspect of human movement, changing the nature of perceptions from the place of dwelling; that it was rather like magic. As such I found transforming potential in the activity. *Learning to play* a language, engaging in deep play, rehearsing and performing for tourism, in the present with an eye to the future as a tourist language learner, I argued, involves the commitment of the whole person to this activity and this dialogical commitment to conversation opens new spaces for hope, new communities and networks of practice.

I have argued that tourist language learners, through their languaging activities and through aspects of their reasons for learning a language are breaking the dominant hold of English. As such, I suggested, they are acting out of courtesy and charity, as well as being involved in diagonal activities that take them traveling and unravel their identities, remaking them in other contexts – global and local – as tourist language learners and languagers.

Courtesy and the motivation of tourists to be 'good' guests, capable of communicating clearly, effectively and respectfully with their future hosts returns us to the partial, messy aspects of languaging activity. All social practices are bound into discursive frameworks of subjection, domination and power in subtle and illusive ways. We live in supercomplex worlds (Barnett, 2001). To deny this is to seek to 'mend' Rose's broken middle. Through this chapter, I seek to draw some conclusions to the threads of this argument and to the concerns that have detained me in this book. I argue that the apparently opposing aspects of tourist language learning – the concern with educational desire, risk, linguistic currency, way finding and pronunciation, the concern with conversation, play, performance, courtesy and charity, languaging practice – may be understood as learning the arts of survival.

Basic Human Needs

> *I want to be able to get by, to make myself understood, to be able to speak to people in shops, chemists, doctors. I want to be able to get a bed for the night, order food, to arrive in the right place at the right time. And I want to understand what is happening on the streets around me, to ask people to help me and to be able to communicate. I want to understand what a police officer says to me. I want to be able to buy presents to take home. Basically, I want, to survive.*

I want to survive. In the compilation above of the desires for learning expressed by tourist language learners we find a list of tourist needs. These needs are no different from the basic human needs elaborated by Abraham Maslow in 1943 in his now seminal *Theory of Human Motivation* (Maslow, 1943). In his treatise, Maslow listed a hierarchy of needs. At the apex of his pyramid is *actualization* followed by, *esteem, love/belonging, safety, physiological need.*

Although the subject of dispute and debate and revision since 1943 this taxonomy remains the starting point for discussions of what human beings need to survive. In recent years this has been discussed in the context of language learning as well as in discussions of peace and justice (Canning, 2005; Staub, 1999; Staub, 2003). Survival language for tourists indexes each of these dimensions: food, shelter; risk avoidance; relation, connection, meeting and greeting; comprehension, understanding, converstation; successful languaging. Although these could be described hierarchically, as Maslow does, the more fluid, interplay of these elements is now accepted wisdom. Food entails conversation, conversation entails languaging.

The actual needs presented in the tourist language classes, as curricula, pointed to food, drink, shelter and safety – risk avoidance and way finding – as the seemingly most important dimensions. They took the form of actual lessons, handouts, text book chapters, in the classes themselves. But, as I have demonstrated throughout this book, other, less tangible aspects of life and need were present in the class which do indeed relate to love, esteem, actualization, in Maslow's terms, and these would be present at the same time as actual and imagined physiological aspects. Jelly babies accompanied conversation, booking hotel rooms came with laughter and play.

Tourist language learning focuses, through a *curriculum-as-designed-and-desired*, on a certain sense of survival for a body that is mobile and unhabituated to life in a new environment. The focus, the dominant phenomena for material survival for tourist language learners involve food, shelter, medical supplies, clothing and gifts. These articulate with other dimensions of the human needs taxonomy. In each case they involve bodily perception: 'our body' says Merleau-Ponty (2002: 169) is our general medium for 'having the world'. Each of these aspects of consumption, consumed in and through a halting conversation, are related to what Merleau-Ponty terms 'actions necessary for the conservation of life' (p. 169). But each of these aspects is in term mediated, experienced through the tourist's languaging body as it works 'to have the world' – in this respect food, shelter, clothing and gifts.

The sensory perception discussed in Chapter 4, the body attuning itself to its environment, is also in play in the domains of survival, as an attention to matter, and as a mode of learning in itself. Ingold, drawing on Lave (Lave & Wenger, 1991), refers to this as follows: '"Understanding in practice" [...] is a process of *enskilment*, in which learning is inseparable from doing, and in which both are embedded in the context of a practical engagement in the world – that is, in dwelling' " (Ingold, 2000: 416).

The learning of the language and its practice through 'hands-on training' in the everyday tasks of consumption – of food, clothing, shelter and relation – is where the tourist languager learns to respond, with ever increasing fluency, to the way in which life is lived in a new environment. And one of the media for this hands-on work of survival, this education of attention, occurs through the language being learned and through a constant attunement to language, dialect and accent. It is important to listen, to look and to learn how it is that goods are purchased, how or whether queues form, what the courtesies are that accompany the purchasing. For learning to survive as a tourist means learning to consume – in the widest sense of the word – in a new language and in a new environment. Let us

examine this aspect by focusing in particularly on the physiological dimensions and how they interweave with other elements of human need.

A Cup of Coffee

So you are in a restaurant and you want to order food politely. The waiter might come
up to you and say in Italian:

Scusi

Desidera?

Dica?

Cosa Prende?

Prego

And you would then reply:

Vorrei un caffè per favore

Prendo un caffè

Per me un caffè

When you are in Italy you'll find you automatically get an espresso if you ask for a
caffè. And there is no such a think as a café latte, it would be a caffè macciato, or a
latte macciato, depending on how strong you wanted the coffee. 'What does macciato
mean?' someone asks – 'It means stained.' Also, you don't usually get tea with milk
automatically so English tourists will have to ask for it.

So then the waiter would come back and say:

Ecco – here it is

Ecco (a lei, a voi) – if it is specifically for you alone or for you plural – 'yous, as we say
in Glasgow'.

To survive, in any phrase book or guide book, means knowing how to
order that perennial cup of coffee. Coffee, ordering and drinking it, partic-
ipating in this rituals, for the Italian and Portuguese tourist language
learners, was of fundamental importance and one of the first lessons
learned. In fact, it was a lesson that had already been learned by many as
part of social being, not as part of structured curriculum, but in everyday
interaction, consumption, films, life.

But, as we noted earlier in the book, being able to order a cup of coffee
in another language is also the lowest of the low for language professionals. It is the one thing that language professionals thoroughly despise as a
'competence' or 'skill', rather than seeing it as 'understanding in practice'

and as 'enskilment' (Ingold, 2000) – as a way of getting on with life, as a way of integrating the human need for drink with the meeting and the greeting. Often, it has to be said, it is the mainstream language professionals who hold such views, those in the steady jobs that don't depend so acutely on the seasonal reviews that come to so many of the hourly paid, or temporary language teachers who teach 'basic survival'. Let's buy that coffee again:

I found a stand to buy coffee and stood talking for ages with someone from Brazil and someone who speaks German – Marcelo both of them. They were struck by my use of uma bica – it clearly marked me as a foreigner who knew something about the language and who cared about the language. I managed to tell them lots about the language I speak – languages are really the constant subject of conversation…words flow between us all the time. Much of my conversation was oriented towards home and their questions were about where I was from not about where I was going or even so much why I was here. It was a real boost to have such attentive listeners and helpers with the language.

Buying that infamous coffee, repeated here because it is a repeated action, is a case in point. The first time my sentences are formulaic, awkward, rehearsed from a note book or phrase book: 'Uma bica se faz favor.' The response, the welcoming response that notices that I'm really trying, helps me understand a little more about how this works – how I stand and wait for the drink, how others do this too, how the coffee is made, served up, how I can stand at the bar – not just go and find a table – how my attempt invites further conversation, opens up a conversation about good coffee, how I can ask if I got it right, how other names for different coffees are shared. And through the course of a language holiday in Lisbon I notice that our afternoon trips out to visit the sites are partly an education of attention broadly conceived, but also an education of consumption attention. Our guide goes up to the kiosk first, or speaks to the waiter first, we hear him order different drinks – 'um galão, um cerveja, uma água mineral con gás, uma bica cheia'.

One kiosk becomes my favourite. And I noticed that at 4 o'clock after a long morning of hard classes, after the hot midday sunshine and after visiting museums, churches, cathedrals and Roman remains I'm ready for the thick, hot strong coffee as they make it here. What is learned – in body and speech – is what is consumed. My education of attention increases in fluency as an attention to the needs of my body in this hot place, and my tongue too – as it becomes familiar with the taste also adapts to the flow of the language of its consumption. I say the phrase more readily, *fluently* now. Fluency is the bedding of rehearsals – practices – into the body and material life. It is an accumulation of stories, connection, memory, material, history, routine and ritual, work and reflection. And that is learned, developed in the context of languaging as opposed to mere language acquisition.

> *We put together a list of food to order from a shop as a class. It's a bit like playing 'my aunt went to Paris'. My tutor begins and then we each add an item, listing all the others that went before. It's an odd selection that we come up with, but it represents what we have learned thus far, and what we hope we might be able to purchase:*
>
> *Queria comprar – I'd like to buy…*
>
> *um meio quilo de tomates*
>
> *um quilo de peixe*
>
> *uma alface*
>
> *um meio quilo de queijo*
>
> *um bolo*
>
> *dois quilos de patatas*
>
> *três alhos*
>
> *uma sandes*
>
> *dois quilos de morangos*
>
> *um ganso*
>
> *um perú*
>
> *meio litro de leite*
>
> *um frango.*

As we get to the goose (*ganso*) and the turkey (*perú*) there is great laughter. Its actually March, but this takes us back to immediate post-Christmas class when my companion and I made much of our turkey and goose con-sumption – much to the hilarity, the remembered hilarity, of the rest of the group. In fact, looking over the list, these two items are the ones which stand out as the ones we do not seriously imagine consuming in Portugal or Brazil. The rest – we can taste and smell them already – the heat, the difference between food in the North of Europe and food from the South. It is whetting our appetites, simulating the experience known to us through embodied memories of being there and tasting the place.

The food and drink we imagine, we remember and we practise buying represent fun, memory, survival – needs meet on many different levels and are present in the tourist language class. The education of attention to food is a sensuous experience, it is fun, and it involves turning our tongues to words as well as to flavours.

Gifts

Gifts and rituals of exchange have long been a focus of anthropology and other disciplines, most notably, though far from exclusively, through the work of Mauss (1990). In tourism studies too, in recent years, gifts and the biographies of objects and souvenirs have received attention (Jack & Phipps, 2005; Lury, 1996). I do not wish to dwell on the aspects of gifting behaviour here, but rather to point to the way in which gifts, as material objects, symbolise both the meeting of a variety of human needs. These may indeed be physiological – for the receiver – but invariably they symbolise love, esteem, actualization of a thought, a duty, an exchange through language and transformed into an object. The verbal exchange of stories works in a slightly different way (Bendix, 2002; Cronin, 2000; Jack & Phipps, 2005) but it nonetheless points also to the physiological efforts in language. 'Only humans narrate', says Ingold '[b]ut to construct a narrative one must already dwell in the world and, in the dwelling, enter into relationships with its constituents, both human and non-human' (Ingold, 2000: 76).

> In between our classes and the afternoon trips we go shopping. In the early stages of the course we do this alone, or with the companions who have joined us on this language holiday. But as the week progresses and we form a more cohesive social group we shop together, consume together. We go into bars and buy bottles of water, together, we have lunch or coffee together, rehearsing the rituals we have learned earlier in the week, sharing the different knowledge we now have in our bodies, from the things we have bought and the places we have been. We do this in Portuguese, but also – as this is time 'off' – we do this in the languages that level out as easiest for us, sometimes German, sometimes, French, English, Italian.

> Anja is in her late fifties. She has small grandchildren and she has just met me having been to the bookshop I'd told her off in the Prato – the shopping centre in the heart of the business district of the town. She shows me her purchases – a copy of St Exupery's Le Petit Prince *in Portuguese. I read this story to the grandchildren, she says, but I'd like to try it myself in Portuguese. And she is excited. She's found the name of a good music shop. She is a passionate musician, and music teacher, of drumming in particular. Her love of world music has led her to travel and to learn other languages. She urges me to join her in her quest for Portuguese music. And off we go. As she explains how the music works and talks to me of her love of it, a new area of life is opened out. We both buy CDs as gifts for those back home, a link created through language and music and consumption here between each other, and the sharing of knowledge and passions, and those we are connected to in our everyday lives.*

'What we call consumption rituals are the normal marks of friendship' says Mary Douglas in her new introduction to the 1996 version of the now seminal *World of Goods* (Douglas & Isherwood, 1996). 'The patterned flow of consumers goods would show a map of social integration' (p. xxii). This map of social integration is not, any longer, if it ever really was, an easily bounded one under the conditions of liquid modernity and social mobility. In *Sociology beyond Societies*, Urry (2000) maintains that sociology can no longer be of any relevance unless it abandons its view of bounded social institutions and concerns itself with the flows of objects, messages, people, ideas and images and looks at the implications and consequences of these mobilities for the experiences of human life: time, space, dwelling and citizenship. His argument rests on the way in which '*inhuman* objects' – what Ingold perhaps preferably terms 'non-human' objects (Ingold, 2000) – are what reconstitute social relations in the world of global complexity: 'Such relations are made and remade through machines, technologies, objects, texts, images, physical environments and so on. Human powers increasingly derive from the complex *interconnections* of humans with material objects' (Urry, 2000: 14).

And so it is, as tourist language learners, be it through our text books and phrase books, or through our purchase of bottled water or drumming CDs, that relations are made. Urry is right, but only so far; for us the relation was also being made through languages which we were learning to practise, which were becoming part of our mode of dwelling. What the material objects symbolised were a solid aspect of conversations about music and home and thirst and heat, and the finding of that great book shop and the place to buy stamps. Language is not an inhuman object and for tourist language learners it was the source and the medium relation – language as object in the form of Portuguese song, or Portuguese story books – and also language as the way to the object, the stories told that led to these desired objects.

Courtesy and Charity

When we speak of gifts in the context of languages and language learning, our words shift a little semantically and become Pentecostal. 'She has a gift for languages', rather like 'a gift' for music. This sense of gifting brings us into other senses of survival – those that relate not to individual human needs to but to a collective sense, those that relate to the activities and relations formed in common through meeting human needs together. They return us to courtesy and charity and as such, I would argue, they point to the relationship between languages and life:

> Life and Language are moving things. They are not static. Nor are they mono-
> lithic, they are flawed and ambiguous and the art of dealing with circum-
> stances [...] involves adaptation to the resources of the system in innovative

ways. The real political question is how do we relate to others in the inter-making of this reality. Do we enhance the space for life, joy, love and pleasure for all or only for ourselves? To put it another way: Is it possible to have a form of human flourishing to which the oppression of others is *intrinsic* rather than accidental? (Young, 1996: 88)

Young's answer to his own questions is a hermeneutics of hope, present for him in conversation, in Williams' social miracle, present in the attempts, the broken attempts, to try, to commit, to understand and to try again. For tourist language learners – social actors making changes in the status quo of their language habits – the new language is a sign that they have some common feeling with others, that they are not content to operate according to the dominant, easy modes suggested by tourism and that as tourists themselves they are prepared to operate a very significant inversion:

> The institution / ritual of charity tells us that to have a language to negotiate or quarrel *in* is already to presuppose the social miracle, the fact of linguistic sharing. Charity uncovers the bedrock of speech: sheer converse, the exchange of sounds in codified patterns and the peculiar exhalation that attaches to just that (Williams, 2000a: 87–8).

Courtesy and *charity* are somewhat old fashioned words. Both have particular associations. *Courteous* behaviour is defined by the *Oxford English Dictionary* as 'polite, kind, considerate in manner or approach'. Of course, the manner of approach chosen in another language can indeed be aggressive, disrespectful, impolite. Often tourist's attempts at languaging will just come out 'wrong' and perhaps add more weight to views of tourists, from certain social or national groups, as ignorant, rude and pushy. But in the context of tourist language learning the motivations – the manner of approach is indeed practically courteous and imagines tourist – host encounters as operating with, among other things, charity: 'It affirms what it is in language that is 'there' before and after argument and context – which is not self-expression (a meaningless idea outside the frame of converse) but the possibility of recognition' (Williams, 2000a: 86).

Inversions and their discussion are a key feature of the literature on tourism. In this literature, tourism, it is claimed, turns the everyday world upside down and inside out. For the most part these inversions are righted upon return, they are temporary and pose no risk. But to choose not to speak in ways which are powerful, comfortable, which get things done and done quickly in the world, to refuse the dominant way of things and to speak from a counter-script is, I would argue, to do more than just be king or queen for a day. It is not just playing but transforming the self with words enfleshed, enskilled. Such courteous action, is a strange and perhaps, at face value, unthreatening assault on the dominant ways in which we are told that the world works, and acknowledges other ways in which other worlds work.

This is particularly true in the context of tourism where the horror stories about tourists' discourteous behaviour amplify the already negative, *discourteous, uncharitable* practices that can be spawned through tourism, as they can through other human practices. Unlike the asceticism of the rich, the rejuvenation for the old or the parties for the poor that are well-documented inversions in the tourist literature as I noted earlier, the inversion of the self requires a more primary inversion. It requires an inversion of the whole person – from fluency to stuttering speech, from English to a tacit attempt at articulating a respect for other ways of playing life in language. It requires a particular humility and a full release of the powers and forms of capital that attach to English.

Paulo Freire, the Brazilian critical pedagogue, maintains that it is only through dialogue – through courteous, charitable conversation – that the world can be named and transformed. Dialogue he maintains, 'cannot exist without humility' (Freire, 1970: 71). He goes further, however, in the context of domination, to incorporate the need for a love of people and the world. This sense of love is related in English to the idea of charity, the old term used for what is now translated from the Greek, as love:

> Because dialogue is an encounter among women and men who name the world, it must not be a situation where some name on behalf of others. It is an act of creation, it must not serve as a crafty instrument for the domination of one person by another. [...] The naming of the world, which is an act of creation and recreation, is not possible if it is not infused with love (Freire, 1970: 70).

The dialogic, conversational, diagonal movement made by tourist language learners is not a pure, charitable, courteous action. To claim this would be to over-simplify a complex practice. Of course there are all kinds of negative motivations and practices that are worked out in the course of the time spent learning and not every interaction will correspond to ideals we may have in mind. But it is nonetheless an act of creation and recreation that is indeed attempting to dialogue with others, without English, in situations of domination, in ways that help, are charitable – sometimes with self-interest – but often with the social miracle in mind. I also do not want to argue that this is a somehow transcendental action, detached from the 'quick' of human life. It is not. In fact it is precisely in the 'quick' of face-to-face encounters with others, in ordinary, material tasks, over time, that this work of speaking differently proceeds.

Cosmopolitan Tourist People

I am aware that the notes sounded in this book move us through a variety of harmonies but that overall the tone is hopeful, optimistic. At this juncture the argument has taken us through risk, danger and survival as motivations for tourist language learning, into a view of the activity of tourist language learning as gesturing, in its own particular ways, towards more generous manifestations of the human spirit, of neighbourliness and the social bond. As such, this work is a quest for hope. It reflects Bauman's view, expressed in *Liquid Life* that: 'Adorno's precept – that the task of critical thought "is not the conservation of the past, but the redemption of the hopes of the past" – has lost nothing of its topicality' (Bauman, 2005).

Throughout the discussions in this book I have insisted on the awkward, even disquieting terms of 'tourist language learners' and 'languaging' in order, I have argued, to open a space in which the subtleties of human movement in these activities can be traced. I have wanted to explore the dynamic patterns that emerge out of the myriad relationships and changes that such activities entail. I have been interested in the interplay of material and social worlds in both the space of the classroom and in the whole social world. I have pondered over the ways in which tourist language learning brings touristic imaginings into its midst as memories or hopes for future encounters. I have then reflected on languaging and the way tourist languagers add to the multilingual, intercultural concentration which, I have insisted, is a distinguishing characteristic of tourism and tourist sites.

Of course multilingualism and intercultural encounter are concentrated in other domains of life. In a cosmopolitan city such as London, for instance, public space is thick with languages of all kinds produced by tourists, temporary and permanent residents of that city alike. Language learning goes on in London, as in other cosmopolitan places, but language learning for 'cosmopolitan dwelling' is largely the language of the state, English for London, learned by those now resident, but with other language roots. Some of these cosmopolitan people may also engage in tourist language learning, but this is a different issue.

There are important differences between such cosmopolitan experience and tourism as a cosmopolitan experience. These do not so much equate to the temporary nature of tourism. Multilingualism is indeed a permanent feature of many tourist sites – the people and some of the language sounds they bring with them may change subtly, or even dramatically over time – but the multilingualism remains, becoming ever more unscripted and inscripting as signs and guides and books are offered in translation.

It is no longer possible to speak easily of permanence in terms of our homes and our residency. Much of life has taken on a temporary nature, a mobility, a liquidity that some celebrate and others condemn:

> Life in liquid modern society is a sinister version of the musical chairs game, played for real. The true stake in the race is (temporary) rescue from being excluded into the ranks of the destroyed and avoiding being consigned to waste. And with the competition turning global, the running must now be done round a global track (Bauman, 2005: 3).

Those who are permanent residents of a place are also tourists, moving, consuming, changing aspects of their life. And ordinary life too has multilingual, intercultural dimensions to it and always as had. I do not wish, in speaking of tourism as a multilingual, intercultural concentrate, to deny the aspects of heterogeneity found in everyday life and in cosmopolitan sites in particular. I do not even wish to suggest, returning to Bauman's definition of tourists as 'temporarily leisured people' (Bauman, 1996), that the temporary nature of dwelling that is tourism, is particularly defining any longer. Bauman himself, I believe, has moved to consider the temporary nature of tourism of 1996 to be an aspect of liquid life, and to be inherent in the lives of those who live 'closest to the top of the global power pyramid' (Bauman, 2005: 3–4).

The tourists I encountered were temporarily leisured both at home and on holiday, playing in the interstices of the local and the global, often at one and the same time. The situation is not quite as clear-cut as Bauman describes it. Some of those I encountered were indeed part of the global class, others were definitely not. Their classes were paid for in many cases by the state. They were rooted people with a strong sense of home and of belonging, having lived all their life in one city and having spent their holidays, in some cases, living life in similar rooting ways, which had brought then to the point of wanting to speak to others in this language.

The distinguishing factor that leads me to continue to insist on tourism as being different, what for me defines tourism as different from everyday life, is that it represents a break from daily routine and habit. In cosmopolitan places and in everyday life there may indeed be extrinsic multilingual and intercultural dimensions but in tourism these are *perceived* in different ways, experienced as a rupture, a break with routine. The habits, the familiarity that accrues to dwelling in one place changes when one becomes a tourist and breaks with those habits (Jack & Phipps, 2005: 169).

Tourist language learning is language learning *for* tourism. It may be possible to argue that some of the experiences and descriptions and even conclusions I have drawn here also apply and could be mined from other language classes: languages for engineering, languages for business, languages for aid, languages for literary study, languages for translation and interpreting, languages for the military, for spying, for global trade. Indeed the Rosetta Stone – the vast, growing 'instant' language company – boasts on its website an unholy alliance, which includes the following 'users': NASA, The Saudi Royal Airforce, British Airways, US State Department, Amoco Corporation, Indianapolis public schools, Johns Hopkins University, Coca Cola, Union Carbide, American Embassy Mozambique, Chernobyl Decommissioning Project, Fort Dix, Fort Meade Naval Security, UN High Commissioner for Refugees, US Air Force Band, Médicins sans Frontiers, Salvation Army, Order of Cistericans (Vatican City) (http://www.rosettastone.com).

What distinguishes tourist language learning from those in this list is that they express a quest for, yes, survival that others may share, but more importantly for (re)creation. They entail a quest for forms of rest, for time that represents a break form habituated daily action. Such time is physiological survival time as much as it is time that enables belonging – to communities of practice, as tourists – and it also allows a certain actualisation through which the self may survive-through-becoming. As such, my insistence upon the term of tourist language learning, brings us back to perennial themes in the tourism literature. For if tourist language learning represents a quest, ultimately, for (re)creation, it is not a quest which is liquid or light, to use Bauman's terms, for those who are its survivors and who stick it out and who actually do language. Tourist language learning, survival indeed we might begin to say, involves, as we have seen throughout this book, what Cronin terms 'kinetic resistance' (Cronin, 2000: 116). 'We learn each other, we cope with each other, in the trials and errors, the contests and treaties of speech; which takes time, and doesn't quickly or necessarily yield to communion' (Williams, 2000a: 86).

Tourism remembers the Sabbath, for those able to enjoy its goods, in new ways. It has long been seen as a sacred journey. There is a vast literature, following Graburn's first exposition of the theme (Graburn, 1978), on pilgrimage and festivals and on sites of heightened experienced of worship to which pilgrims and tourists are attracted (Eade & Sallnow, 2000; Ross-Bryant, 2005; Westwood, 2003). What much of this literature misses is the ordinary, everyday nature of sacred activity, even the boring quality. Tourism as a sacred journey should not just be understood as sacred in some transcendental, spiritual sense, where spirit is detached from everyday life and human needs, rather, I would argue that tourism as a sacred journey, as something as odd and ordinary as tourist language learning, is an incarnational journey. It is about the perception of the world from its places of dwelling, in everyday life and its habits.

But – and this warning note is important – there is much debate about the place of the 'sacred' within tourism. In *Is the Sacred for Sale?*, Alison Johnston makes a strong plea, on behalf of indigenous peoples, for an end to the vast majority of tourism – particularly ecotourism – seeing it as destructive in environmental and cultural terms and as selling all that is sacred: 'Only a minority of travelers opt for ecotourism because of the possibility of profound learning and growth. These rare individuals are in search of a personal experience that will touch them on multiple levels' (Johnston, 2006: 17). It is this minority – the tourist language learners, ordinary, everyday folk – who bother with often profound and relational learning – who, though in no way perfect and often embedded in the conflicting and contradictory aspects of tourism on a macro scale, also, at one and the same time, *take time* in small ways, slow things down.

In many world religions and in the Judaeo-Christian traditions of my own, 'kinetic resistance' was built in to the precepts for living life together. The Hebrew text for the Ten Commandments is sparse and direct in its expression of the Law. There are no comforting 'thou shalt nots' for the Israelites. The Hebrew word for no is *lo*: No other Gods, no graven images, no wrongful use of my name, no acquisitive coveting, no stealing, no killing, no adultery, no crooked courts...honour your parents and at the heart, the pivot of the text: Remember the Sabbath day by keeping it holy' (Exodus 20: 21).

Tourist language learners are engaged, in some respect, not in a perfect, utopian life, but in remembering the Sabbath through the regular, routine inscription of other ways of speaking from the body into their place of dwelling. They are involved in kinetic resistance; resistance to English as a dominant language; resistance to easy consumption through the slow learning of language; resistance to alienation, through the imagination and enactment of courtesy and charity, through the commitment that grows from intercultural speaking and listening to the social miracle of conversation. Such kinetic resistance is also at root, a way of enabling the self, its practices and communities, to survive and be revived and be renewed. It enables the vitality of the 'quick' to re-emerge, and even to linger:

Human doing and making has a 'conversational' dimension in its calling forth unceasing response and reflection in the form of further doing. Can you imagine a situation in which it could be said: 'We have now discovered how to cook a meal, bring up a child, build a house, plan a taxation system, bury the dead', so that there would be no comment possible, no engagement with what has been done except to imitate it? (Williams, 2000b: 198).

Tourism, is human doing and making. For good and for ill. It is special, it institutes rest, and it is everyday. It is consequently always moving, though with some enduring aspects that mean that for some, for those who try, it can be more than Bauman's dystopia of liquid life. In *Liquid Life* (2005) Bauman choses the city of Eutoria from Calvino's *Invisible Cities*, the city where everyone is always moving on to the next place, and where the Devil takes the hindmost, where no one stays for any time at all, as symbolising the world of global power and its players. He may be right, but I suspect that maybe all is not lost. For my part, I would choose not one of Calvino's many cities but the description given of the conversations between Marco Polo and Kublia Khan:

The inferno of the living is not something that will be; if there is one, it is what is already here, the inferno where we live every day, that we form by being together. There are two ways to escape suffering it. The first is easy for many: accept the inferno and become such a part of it that you can no longer see it. The second is risky and demands constant vigilance and apprehension: seek and learn to recognize who and what, in the midst of the inferno, are not inferno, then make them endure, give them space (Calvino, 1979: 129).

This, perhaps, is why we bother to learn other languages against all the odds and when we cannot learn every language in the world. It is perhaps a gesture of survival towards life and languages. The survival of poetry, conversation, beauty and possibility – of all that makes for and is made from the 'quick'. There is something to be gained by living the paradoxes offered by understanding tourism as a sacred journey where bothering with languages is courteous, charitable and may be seen as being for the sake of life, so that the conversation may go on between us.

Afterword

I'm still learning Portuguese. The social bond is much stronger now. The relationships and links I have with countries where Portuguese is spoken have increased. I have a friend who was born in Mozambique. I have strengthening relationships with a research centre in Portugal and with several different Portuguese and Brazilian universities. I have Brazilian friends. I am going to Mozambique this year and no doubt I'll travel to Brazil most likely with work, but also as a tourist, in the coming years. One of the Portuguese classes I joined is still meeting. We no longer have a teacher, our level 2 course – the post-beginners course never got off the ground – the bureaucrats said that there weren't enough people wanting to take the course – but we met anyway, with a great teacher who we paid privately. And now, in the absence of any teacher at all we are still meeting, a few of us – a growing number. But we take it in turns to bring along texts to read and to talk for 2 hours a week to each other in Portuguese. Perhaps we do need a teacher – we are spending a lot of time with dictionaries and grammar books together, asking each other questions about language and culture and resting in English to tell stories, or laugh.

Meeting, greeting and eating and languaging. The space between, the space of language learning, not of languaging, the determination to try and language, to persevere because of the sense of the rewards of this *linguistic currency*, is one where we maintain our social bondedness. The language holiday came together for a short, intense period, and then dwindled away – the market was not able to provide the kinds of conditions in which the bonds might continue. Sometimes I see people who were on the first course with me in town, as I walk the streets and we smile at each other.

Learning Portuguese has changed my life. Six weeks of Italian has added an accent, whetted an appetite. But I cannot learn every language in the world, and the ones I am learning open me out to all manner of accusations and ethical dilemmas. How can I learn Portuguese when, as Cronin, notes:

> [t]he arrival of Portuguese in Brazil led to the disappearance of 75 percent of the languages spoken in the country, and, of the 180 indigenous languages still remaining, few are spoken by more than 10,000 speakers. Language

change is a constant feature of human history but the rate of language loss in more recent centuries is distinctly alarming (Cronin, 2000: 118).

To even suggest here that there is goodness or courtesy in my own guesting is surely to claim to much and to wilfully ignore my own complicity in what some term language death or extinction and others, more chillingly, call language genocide.

Obviously, the solutions cannot lie just with one person. Indeed to suggest that they do is to allow the collective, societal and political responsibility to be abdicated and to pretend that there is no way, in educational structures, in the regulation of tourism, in the distribution of resources, in the detaching of languages and their commodification through textual practices, for languages to saved. It is to believe that Babel must be rebuilt.

But equally, and in the midst of this supercomplex moral impasse, in the limitation of knowing that I cannot learn every language in the world, that the world is not mine to speak to, languages are indeed thrown across my path, urging me into relationship – not letting me just look through the windscreen at the sites but asking me to hear, to listen and to speak back, to engage in conversation.

And that, indeed, is what I have done. I go in and out of homes in Portugal. I spend holidays there. I meet people in other places who speak with me in Portuguese. Brazil and Mozambique are beginning to beckon, to call me through the main language that is spoken there. I am already able to sense and hear and even, at times, to use the different accents that differentiate the one accent from another. I am attuned to the language, I am moving vertically, horizontally and most of all diagonally. I savour the sensual experience of being in Portuguese and surrounded by the somatic dimensions of its life, concentrated for me to date, in memories and experiences of Portugal. For those who accompany me in my learning journeys, other worlds are brought into my hearing: Brazil, Mozambique.

And Glasgow itself, the city where I live, has had a new map traced upon it. The locations of learning are vivid for me – the drafty, cold, steamed up classroom on a Monday night, the six weeks of a warm summer spent in the light and airy space of a refurbished room for adult learners, the flat generously given over to us by a member of the course. But other locations have come into view. Concert venues, some bars, theatres are now entering my life through the attractions of Portuguese language, of the cultures that attach to this language, to the poetry, the literature, the magazines. In the bookshop in town I now know where to buy the Portuguese press. Interlingual travelling, as Cronin terms it, is becoming mine across this language.

Tourist language learning may be popular but it is also precaricous. The wages paid to those who teach are minimum, and it is a highly, highly gendered activity. It is casualised and also seasonal with little hope of permanency for those who wait anxiously in September to see if their quota will be reached. I received three letters from course providers informing me that the course I had enrolled in had not reached its necessary quota and returning my cheque. Another language teacher with less to live on than before.

Last night some of us who are still learning Portuguese gathered in my lounge. The talk was of Scots, of Spanish, of German, of French and again and again of Portuguese, of Brazil and of Portugal. We read poetry, listened to music, lingered over learning from extracts of text. At one point we even sang...*playing* the language to music from within. We have reached a stage where we can sustain a conversation and begin to explore the things of life that delight us. Graham had brought along a tape on to which his Brazilian partner and her niece had generously recorded extracts of a passage that we had chosen to read together. We drank hot ginger and ate scones. It was warm. We were both here and there, between now and then.

Bibliography

This bibliography is an indicative compilation of those references directly cited in the body of this work, and those which have informed its writing.

Abram, D. (1997) *The Spell of the Sensuous: Perception and Language in a More-than-human World*. New York: Vintage.

Adams, D. (1979) *The Hitchhiker's Guide to the Galaxy*. London: Macmillan.

Adejunmobi, M. (2004) *Vernacular Palaver: Imaginations of the Local and Non-native Languages in West Africa*. Clevedon: Multilingual Matters.

Agar, M. (1994) *Language Shock: Understanding the Culture of Conversation*. New York: William Morrow.

Anderson, B. (1991) *Imagined Communities: Reflections on the Origin and Spread of Nationalism*. London and New York: Verso.

Austin, J.L. (1975) *How to do Things with Words*. Cambridge, MA: Harvard University Press.

Balibar, E. (2003) *We, The People of Europe?: Reflections on Transnational Citizenship* Princeton, NJ and Oxford: Princeton University Press.

Barnard, A. and Spencer, J. (1996) *Encyclopaedia of Social and Cultural Anthropology*. London: Routledge.

Barnett, R. (1994) *The Limits of Competence: Knowledge, Higher Education and Society*. Buckingham: Open University Press.

Barnett, R. (1997) *Higher Education: A Critical Business*. Buckingham: Open University Press.

Barnett, R. (2001) Crises of the humanities: challenges and opportunities. In R. Di Napoli, L. Polezzi and A. King (eds) *Fuzzy Boundaries? Reflections on Modern Languages and the Humanities* (pp. 25–42). London: CILT.

Barnett, R. and Coate, K. (2005) *Engaging the Curriculum in Higher Education*. Maidenhead: Open University Press.

Barton, D. (1994) *Literacy: An Introduction to the Ecology of Written Language*. Oxford: Blackwell.

Barton, D. and Tusting, K. (2005) *Beyond Communities of Practice: Language, Power, and Social Context*. Cambridge: Cambridge University Press.

Bauman, Z. (1996) From pilgrim to tourist – or a short history of identity. In S. Hall and P. du Gay (eds) *Questions of Cultural Identity* (pp. 18–36). London: Sage.

Bauman, Z. (2000) *Liquid Modernity*. Cambridge: Polity.

Bauman, Z. (2002) *Society under Siege*. Cambridge: Polity.

Bauman, Z. (2005) *Liquid Life*. Cambridge: Polity.

Bausinger, H.e.a. (1991) *Reisekultur: Von der Pilgerfahrt zum modernenen Tourismus.* Munich: C.H. Beck.

Baysan, K. (2001) Perceptions of the environmental impacts of tourism: A comparative study of the attitudes of German, Russian and Turkish tourists in Kemer, Antalya. *Tourism Geographies* 3 (2), 218–35.

Beck, U. (1986) *Risikogesellschaft. Auf dem Weg in eine andere Moderne.* Frankfurt am Main: Suhrkamp.

Beck, U. (1992) *Risk Society: Towards a New Modernity.* London: Sage.

Beck, U. (2002) The cosmopolitan society and its enemies. *Theory, Culture and Society* 19 (1–2), 17–44.

Bendix, R. (2002) Capitalizing on memories past, present and future; observations on the intertwining of tourism and narration. *Theory, Culture and Society* 2 (4), 469–87.

Benjamin, W. (1973a) The task of the translator. In *Illuminations.* London: Fontana.

Benjamin, W. (1973b) *Illuminations.* London: Fontana.

Bhabha, H. (1994) *The Location of Culture.* London: Routledge.

Blanche-Benviste, C. and Valli, A. (1997) *L'intercomprehension: le cas des langues romanes.* Paris: Le Francais Dans le Monde.

Boorstin, D. (1961) *The Image: A Guide to Pseudo-events in America.* New York: Harper Row.

Bossy, J. (1984) *Christianity in the West 1400–1700.* New York: Oxford University Press.

Bourdieu, P. (1977) *Outline of a Theory of Practice.* Cambridge: Cambridge University Press.

Bourdieu, P. (1991) *Language and Symbolic Power.* Cambridge: Polity.

Bourdieu, P. (2000) *Pascalian Meditations.* Cambridge: Polity.

Brameld, T. and Matsuyama M. (1977) *Tourism as Cultural Learning. Two Controversial Studies in Educational Anthropology.* Washington, DC: University Press of America.

Brutt-Griffler, J. (2002) *World English: A Study of its Development.* Clevedon: Multilingual Matters.

Buber, M. (1958) *I and Thou.* Edinburgh: T&T Clark.

Burns, P.M. (1999) *Tourism and Anthropology.* London and New York: Routledge.

Byram, M. (1997) *Teaching and Assessing Intercultural Communicative Competence.* Clevedon: Multilingual Matters.

Byram, M. and Fleming, M. (1998) *Language Learning in Intercultural Perspective: Approaches through Drama and Ethnography.* Cambridge: Cambridge University Press.

Calvino, I. (1979) *Invisible Cities.* London: Picador.

Canagarajah, A.S. (1999) *Resisting Linguistic Imperialism in English Teaching.* Oxford: Oxford University Press.

Canning, J. (2005) *Global Issues, Local Responses: Engaging with Environmental Issues Through Languages and Area Studies Curricula.* Southampton: Subject Centre for Languages, Linguistics and Area Studies.

Carrithers, M. (1992) *Why Humans Have Cultures: Explaining Anthropology and Social Diversity*. Oxford: Oxford University Press.

Chambers, G. (2000) Motivation and the learners of modern languages. In S. Green (ed.) *New Perspectives on Teaching and Learning Modern Languages* (pp. 46–76). Clevedon: Multilingual Matters.

Chaney, D. (1993) *Fictions of Collective Life: Public Drama in Late Modern Culture* London: Routledge.

Clifford, J. (1997) *Routes: Travel and Translation in the Late Twentieth Century* Cambridge, MA: Harvard University Press.

Coleman, J. (1999) Stereotypes, objectives and the Auslandsaufenthalt. In R. Tenberg (ed.) *Intercultural Perspectives: Images of Germany in Education and the Media* (pp. 145–59). Munich: Iudicium.

Coleman, S. and Crang, M. (2002) *Tourism: Between Place and Performance*. Oxford: Berg.

Colomer, J. (1996) To translate or to learn languages? An evaluation of social efficiency. *International Journal of the Sociology of Language* 121, 181–97.

Cook, G. (1994) *Discourse and Literature: The Interplay of Form and Mind*. Oxford: Oxford University Press.

Corbett, J. (2003) *An Intercultural Approach to English Language Teaching*. Clevedon: Multilingual Matters.

Crawford, J. (2000) *At War with Diversity: US Language Policy in an Age of Anxiety* Clevedon: Multilingual Matters.

Crik, M. (1996) Representations of international tourism in the social sciences: Sun, sex, sights, savings, and servility. In Y. Apostolopoulos (ed.) *The Sociology of Tourism* (pp. 15–50). London and New York: Routledge.

Cronin, M. (2000) *Across the Lines: Travel, Language and Translation*. Cork: Cork University Press.

Cronin, M. (2003) *Translation and Globalization*. London & New York: Routledge.

Cronin, M. and O'Connor, B. (2003) *Irish Tourism: Image, Culture and Identity*. Clevedon: Channel View.

Crouch, D. (2002) Surrounded by place: Embodied encounters. In S. Coleman and M. Crang (eds) *Tourism: Between Place and Performance* (pp. 207–18). Oxford: Berg.

Crowther, J., Martin, I. and Shaw, M. (1999) *Popular Education and Social Movements in Scotland Today*. Leicester: NIACE.

Crystal, D. (1997) *English as a Global Language*. Cambridge: Cambridge University Press.

Dann, G. (1996) *The Language of Tourism: A Sociolinguistic Perspective*. Wallingford: CAB International.

Dann, G. (2004) (Mis)representing the other in the language of tourism. *Journal of Eastern Caribbean Studies* 29 (2), 76–94.

de Botton, A. (2002) *The Art of Travel*. London: Hamish Hamilton.

de Certeau, M. (1984) *The Practice of Everyday Life*. Los Angeles and London: University of California Press.

Derrida, J. (1996) *Monolingualism of the Other or the Prostheis of Origin*. Stanford, CA: Stanford University Press.

Di Napoli, R., Polezzi, L. and King, A. (2001) *Fuzzy Boundaries? Reflections on Modern Languages and the Humanities*. London: CILT.

Dörnyei, Z. (2000) *Teaching and Researching Motivation*. Harlow: Longman.

Douglas, M. (1966) *Purity and Danger: An Analysis of the Concepts of Pollution and Taboo*. London and New York: Routledge.

Douglas, M. (1994) *Risk and Blame: Essays in Cultural Theory*. London and New York: Routledge.

Douglas, M. and Isherwood, B. (1996) *The World of Goods: Towards an Anthropology of Consumption* (2nd edn). London and New York: Routledge.

Dunbar, R. (1996) *Grooming, Gossip and the Evolution of Language*. London and Boston: Faber and Faber.

Eade, J. and Sallnow, M. (2000) *Contesting the Sacred: The Anthropology of Christian Pilgrimage*. Chicago: University of Illinois Press.

Edwards, J. (1995) *Multilingualism*. London: Penguin.

Farnell, B. (1994) Ethno-graphics and the moving body. *Man* 29 (4), 929–74.

Farnell, B. (2000) Getting out of the *habitus*: An alternative model of dynamically embodied social action. *The Journal of the Royal Anthropological Institute* 6 (3), 397–418.

Featherstone, M. (2002) Cosmopolis: An introduction. *Theory, Culture and Society* 19 (1–2), 1–16.

Fighiera, C. and Harmon, L. (1986) Le probleme des languages dans le tourisme. *Documents sur l'Esperanto* 21, 1–24.

Fishman, J. (2001) *Can Threatened Languages be Saved?* Clevedon: Multilingual Matters.

Fordham, T. (2005) Pedagogies of cultural change: The Rotary International Youth Exchange Program and narratives of travel and transformation. *Journal of Tourism and Cultural Change* 3 (3), 143–59.

Foucault, M. (1980) *Power/Knowledge*. New York: Pantheon Books.

Freire, P. (1970) *Pedagogy of the Oppressed*. London: Penguin.

Gallagher-Brett, A. (2004) *Seven hundred reasons for studying languages*. Southampton: University of Southampton, Subject Centre for Languages, Linguistics and Area Studies.

Geertz, C. (1973) *The Interpretation of Cultures*. London: Fontana.

Gibson, J.J. (1979) *The Ecological Approach to Visual Perception*. Boston: Houghton Mifflin.

Giroux, H. (2001) *Theory and Resistance in Education*. Westport, CT: Bergin and Garvey.

Graburn, N. (1978) Tourism: The sacred journey. In V. Smith (ed.) *Hosts and Guests: The Anthropology of Tourism* (pp. 17–31). Oxford: Blackwell.

Greenwood, D. (1978) Culture by the pound: An anthropological perspective on tourism as a cultural commoditization. In V. Smith (ed.) *Hosts and Guests: The Anthropology of Tourism* (pp. 129–38). Oxford: Blackwell.

Guilherme, M. (2000) Critical cultural awareness: The critical dimension in foreign culture education. PhD thesis, University of Durham.

Guilherme, M. (2002) *Critical Citizens for an Intercultural World*. Clevedon: Multilingual Matters.

Hall, S. and du Gay, P. (1996) *Questions of Cultural Identity*. London: Sage.

Hannerz, U. (1996) *Transnational Connections*. London and New York: Routledge.

Hecht, Anat (2004) Past, place and people: An ethnography of museum consumption. PhD thesis, University College London.

Heidegger, M. (1971) *Poetry, Language, Thought*. New York: Harper Colophon Books.

Hennig, C. (1997) Touristenbeschimpfung: Zur Geschichte des Anti-tourismus. *Zeitschrift für Volkskunde* 93 (1), 31–41.

Hennig, C. (1999) *Reiselust – Touristen, Tourismus und Urlaubskultur*. Frankfurt am Main: Suhrkamp.

Hofstede, G. (1996) *Cultures and Organizations, Software of the Mind: Intercultural Cooperation and Its Importance for Survival*. New York: McGraw Hill.

hooks, b. (1991) *Race, Gender and Cultural Politics*. London: Turnaround.

Ingold, T. (1993) The art of translation in a continuous world. In G. Pálsson (ed.) *Beyond Boundaries: Understanding, Translation and Anthropological Discourse* (pp. 210–30). Oxford: Berg.

Ingold, T. (2000) *The Perception of the Environment: Essays in Livelihood, Dwelling and Skill*. London & New York: Routledge.

Jack, G. and Phipps, A. (2003) On the uses of travel guides in the context of German tourism to Scotland. *Tourist Studies* 3 (3), pp. 281–300.

Jack, G. and Phipps, A. (2005) *Tourism and Intercultural Exchange: Why Tourism Matters*. Clevedon: Channel View.

Jaworski, A. and Pritchard, A. (2005) *Discourse, Communication and Tourism*. Clevedon: Channel View.

Jaworski, A., Thurlow, C. and Lawson, S. (2003) The uses and representations of local languages in tourist destinations: A view from British TV holiday programmes. *Language Awareness* 12 (1), 5–29.

Johnston, A.M. (2006) *Is the Sacred for Sale? Tourism and Indigenous Peoples*. London: Earthscan.

Keating, M.C. (2005) The person in the doing: Negotiating the experience of self. In D. Barton and K. Tusting (eds) *Beyond Communities of Practice: Language, Power, and Social Context* (pp. 105–38). Cambridge: Cambridge University Press.

Kelly, M. and Jones, D. (2003) *A New Landscape for Languages*. London: Nuffield Foundation.

Kelly-Holmes, H. (2005) *Advertising as Multilingual Communication*. London: Macmillan.

Kirschenblatt-Gimblett, B. (1998) *Destination Culture: Tourism, Museums and Heritage*. Berkeley: University of California Press.

Koshar, R. (2000) *German Travel Cultures*. Oxford and New York: Berg.

Kramsch, C. (1993) *Context and Culture in Language Teaching*. Oxford: Oxford University Press.

Kramsch, C. (1998) Constructing second language acquisition research in foreign language departments. In H. Byrnes (ed.) _Learning Foreign and Second Languages: Perspectives in Research and Scholarship_ (pp. 23–38). New York: Modern Languages Association of America.

Lave, J. and Wenger, E. (1991) _Situated Learning: Legitimate Peripheral Participation._ Cambridge: Cambridge University Press.

Laver, J. and Roukens, J. (1996) The global information society and Europe's linguistic and cultural heritage. In C. Hoffman (ed.) _Language, Culture and Communication in Contemporary Europe_ (p. 27). Clevedon: Multilingual Matters.

Law, J. (2004) _After Method: Mess in Social Science Research._ London & New York: Routledge.

Leclerc, D. and Martin, J.N. (2004) Tour guide communication competence: French, German and American tourists' perceptions. _International Journal of Intercultural Relations_ 28 (3–4), 181–200.

Love, L.L. and Kohn, N. (2001) This, that and the other: Fraught possibilities of the souvenir. _Text and Performance Quarterly_ 21 (1), 47–63.

Lury, C. (1996) _Consuming Culture._ Cambridge: Polity.

Lyotard, J.-F. (1984) _The Postmodern Condition: A Report on Knowledge._ Manchester: Manchester University Press.

MacCannell, D. (1973) Staged authenticity: Arrangements of social space in tourist settings. _American Journal of Sociology_ 79 (3), 589–603.

MacCannell, D. (1975) _The Tourist: A New Theory of the Leisure Class._ New York: Schocken Books.

MacDonald, S. (1997) _Reimagining Culture: Histories, Identities and the Gaelic Renaissance._ Oxford & New York: Berg.

Mcfague, S. (1975) _Speaking in Parables: A Study in Metaphor and Theology._ London: SCM Press.

MacIntyre, A. (1985) _After Virtue: A Study in Moral Theory._ London: Duckworth.

Maslow, A.H. (1943) A theory of human motivation. _Psychological Review_ 50, 370–96.

Mauss, M. (1990) _The Gift: The Form and Reason for Exchange in Archaic Societies._ New York and London: Routledge.

Meethan, K. (2001) _Tourism in Global Society: Place, Cultural Consumption._ Basingstoke: Palgrave.

Méndez García, María del Carmen (2005) International and intercultural issues in English teaching textbooks: The case of Spain. _Intercultural Education_ 16 (1), 57–68.

Merleau-Ponty, M. (2002) _Phenomenology of Perception._ London: Routledge.

Mühlhäusler, P. (2003) _Language of Environment. Environment of Language: A Course in Ecolinguistics._ London: Battlebridge.

Nash, D. (1978) Tourism as a form of imperialism. In V. Smith (ed.) _Hosts and Guests: The Anthropology of Tourism_ (pp. 33–47). Oxford: Blackwell.

Nash, D. (1996) _Anthropology of Tourism._ New York: Elsevier Science.

Nuñez, T. (1977) Touristic studies in anthropological perspective. In V. Smith (ed.) _Hosts and Guests: The Anthropology of Tourism_ (pp. 207–16). Philadelphia: University of Pennsylvania Press.

Ong, W.J. (1982) *Orality and Literacy*. London and New York: Routledge.

Pearce, P. (2005) *Tourist Behaviour: Themes and Conceptual Schemes*. Clevedon: Channel View.

Pfaffenberger, B. (1983) Serious pilgrims and frivolous tourists: The chimera of tourism in the pilgrimages of Sri Lanka. *Annals of Tourism Research* 10 (1), 57–75.

Phillipson, R. (1992) *Linguistic Imperialism*. Oxford: Blackwell.

Phipps, A. and Gonzalez, M. (2004) *Modern Languages: Learning and Teaching in an Intercultural Field*. London: Sage.

Pi-Sunyer, O. (1978) Through native eyes. Tourists and tourism in a Catalan maritime community. In V. Smith (ed.) *Hosts and Guests: The Anthropology of Tourism* (pp. 149–55). Oxford: Blackwell.

Pourhashemi, P. (2005) Travelling light with heavy cultural baggage. PhD thesis, University of Glasgow.

Ricoeur, P. (1974) Listening to the parables of Jesus. *Criterion* 13 (Spring), 18–22.

Ricoeur, P. (1984) *Time and Narrative*. Chicago: University of Chicago Press.

Ricoeur, P. (2004) *Sur la Traduction*. Paris: Bayard.

Robinson, M. and Andersen, H.C. (2002) *Literature and Tourism*. London: Continuum.

Rose, G. (1992) *The Broken Middle: Out of Our Ancient Society*. Oxford: Blackwell.

Rose, G. (1996) *Mourning Becomes the Law*. Cambridge: Cambridge University Press.

Ross-Bryant, L. (2005) Sacred sites: Nature and nation in the U.S. national parks. *Religion and American Culture* 15 (1), 31–62.

Russell, A. and Wallace, G. (2004) Irresponsible ecotourism. *Anthropology Today* 20 (3), 1–3.

Russell, H. and Leslie, D. (2004) Foreign languages and the health of UK tourism. *International Journal of Contemporary Hospitality Management* 16 (2), 136–8.

Said, E. (1999) *Out of Place: A Memoir*. London: Granta.

Schechner, R. (1985) *Between Theater and Anthropology*. Philadelphia: University of Pennsylvania Press.

Schechner, R. (2002) *Performance Studies: An Introduction*. London and New York: Routledge.

Scott, J.C. (1990) *Domination and the Arts of Resistance: Hidden Transcripts*. New Haven: Yale University Press.

Shaules, J. (2004) Explicit and implicit cultural differences in cultural learning among long-term expatriates. PhD thesis, University of Southampton.

Skutnabb-Kangas, T. (2000) *Linguistic Genocide in Education – or Worldwide Diversity and Human Rights?* Mahwah, NJ: Lawrence Erlbaum.

Smith, V. (1977) *Hosts and Guests* (1st edn). Philadelphia: University of Pennsylvania Press.

Snow, P. (2004) Tourism and small-language persistence in a Panamanian Creole village. *International Journal of the Sociology of Language* 166, 113–29.

Spivak, G. (1999) Translation as culture. In I. Carrera Suarez, A. Garcia Ferandez and M.S. Suarez Lafuente (eds) *Translating Cultures* (pp. 17–30). Hebden Bridge: Dangaroo Press.

Sproull, A. (1996) Regional economic development and minority language use: the case of Gaelic Scotland. _International Journal of the Sociology of Language_ 121, 93–117.

Staub, E. (1999) The roots of evil: Social conditions, culture, personality, and basic human needs. _Personality and Social Psychology Review_ 3 (3), 179–92.

Staub, E. (2003) Notes on cultures of violence, cultures of caring and peace, and the fulfillment of basic human needs. _Political Psychology_ 24 (1), 1–21.

Steiner, G. (1998) _After Babel: Aspects of Language and Translation_ (3rd edn). Oxford: Oxford University Press.

Taussig, M. (1993) _Mimesis and Alterity: A Particular History of the Senses_. New York: Routledge.

Thurlow, C., Jaworski, A. and Ylänne-McEwen, V. (2005) 'Half-hearted tokens of transparent love'? 'Ethnic' postcards and the visual mediation of host-tourist communication. _Tourism, Culture and Communication_ 5 (2), 93–104.

Turner, V. (1982) _From Ritual to Theatre: The Human Seriousness of Play_. New York: Performing Arts Journal Publications.

Turner, V. (1995) _The Ritual Process: Structure and Anti-Structure_. New York: de Gruyter.

Turner, V. and Turner, E. (1978) _Image and Pilgrimage in Christian Culture; Anthropological Perspectives_. New York: Columbia University Press.

Turton, D. (2004) Lip-plates and 'the people who take photographs': Uneasy encounters between Mursi and tourists in southern Ethiopia. _Anthropology Today_ 20 (3), 3–9.

Urry, J. (1990) _The Tourist Gaze: Leisure and Travel in Contemporary Societies_. London: Sage.

Urry, J. (2000) _Sociology beyond Societies: Mobilities for the Twenty-first Century_. London & New York: Routledge.

Urry, J. (2002) Mobility and proximity. _Sociology_ 36 (2), 255–74.

van Wolde, E. (2000) The earth story as presented by the Tower of Babel narrative. In N.C. Habel and S. Wurst (eds) _The Earth Story in Genesis_ (pp. 147–57). Sheffield: Sheffield Academic Press.

Vygotsky, L.S. (1978) _Mind in Society_. Cambridge, MA: Harvard University Press.

Waller, J. and Lea, S. (1999) Seeking the real Spain? Authenticity in motivation. _Annals of Tourism Research_ 26 (1), 110–29.

Wenger, E. (1999) _Communities of Practice_. Cambridge: Cambridge University Press.

Westwood, J. (2003) _On Pilgrimage: Sacred Journeys around the World_. Mahwah, NJ: Hidden Springs.

Wiley, E. (2005) Romani performance and heritage tourism: The pilgrimage of the gypsies at Les Saintes-Maries-de-la-Mer. _The Drama Review_ 49 (2), 135–58.

Willett, J. (1964), _Brecht on Theatre: The Development of an Aesthetic_. London: Methuen.

Williams, R. (1977) _Marxism and Literature_. Oxford: Oxford University Press.

Williams, R. (2000a) _Lost Icons: Reflections on Cultural Bereavement_. London & New York: T&T Clark.

Williams, R. (2000b) *On Christian Theology*. Oxford: Blackwell.

Winslow, J.D. (1997) Languages and tourism: Raising the standards. *Linguist* 36 (4), 94–8.

Wittgenstein, L. (1953) *Philosophical Investigations*. Oxford: Blackwell.

Yamashita, S. (2003) *Bali and Beyond: Explorations in the Anthropology of Tourism*. New York and Oxford: Berg.

Young, R. (1996) *Intercultural Communication: Pragmatics, Genealogy, Deconstruction*. Clevedon: Multilingual Matters.

Index

Abram, D. 59, 136, 145-6
activity holidays 78
affective risk 52-3
agency 54-5
agents 12
alphabet pronunciation 81-2, 86
anthropology
– of perception 53-7
– of tourism 9-10, 49, 85
anti-structure, structure and 83, 84-7, 97
artefacts, tourist maps as 71
attaching process 88, 97, 102
attention, education of 19, 55, 175, 176-7
attentive action 124, 133
auto-anthropology 8
autonomous language 135

Babel 89
Babel fish 154
Balibar, E. 151-2
banal cosmopolitanism 50, 63
Barnett, R. 123, 169, 172
Barnett, R. & Coate, K. 36-9, 53, 66
Barton, D. 35, 161-2
bauen 20
Bauman, Z. 10, 16, 27, 60, 143-4, 181-3, 185
Beck, U. 46, 49, 50, 57, 63, 157-8, 160
being, through perception 92
being lost 74, 75
being-in-the world 83
Bendix, R. 50, 70, 75, 177
Benjamin, W. 29, 139
bilingual individuals 17
bodily hexis 54, 55, 57, 59, 63, 86
body
– demands of language learning on 132
– tourist language learners 83
    see also tourist body
bodying-forth 65, 70
Bourdieu, P. 8, 52, 54-5, 59-62, 70, 86, 108,
    111, 118
breaking English 142-55
broken fragments 151-3
broken middle 148-9, 150, 152-3, 172

Brutt-Griffler, J. 143
Buber, M. 118, 151
Building, Dwelling, Thinking 20, 43
business, language learning for 32
Byram, M. 6, 22-3, 31, 99, 139

Canagarajah, A S. 143, 148, 168
capital 60
Cartesian dualism 53-4
charity 104, 105, 178-81
Clifford, J. 65, 116
cock fights, Balinese 116-20
colonialism 24
common tongue 168-9
communication, impulse for 23
communicative approach, language
    learning 33
communitas 43, 85, 103-4, 118-19
communities of the perfect 148
competency 23
comprehension 98, 99, 103
comprehension-for-conversation 100, 111
conceptual terrain, language learning 11-13
consumer capitalism, intercultural training
    22-3
consumer models, tourism 9
consumption rituals 178
conversations 97-112
– desire for 110
– from comprehension to 99-104
– gratuitous speech 106-7
– miraculous aspect 104-6, 110
– pain and pleasure in 120
– reasons for bothering 109-10
– sustained by games 114
– theological perspective 107-9
– tourist orality and literacy 97-9
cosmological shift 75, 79
cosmopolitan tourist people 181-5
cosmopolitanism 30, 151, 157-8
    see also banal cosmopolitanism
Council of Europe 25, 26
countercultural procedure, language
    learning as 132

courtesy 144, 151, 172, 178-81
creative acts of discovery 55, 56
creative acts of imagining 57
creativity 44
critical literacy 63, 163
critical thought 181
Cronin, M. 10, 16-7, 69-70, 74, 143-4, 146, 157, 159-166, 177,183, 186-7
cultural advice 24
cultural change 19-20, 128-9
cultural difference 169
cultural learning 155
cultural legacies, languages as carriers of 24
cultural resistance/revolution 151-2
cultural tourist 30
culture, and tourism 29, 30
curricula, tourist language courses 36-43
curriculum design 36-7
curriculum-as-designed 37, 39, 40, 46, 53, 66, 122, 173
curriculum-as-desired 39, 40, 42, 43, 44, 46, 47, 99, 122, 173
curriculum-in-action 37, 38-43, 53

Dann, G. 10, 21, 94
de Certeau, M. 19, 39-40, 71-4, 78
deep play 117, 118, 120-3, 124, 126
democratic dialogue 168-9
Derrida, J. 62, 65, 86, 180, 125-6, 17, 153
desires, tourist language learning 41, 43, 110
dialogue 180
  see also democratic dialogue; intercultural dialogue
direct perceptions 55, 56
directions 66, 67-71
diremption 148
discourse analysis 21, 22
discourse(s)
– functionalist 6, 109, 144
– of risk 49, 50
– two level 110
discursive disciplining, tourist body 50-1
displacement 69
distanciation 139
documentation, risk concerns 52
dominant languages
– neo-Babelian scenarios 165-6
– reasons for learning 143
dominant tongue, break with 143
double break 8, 143
Douglas, M. 16, 49, 53, 62-3, 178
dwelling 154-5
– language, building and 20-1

– languaging as an act of 12, 19, 147, 155
– 'letting dwell' 11, 43, 65
– as movement 120
– in travel 65
– in the world 7

ecological psychology 54
economic power 17
ecotourism 184
education of attention 19, 55, 175, 176-7
educational tourism 29-32
emplotting 68
employability 23, 35
enchantment metaphor 137
enculturation 7
engagement 90
enskilment 7, 19, 58, 123, 173
entertainment, tourist speech as 141
entre-deux of human-relatedness 159, 165
environment, relational model 66-7
epistemological risk 51-2
ethnography 7-8, 9
European Union 90
everydayness, language learning as quest for 18-20
expectation, language rehearsal 130

Farnell, B. 54-5, 59, 63, 70, 83, 105
Featherstone, M. 30, 158
fellow-feeling 29-30
fixing process 102
fluency 126, 175-6
foolish feelings, language rehearsal 131
Foucauldian interpretation, risk concerns 50-1
Freire, P. 94-5, 123, 180
functionalist discourse, language learning 6, 109, 144
future present tense, tourist learning 48

game playing 105, 106
games 113-27
– cock fights 116-20
– deep language play 120-3
– language games 114-16
– learning and lassoing 124-6
– in tourist language class 113-14
gathering process 88, 97, 102
gaze *see* tourist gaze
Geertz, C. 53, 116-8, 120-4
gender relations 138
geography *see* place
gifts 177-8
Giroux, H. 36, 62-3, 163

global communication, tourism as 22
global democratisation 157-8
global risk society 49
globalisation 25, 151, 165-6, 167, 168
globe perspective 66-7, 74
Graburn, N. 49, 85, 183
graphism 101
guide books 24, 52, 65, 147, 161
guides 160, 166

habitus 54, 55, 57, 59, 63, 70
halting aspect, tourist language
   performances 139, 141
handouts 41-2
hands-on training 116
happiness, risk concerns 52-3
Heidegger, M. 10-11, 20-1, 3, 65, 80
hidden curriculum 36
hierarchy of needs 172
higher education, lifelong learning
   elements 37
'holy social actors', language learners as
   150
home learning 34
hopelessness, language learner's enterprise
   150
'hoping creatures' 144
horizontal travel 163
host communities 93, 166
host languages, limited opportunities for
   speaking 16, 17
host-guest relationships 17
human-relatedness
– Babel as story of 89
   see also entre-deux of human-relatedness;
   quick of human-relatedness;
   relationships
'humane attempts at living', pronunciation
   as 94

imagined presences 49, 50, 56
improvisation, language rehearsal 131
'in the middle of things' 149-51
in-betweenness 30, 36, 158, 160-1
Ingold, T. 7, 10-11, 19, 21, 41, 53-8, 61-2,
   66-9, 71, 74, 88, 97, 101, 111, 116, 120,
   123-6, 145-6, 154, 173, 175, 177, 178
inhuman objects 178
intentional movement, perceptual activity
   as 55, 61
interagent interaction 41
intercultural awareness 26
intercultural being 91
intercultural communication 11, 111-12, 168

– as an everyday quest 18-20
– curriculum-as-desired 47
– languages as functional necessities 6
– as struggle to make meaning 26
– tourism as 21-5
intercultural communicative competence 2,
   22, 30-1
intercultural dialogue 25-7
intercultural learning 19
intercultural speaking 99
intercultural technologising 154-5
intercultural training 22-4
interlingual travelling 187
inversions, in tourist literature 179-80
irrational nature, deep play 117, 118

kinetic resistance 159, 162, 183, 184-5
kinship 120
knowledge, relational form of 66

language
– building and dwelling 20-1
– as embodied 54
– and geography 145-6
– inhabiting 115-16
– magical role 59
– 'moving around' in 66, 70
– rehearsal see speech rehearsal
   see also languages; playing a language;
   spoken language
language activists 12
language autonomy 160, 161
language death 24, 187
language dependency 160
language destinations 42, 47
language ecologies of tourism 24
language economies 24
language of Europe, translation as 151-2
language games 114-16
language holidays 33, 37, 40, 42
language learning
– change in 2
– dominant approach to 33
– functionalist discourse 6, 109, 144
– materials 34-5, 37, 42
– need for a different perspective on 2
– process of 7
– terminology 11-12
   see also tourist language learners; tourist
   language learning
language professionals 174-5
'language of a thinking body' 75
language wounds 125-6, 136
language-world 115

languaged 9
languagers 12, 46, 91, 136-8, 141
languages
– as carriers of cultural legacies 24
– as inalienable goods 107
– as markers of identity 11
– as new places to dwell 19
– as 'out of place' 16
– politics of 62-3
– research 21-2
– sustained by tourism 144
  see also dominant languages; host
  languages; modern languages
languaging 3, 7, 166, 170
– as an act of dwelling 12, 19, 147, 155
– as being able to comprehend 109
– critical literacy 63
– in-betweenness 30
– lack of literature on 1
– lifeworld perspective 78
– as negotiation of self 162
– rest and moments of generosity in 27
– terminology 12
Lave, J. & Wenger, E. 46, 173
Law, J. 8-9, 94-5, 137
law, risk concerns 52
learned dispositions 54
'learning is kinship' 120
'least rejected object' 134
leisure, locus of learning needs 32
'lengthening strip' of action 58
'letting dwell' 11, 43, 65
lifelong learning 37
lifeworld perspective 66, 67, 74, 76-9
liminality 85, 90, 128
liminoid 90, 128, 140, 141
linguistic acculturation 17
linguistic capital 52, 55, 60-2, 62-3, 86, 119
linguistic currency 52, 55, 60-2, 63
linguistic diversity 167
linguistic guest 139
linguistic guesting 9, 10, 18, 86-7
linguistic host 139
linguistic hosting 118
linguistic power 17
linguistic research 8
liquid modernity 27-8, 60-1, 111, 178, 182
literacising orality 111
literacy ecology 35
literacy practices 34-6, 162
  see also tourist literacy
little deaths 49
live performance, simulation of 116
local forms of community 27

loss
– in the context of way finding 70, 73, 74
  see also being lost
Lyotard, J. 25, 132, 166, 170

MacCannell, D. 10, 18, 93, 128
MacIntyre, A. 25-7, 94, 122, 144
magic, language learning equated with
  59-60
magic metaphors, languagers and 136-8
maps *see* tourist maps
marketing models, tourism 9
material break 144-7
material risk 52
Mauss, M. 111, 177
Mcfague, S. 75, 83, 97
meaning-making 26, 104-5
memory, language rehearsal 130-1
Merleau-Ponty, M. 66, 83, 92-5, 115, 124, 173
metaphorical thinking 75
mimesis 91, 92, 134
mind-broadening 30, 31-2
miraculous aspect, conversation 104-6, 110
mobility, course books designed for 37
mode of action, perception as 55, 56, 57
model-based research 21, 22-4
modern languages
– crisis in 4-6, 35
– intercultural dialogue 25
– intercultural literature 23
modernity 60
  see also liquid modernity; postmodern
  society
monolingualism 65, 86
moral imperative, intercultural dialogue
  25-6
moral questions 122
moral sense, linguistic guesting 86-7
motivation
– to be good guests 172
– tourist language learning 10, 32, 41, 158
'movement of becoming' 11
moving around, through language 66, 70
multilingual tourism 16
multilingualism 181, 182

narration, and tourism 70
native speaker status 139
negotiation of self 162
neighbourliness 26
neo-Babelian scenarios, dominant
  languages 165-6
non-human agency 41
non-human objects 178

novel perceptions 55, 56

'on the hither side' 111
Ong, W. 53, 59, 98-103, 105-6, 110-1, 162
ontological risk 51, 109
oral comprehension 98
oral tradition, travel narrative 69
oral/written modalities, shift between 84
oralising literacy 111
orality
– and geography 146-7
– tension between literacy and 35, 36
    see also tourist orality

pain
– in conversation 120
– deep language play 120-3
parables, place-space 74-6, 79-80
paradox, tourist language learners 16, 89-91
passports, risk concerns 52
perception 53-7, 61, 92
performance
– as a form of magic 137
– language learning for 23
– least rejected object 134
– as restored behaviour 132-3
– simulation of live 116
– as twice-behaved behaviour 134, 135
    see also social drama; tourist language
    performances
Phillipson, R. 143, 148
photography 101-2
phrase books 24, 34, 81
physical gestures 115
physicality, production of language 105-6
place
– connection between language and 145-6
– distinction between space and 73-4
– and orality 146-7
– significance of, through relational context
    88
– in tourist studies 17-18
place name translations 146
place-space parable 74-6, 79-80
play, tourist language class 119
playfulness, language rehearsal 141
'playing a language' 125-6, 134
pleasure
– in conversation 120
– deep language play 120-3
politics of languages 62-3
possession, language rehearsal 131
postcard writing 102
postcolonialism 24

postmodern society 49
power 17, 40, 122, 150-1
practiced place 73
pre-existing templates, curricula 37-8
pronunciation 81-96

quick
– of human-relatedness 1, 2, 6, 26, 91, 94, 97,
    102, 103, 105, 111, 138, 151, 158
– of tourist language learning 1, 3, 9, 27, 33,
    36, 58

rationalism 26
recording 144-5, 147
reflexive risk society 49-50
reflexivity, tourist language performances
    141
rehearsal see speech rehearsal
rehearsal space 58, 103, 130
relational activity, language learning as
    90-1, 170
relational models 66-7
relationships
– language learning for 33
– tourist language classes 68
    see also host-guest relationships;
    human-relatedness; tourist-host
    relationship; tourist-human relationship
(re)creation, language learning as quest for
    183
research
– language learning 2
– linguistic 8
– tourism 1, 10, 17-18, 21-3, 31, 177
resistance 40, 42, 122, 166
respect, language learning as 91-5
restored behaviour
– language performance 138
– language rehearsal 133-6
rehearsal as process of 132-3
Ricoeur, P. 18, 68, 75, 86, 114
risk society 49, 64
risk(s) 48-64
– affective 52-3
– analysis 49
– concerns, Foucauldian interpretation 50-1
– in the context of way finding 73
– discourses 49, 50
– epistemological 51-2
– management 50
– material 52
– minimisation
    language learning 55-7, 63
    linguistic currency 61

magical role of language 59-60
politics of languages 62-3
– ontological 51, 109
– perception 49, 53-7
– real and imagined 57-9
– to status 118, 119
– tourist language learning 50, 90
ritual function, tourism as 85
ritual process, of society 85
role play 58, 59, 72, 73, 105, 106-7, 120
Rose, G. 148-51, 153, 172

the 'sacred', in tourism 184
sacred journey, tourism as 85, 183-4, 185
Schechner, R. 58, 129, 132-5, 138, 140, 142
self-relation 150
sense potential 93
sensuous aspects, tourism 146
shamans 59
skills discourse 2, 25, 26, 35, 123
Skuttnabb-Kangas, T. 24, 143, 148, 167
Smith, V. 18, 85, 91
social bonding/bondedness 43, 120, 153, 154
social drama, speech rehearsal as 140-1
social inequality, linguistic capital 62
social integration, flow of consumer goods 178
social interaction 41
social learning 131, 154
social relations 63, 178
sociality 106, 124
society 85
sojourners 31, 95
sound 84, 101, 102
souvenirs 177
space
– distinction between place and 73-4
– tourist studies 17-18
   see also place-space parable; rehearsal space
spatial stories 73-4, 78
speech, gratuitous 106-7
speech acts 106
speech rehearsal 128-41
– aspects of 130-1
– languagers as magicians 137-8
– as modes of language performance 138-9
– as restored behaviour 132-6
– as social drama 140-1
spoken language 102, 105-6
stagecraft 137
staged authenticity 128-9
status 117, 118, 119

stories
– verbal exchange of 177
   see also parables; spatial stories
strategies 39, 40
strips of behaviour 133, 138, 139, 152
structure, and anti-structure 83, 84-7, 97
subjectivity, risk concerns 51
subjunctive mood 147, 151
supply and demand models, intercultural training 23-4
surprise, language rehearsal 130
survival 171-85
– basic human needs 172-7
– courtesy and charity 178-81
– gifts 177-8
symbolic violence, linguistic capital 62-3

tactics 39, 40
talisman, language learning as 53
techne 80
technological fix, intercultural dialogue as 25-7
'temporary leisured people', tourists as 16, 182
text books, low-status 41
texts 35, 101, 161-2
theology 107-9
'third term' 108
tidying up, for tourists 93
timetables 65
tongue twisting 87-9
totalising aspect, tourist maps 71
tourism
– anthropology of 9-10, 49, 85
– connection between language and place 145-6
– cultural continuity 129
– democratisation 111
– educational 29-32
– as form of non-human agency 41
– as intercultural communication 21-5
– language sustained by 144
– lifeworld perspective 67, 76-9
– liminal dimensions 85
– 'little' deaths 49
– marketing and consumer models 9
– multilingual 16
– and narration 70
– negative representations 31
– research 1, 10, 17-18, 21-2, 31, 177
– as a sacred journey 85, 183-4, 185
– as staged phenomenon 128-9
tourist body 50-1, 153, 173
tourist destinations 16, 97

tourist gaze 10, 69
tourist imagination 95-6
tourist industry 16, 17, 18, 23-4, 142
tourist language classes
– alphabet and word pronunciation 81-3
– charitable aspect 105
– games in 113-14
– imagined presences 50
– life and freshness in 1
– maps and directions in 66
– meaning-making 104-5
– modified by the presence of tourism 40-1
– needs presented in curricula 173
– perceived risks 55-6
– place name translations 146
– rehearsal space 58, 103, 130
– relationships 68
– resistance and power 122
– restored behaviour 133-4
– sensuous aspects of tourism 146
– social bondedness 43, 154
– status and play in 119
– structure and anti-structure 86
tourist language courses
– cultural advice 24-5
– curricula 36-43
tourist language learners 156-70
– attempt to inhabit language 115-16
– body 83
– as 'holy' social actors 150
– horizontal and vertical travel 163
– interaction 41
– kinetic resistance 184-5
– limits to language knowledge 163-5
– moral sense of linguistic guesting 86-7
– motivation 10, 32, 41, 158
– negotiation of self 162
– paradox of 16, 89-91
– potential to change nature of touristic
    exchange 165-6
– power 150-1
– terminology 12-13
– vocabulary lists 102
– writing 83-4
tourist language learning 2-3
– activities 43-6, 50
– as an act of will 90
– as an everyday quest 18-20
– communicative and experiential
    dimensions 34
– conceptual terrain 11-13
– as countercultural procedure 132
– deep play 120-3, 124, 126
– democratisation in 4

– desires 41, 43
– embodied imagining of being a tourist 43
– equated with magic 59-60
– finding ways of dwelling 21
– gratuitous nature 105
– in-betweenness 30, 160-1
– as magical talisman 53
– playing a language 125-6
– pull to orality 102-3, 112
– purposes 4, 7-9, 15, 33, 42-3, 105, 109,
    149-50
– as quest for (re)creation 183
– quick of 1, 3, 9, 27, 33, 36, 58
– reasons for 109-10
– as respect 91-5
– risk minimisation 55-7, 63
– sense of inadequacy 125-6
– as social drama 140
– texts 161-2
– as a 'way of singing' 124
– as work of relating 90-1, 170
– working against the grain 149
tourist language packages 145
tourist language performances 138-9, 141
tourist language programmes 32-4, 36
tourist literacy 97-9
tourist literature, inversions in 179-80
tourist maps 65, 66, 71-4, 78, 79-80
tourist needs 172-3
tourist orality 97-9, 102-3, 110, 112
tourist purposes, language learning for 4,
    7-9, 15, 33, 42-3, 105, 109, 149-50
tourist-host relationship 119
tourist-human relationship 1
touristic communication, versus literacy
    practices 36
touristic dance 129
tourists
– as culture carriers 30
– distinction between sojourners and 31, 95
– as language carriers and language makers
    24
– as 'out of place' 16
– as semiologists 10
– survival language 172-3
– as 'temporary leisured people' 16, 182
– tidying up for 93
    see also cosmopolitan tourist people;
    cultural tourist
translation
– connection with magic 59
– for easing the process of tourism 93
– globalisation 165-6
– kinetic resistance 159

– as the language of Europe 151-2
– within tourism 16, 166
travel 29-30, 163
travel narratives 69
Turner, V. 43, 83, 85, 90, 103, 118, 128, 132, 137, 140-1, 158
twice-behaved behaviour 134, 135

UNESCO 24, 25, 26, 90
universalism 26
Urry, J. 10, 18, 22, 49, 56, 69, 85, 178

verbal economy 103
Verfremdung 139
vertical travel 163
virtue 121-2
vocabulary lists 102

way finding 65-80
wealth, and risk 49
well being, risk concerns 52-3
Wenger, E. 46, 162
western acting 139
Williams, Raymond 29, 145
Williams, Rowan 104-8, 110-11, 123, 126-7, 148-50, 152-3, 179, 183, 185
word lists 102
wounds, speaking another language 125-6
writing 83-4, 101
writing games 115
written comprehension 98

Young, R. 135, 147, 149, 151, 167-8, 179

zones of proximal development 41, 43